a couple's breakup from
their dog's point of view

IN THE DOGHOUSE

a couple's breakup from
their dog's point of view

IN THE DOGHOUSE

TERI CASE

BZCE PUBLISHING

BZCE Publishing, Clearwater, Florida

Publication Date: April 2019

Hardcover ISBN: 978-0-9997015-2-2

Paperback ISBN: 978-0-9997015-3-9

ebook ISBN: 978-0-9997015-4-6

Cover art by Olya Vynnychenko

In loving memory of Marie, Mama Cat, Dickie Bird, and Kimo

1

SKIP

A DOG'S LIFE

WHOEVER THINKS a dog's life is easy has no idea what they're talking about, and they certainly don't understand a thing about unconditional love.

My Lucy is crying again but with noise this time. Her pain hurts my ears and twists my guts, but her silent tears seemed louder and more painful, if that makes sense to humans. Sometimes she stops breathing and gasps for air, like I do when I don't heel and pull too hard on my leash. Sometimes a groan makes its way from her stomach to her feet, and I swear it vibrates and echoes through the floorboards and into each room. And sometimes I can feel a wave of fresh tears coming like a rainstorm, before Lucy even knows she's going to cry them.

I'm sure the downstairs neighbors can hear her wails through the floor, but they must be used to it after four days. Normally, the teenage boy, Thomas, who lives with his mom, gets upset at loud noises and shouts, "Too loud! Too loud! Too loud!" Maybe crying doesn't count because I haven't heard him complain.

It's eating me up inside that it's my fault John left us. Even if I could find the words, I'd never be able to tell her how sorry I am. And that I'm scared too. Lucy's not the only one John has left behind. She's not the only one praying he'll change his mind and come back to us or wondering what the heck we're going to do without him.

Her blond hair is wet and plastered against the side of her face, where she's been brushing her torrential downpour of tears. I lean forward to lick the tears from her salty cheeks, but she turns me away.

"Not now, Skip," she says.

Even now, she's beautiful to me. I know it's not right to say so when her face is red and her eyes are puffy from too much grief, but it's true. With her face clear of makeup, and her damp hair and rumpled clothes, she reminds me of the many times we've been caught walking in the San Francisco rain. Only then, she laughs. Smiles. She has the best smile in the world.

A walk was the first thing we did together when she and John brought me home seven years ago, and if it hadn't been so late and if the next day hadn't been a workday, I think we could've walked all night long. That was the first time she sat next to me, leaned her forehead against mine, and whispered, "You're perfect for me." I get teary thinking about it. She's been perfect for me too.

Pacing seems to help. Checking her phone, though? Not so much. Because it's not bleeping or dinging, and that silence means no John. I hate those phones and how people are always looking down at them. My paws have been stepped on more than once by a hunched-over human not paying attention to where they are going. But I digress.

A long walk would do us some good. We could both

use some fresh air and activity. We need to burn off some of this pent-up negative energy. And I need to urinate. Heck, we haven't been on a proper walk since John left. Lucy has been opening the back door so I can relieve myself in the complex's backyard. To get there I have to head down four flights of dark, narrow, and steep servant-stairs typical of old San Francisco's apartment-converted Victorian homes. We share the stairs with our top-floor neighbor, "Hoarding Manny." That's what John and Lucy call him. The nickname makes Manny sound older and less handsome than he really is, though. I'm guessing he's about Lucy's age, thirty-two-ish, and he has a strong, confident walk.

Our shared back door steps are riddled with Manny's stacks of dirty terra-cotta pots and bags of potting soil he insists he's going to use someday. That's what he tells the offsite property manager every time John and Lucy complain about his "hot mess all over the place." Right now, the only one using the pots and soil is the damn stray cat that sprays all over them. Pisses John off. No pun intended. Or I guess I should say, *pissed* John off. Still no pun intended.

I'm tired of winding my way down four creaking flights to reach the yard, but I think Lucy feels self-conscious and doesn't want to run into anyone we know at the dog park and answer a bunch of questions, like, "Where's John today?" or "How are the wedding plans going?"

She asks me, "How could he leave us? What will I tell people?"

It's one of the few times I've been glad I can't speak human, so I don't have to answer. Mostly, I'd love to talk a human's ears off. I'm a dog with a lot to say. But just now, I don't need to add lying to my list of how I've been an unfaithful companion.

I've lost count of how many times she's said, "He'll be back," to me, herself, and the empty spot on the couch where John always sat. But she says it more like a question: *He'll be baaaack?* And when the answer isn't forthcoming, I can smell her fear and need for reassurance. Fear and need smell more alike than humans might think. And neither one smells good. They're vinegary. Corrosive. Like you're being eaten from the inside out. Neediness is *no bueno* for the nose.

My natural order of senses is first smell, then sight, and last is sound. Tasting and smelling at once is one of my canine superpowers and usually a good thing. If something smells good about a person, I want to take a deep breath, stick out my tongue, and savor their scent and vibe. If they'll let me, I'll shove my nose deep between their legs and take a good long whiff, but most humans aren't comfortable with such public interest. Plus, humans are backward. They operate in the order of sight, sound, smell. They don't know what they're missing. They really don't.

Sigh.

When someone smells bad or needy or vulnerable, it makes me anxious, like I have to be in charge. Like I'm supposed to do something, only I have no idea what I should do. The pressure makes me defensive, and my white fur will stand up all along my spine. I feel responsible, protective . . . and torn. I'm kind of a two-sided dog. I have the looks and instincts for survival of my Timber Wolf mother but the calm, submissive demeanor of my Labrador father. Mama was a natural leader. My dad was a natural follower. How they met, I have no idea.

I may look like Mama, but I take after my father's side of the family. I'm a cuddler at heart. John was the boss, and I was cool with our arrangement. I'm not alpha-material, but I'm afraid that Lucy is even less alpha-ish than I am. She's not eating. She's not sleeping. And we all know what it means when humans stop eating: she can't take care of herself. A few times, she has reminded me of Soft Voice, my owner when I was born, who had a house and a gigantic yard with Strong Voice. When I was one month old, Soft Voice gave me, Mama, and my brothers and sisters to the pound after Strong Voice "went on to greener pastures" and she couldn't take care of us on her own. That I'm even thinking about Soft Voice and losing my first family is the perfect example of how John's leaving is messing with my head too.

I'm a dog. I'm wired to live in the now. I've got NOW DNA. I'm not supposed to think about the past or the future, but that's all I've been able to do these past four days. Dwelling on yesterday and hoping for tomorrow is something humans love to do, but it's no way for a dog to live. *No, sir.*

Focus on the now, Skip. Focus. I've been mentally coaching myself to take the lead in John's, hopefully temporary, absence. The idea came to me instinctively; not because I want to lead, but I'm a pack animal, and when I see a need, I have to fill it whether I like it or not. It's compulsory. I once heard that females in a wolf pack will all start producing milk when another female has a litter. They do this just in case something happens to the mama or the mama's milk. Amazing, right? They are all for one and one for all.

Lucy's not getting her exercise. *We're* not getting our exercise. I've got to suck it up and do something.

All for one and one for all.

I pick up my leash and carry it to her. Time to take her on a walk. She needs to clear her head and prepare for the workweek to come. Tomorrow is Monday and she starts her new job as the head geriatrics nurse and wellness director at a retirement home. Sure, the timing isn't ideal with John leaving, but she's been waiting to transfer from trauma to geriatrics for a few years. Somehow, I have to help her pull herself together.

"I'll open the back door for you," she says and blows her nose.

Nope. No more backyard. We're going for a walk. I yip and drag my leash to the front door, the clip scraping annoyingly against the hardwood floor. When I reach the door, I get my bark on. I'm annoying enough that after a few attempts, she stands up and says, "Okay, give me a minute."

The bathroom door closes behind her. I drop my leash, confident she is getting ready to go out with me. I'm not letting her off the hook. Through the door, I hear her sniffle and open the medicine cabinet. The distinct rattle of pills catches my attention. She always says, "Nothing gets past you." Nope it doesn't, not when it comes to sound anyway.

I'll just get her fleece and put it by the door for her. As I return to the hallway with her favorite pullover, I hear her turn the knob. Unfortunately, at the same time I hear the key sliding into the front door lock.

Just as Lucy steps into the hall, John opens the front door.

2

SKIP

UNPACKED

WE ALL FREEZE. At first, Lucy and John don't say anything and have eyes only for each other. It reminds me of their silent exchange at the pound when I first met them and when they could read each other's minds. The contrast is startling because they might be staring at each other now, but they're not communicating a darn thing. *Zilch.* They're acting more like wary strangers. It's like they are sizing each other up, the same way I do whenever a new dog shows up at my dog park and I'm not sure if he's a friend or a foe.

And me? I'm standing between them, smack dab in the middle. Unfortunately, it's a place I've been a lot over the past several weeks, polarized by Lucy's hopeful expression and John's scent-de-Cecilia's biscuits, which tells me he hasn't been alone.

Cecilia. Our ruination.

Lucy and I wait together, uncertain if John is coming home or if he's just taking the last of his things and leaving us behind like unwanted leftovers or a forgotten doggy bag.

I know. I know. I sound bitter and hurt, but that's because I am bitter and hurt.

John breaks the silence. "I should've knocked. Sorry, old habit. Skip, come here, buddy."

I wish he would've said Lucy's name first, but the three of us have been this way ever since John's mood changed a few months ago, and it became easier for him to interact with Lucy about me rather than discuss their upcoming wedding and honeymoon or our pack's future together. In the past, John and Lucy have said how sad it is that their married friends who've become parents only talk about their babies. Many times, Lucy has said, "When we have children, we're not going to forget our relationship exists too." And John always said, "That's a deal."

I guess the deal didn't include dogs.

Should I go to him? I'm mad at him for leaving us and putting me in this horrible predicament, but he's making his irresistible cute kissy noises. His thick light-brown bangs slide forward over his forehead as he pats his knee, beckoning me. I'm confused because I've always done what John has told me to do, so I look up at Lucy. *Tell me what to do*, I implore her with my eyes. *Lead me*, I beg.

"Come here, Skip," John says again. "Or are you mad at me too?"

Lucy reaches over and pats my head. "Stay." Only I can't tell if she is telling me to stay or entreating John not to go.

"I'm not mad, John," she says. "I'm confused and hurt."

John clears his throat, and when he speaks, his voice is deep and rough. "Lucy—"

She interrupts. "Have you changed your mind?" The hope in her voice is so heavy I close my eyes, and my long flat tongue goes dry. You know how I feel about negative smells. Her desperation is oozing from her pores. John remains silent. He doesn't know it, but he smells her desperation too. Humans don't like it either. To me, it smells like dried sticky syrup that can get stuck in your fur for days and adheres to the floor when you're napping. Hurts like a son of a bitch when you jump to your feet and lose some hair in the process.

John closes his eyes and squeezes the bridge of his nose. He does this whenever he doesn't want to sneeze or cry. I used to catch him doing this during sad movies. Sometimes, he'd bury his face in my fur, pretending to hug me, but he was really using me as a Kleenex. I never minded. He was the top dog of our pack, and he needed to hide his weaknesses.

"No," he says, "I just need to know you're going to be okay." He takes a step closer.

I stand on all fours, not sure what will happen next when Lucy's energy shifts a bit, but I stay at her side, where I've been for the past four days.

Lucy purses her lips, shakes her head, and puts her hand up, palm forward. She does the same to me whenever she wants me to immediately stop what I'm doing. John knows the signal, so he stops too.

"Why?" she growls. "So *you'll* feel better?" She says it like a question, but she isn't really asking.

If I could talk, I'd warn John: *Back off before she bites you.*

"It's not like that," he says.

"It's exactly like that. You came over here to get *me* to reassure *you* that everything is going to be okay. Well, guess what?" Her arm is shaking as she leans on my head like one of those sticks that old people don't throw but take on walks with them. They're actually called *canes*, but people like to sound hip and healthy, so they call them *sticks*. "It's not okay. I feel stupid, like a fool. I have no idea what has happened between us or why you've changed your mind about us," she says. "Feel better now?"

He leans forward, "You're not a fool. You're amazing. I just need to be alone. I don't want to end up like my parents."

"Your parents? We're nothing like your parents."

John shakes his head. "It's not you. This is my problem."

"Your problem?" Lucy lifts her chin. "Believe me, it's my problem too. What about the past ten years? What about everything we've worked for? Do those years mean so little? So little that 'being alone' sounds better?"

I'm surprised by how strong, clear, and angry her voice is all of a sudden. The kind of angry that makes me tuck my tail, hang my head in shame, and run for another room when it's aimed at me after chewing something I shouldn't have chewed. (Not that I ever do this, mind you. At least not since I was a pup.) If not for Lucy's inflamed face, I'd have a hard time convincing anyone of how fragile she's been.

"What am I missing? What happened?" she asks. "I need a better explanation than you 'want to be alone.' I deserve one. We're supposed to be getting married in five months. Our honeymoon is planned . . ." She lets her sentence trail off as if hoping John will offer a positive ending to it. I hope she doesn't hold her breath for one because John and I know what "wants to be alone" really means.

"Don't you love me anymore?" she asks.

Instead of looking at Lucy, John looks long and hard at me.

Oh shit.

I can read his mind. I can read his slumping shoulders, slack jaw, and heavy lids. They all add up to defeat and his desperate need to confess and be guilt-free.

The hackles on the back of my shoulders and neck rise in alarm.

People think confessing something bad is the right thing to do, but it's not. It's selfish. A confession just helps the person in the wrong feel better while it makes the innocent person feel like a piece of crap. No good comes of confessions. The truth might set John free, but it will destroy my life permanently. He's going to tell Lucy about Cecilia, *she-who-Lucy-knows-nothing-about*, and Lucy will hate us both forever. There will be no second chance for our pack. No possibility of reconciliation even if *he* changes his mind. And she'll take me to the pound for my betrayal, for being the one who introduced him to his new woman.

When John releases a long, slow breath as if he is gearing up for a dogfight, I know what I have to do. I need to make him leave. *Now.* Before he spills the beans and blows our pack and our lives to smithereens.

I start barking like a rabid dog. The more they tell me to be quiet, the louder and faster I bark. I howl until they can't hear themselves think, much less hear each other speak, and I'm not going to stop. I don't even stop when I hear Thomas yell from downstairs, "Too loud! Too loud! Too loud!"

It's one of the hardest things I've ever had to do. But I drive John out the door. Our secret is safe.

3

SKIP

DIRTY DOG

I KNOW what people are thinking even though they haven't heard the whole story yet. They're thinking, *John-the-dirtbag-human-cheater*. They're wrong. He's not a dirtbag. They don't know him like I do. Like Lucy does. He's made some bad choices lately, but we love him, and he's earned our love.

But he strayed. It can happen to the best of us, and if I'd paid more attention the day we met Cecilia two months ago, I could have warned him about the perils of greener grass and avoided this entire mess. Not that I can see green: I only see grays, but I know new grass when I smell it. And who doesn't love a fresh patch of new grass to run in or roll around in? *The old grass, that's who.*

John was working from home that week while his law office was being re-floored, so on an afternoon walk, he took me to a new dog park Lucy had told us about. It was farther away and not our usual path, so I had a lot of marking to do. Every doggone smell, sight, and person was new. I was on sensory overload and loving every minute of it. My nose was to the ground, which meant I was missing John's hand signals and whistles.

"Someone's a little too excited," he said and put on my leash, which he only does when he thinks my safety is at risk or if some silly person who doesn't know the first thing about me drives by and yells, "Leash law!"

When we got to the park, he released me. "Go play."

And that's when I smelled her: a gorgeous well-bred Australian Shepherd.

Love at first scent.

She was the collar to my leash, the marrow to my bone, and the stuffing to my tennis ball. I was in pheromone heaven.

I made a beeline for her and gave her a closer sniff. And just like that, I was under her spell. I climbed on top of her right then and there. Couldn't have stopped myself if I'd wanted to. I was a mounting maniac. Though, for all intents and purposes, I was out of service, if you know what I mean. It was just for show, a natural reflex.

A woman shouted, "Come here, Bunny!"

The Australian Shepherd responded with a bark but didn't move. Her name was Bunny. *Beautiful Bunny.*

John caught up to me and nudged my rump with the toe of his shoe. "Down, Skip. You horndog."

Bunny's woman wagged her finger at me and then at Bunny. "You better watch out for this one, Buns."

At first I didn't notice much about the woman other than she smelled really really really good, like treats, and she was tall, much taller than our Lucy, which isn't difficult.

John introduced himself. "Sorry about that. He's a little fired up today. It's his first time at this park."

"Your first time here, too, then. I thought you were a new face. I'm Cecilia."

They shook hands.

"Well," she asked, "can we trust these two to go play and keep it clean?"

John laughed, but to me there was nothing dirty about how I was feeling. *Dude, blame biology, not the dog.*

"Only one way to find out," John said. "Mind your manners, Skip." He waved toward the field, and Bunny and I took off.

Man oh man, the way Bunny moved when she ran and jumped. The bitch could turn on a dime. *Yowza.* She played hard-to-get at first, but then she started nipping at my hind ankles, and we all know what that means. *Hubba-hubba, baby.*

Now and then, she and I looked over our shoulders to make sure our masters were still there. At the time, it seemed so nice and convenient how John and Cecilia kept each other company while we ran around. I'm not sure how much time passed, even though I'm usually really good about keeping track. But some time later, they called our names. They were ready to go.

"Goodbye, Skip," Cecilia said, offering me one of the best biscuits I'd ever had.

John winked at me and said, "Bow."

I put my right front paw forward and lowered my snout to the ground. John taught me to bow after I refused to learn to shake. Truth is, I *pretend* I don't know how to shake. It's a matter of principle. Until humans start greeting me by turning their backside and letting me stick my nose up their butts, I refuse to shake hands or paws when I meet one of them. So, despite all the treats offered and the entreaties that

Lucy and John have made in my lifetime, I've yet to shake their hands or any other human's.

"Ah-ha," Cecilia smiled and curtsied, pulling her long skirt up at the sides, "handsome and gallant after all, just like your owner."

As far as friendly dog owner banter goes, her comment seemed fairly innocent at the time. And being overstimulated, I ignored the subtle shift in John's behavior and the nuances of chemistry bouncing between him and Cecilia.

In hindsight, I recognize that John swaggered most of the way home that day, but I'd had a swagger of my own, thanks to Bunny. So I guess I had been a bit self-absorbed.

That night when Lucy got home from work and the three of us were relaxing in the living room, John told her we'd gone to the new park. She asked a lot of questions, mostly about me. Did I like it? Was I good with the other dogs?

I cringed, worrying that John would tell her about my surge of hormones and the "humping incident," and then, of course, he did.

Lucy looked at me, squinting, and tried to hide her pretty smile, but she couldn't help herself. In her Chihuahua voice, she sang, "Skip has a girlfriend. Skip has a girlfriend."

John never mentioned Bunny's master.

The thing is, like I've mentioned before, I'm wired to live in the here and now, and when my life is going well, I thrive in the moment. So it shouldn't surprise anyone that the very next day when John and I headed out for our afternoon walk and he gave me permission to walk ahead, I turned toward the new park. I was hot on my own trailblazing from the day before. I had newish territory to

reclaim. A fence post here. A stop sign there. I was off-
leash, so it took me a few sniffs and markings to realize that
John wasn't following me. When I turned to look for him,
he was standing at the crossroad between our usual dog park
and the new dog park.

"Not a good idea, buddy. Let's go to our usual place," he
said.

I walked back to John, and I begged. I begged him to go
to the new park again. The kind of begging a dog can't be
proud about.

Now I know that I mistook his hesitant body language
for laziness.

He finally caved. "I guess you really want to see Bunny
again."

I barked several times. Indeed, I did want to see her
again. Bunny was the first female dog I'd ever felt so drawn
to. Lucy once told me that wolves mated for life, and that
was why she chose me. At the time, I thought Bunny might
be my lifetime mate. Not once did I wonder how that would
work with our current pack.

But back to John and that fateful day.

"Okay, but this is the last time. Trust me. This isn't your
best idea," he said.

Ah, dog's best friend. A true wingman understands we
are all animals at heart. Primal. Always looking to procreate
and sow our oats, even if said oats have been snipped like
mine. I still wanted to go for it and be the alpha to Bunny
like John was alpha to Lucy. John had my back.

Or so I thought.

I didn't have to beg the next three days. My last time at
the new park was TGIF day. All the humans were saying it
to each other: *TGIF! Woo hoo!* A dog really picks up on that

kind of happiness from people. Their tones are lighter. Shoulders relaxed. Heads tilted. Smiles for everyone.

On that last visit, I retrieved Bunny's ball from a bully of a Rottweiler, and I looked over to see John's reaction to my prowess, only to find him standing really, I mean *really*, close to Cecilia and tucking a strand of her curly auburn hair behind her ear. I could read John's thoughts with his broad shoulders rolled back, chest expanded, his head bent intently, and only a handful of inches separating his and Cecilia's noses, lips, and tongues. I stood with the ball between my dumbfounded jaws. My ears began to ring, and my fur rose on my back.

Uh-oh. I knew that stance, that look. I'd seen him stand that way with Lucy. Our Lucy. I knew what John was saying without saying a thing.

Oh no you don't, John. We've got Lucy.

Humans don't share. That's the first rule a dog learns: *humans don't share tail.* They'll share food, clothes, furniture, balls, and blankets, but when it comes to each other, no sharing allowed. Not ever. Look, but don't touch. That's it. I've seen humans get jealous just for looking. One time, John got jealous when he thought Lucy was ogling our neighbor Manny's jeans-covered tuchus during one of the rare moments we were entering the building at the same time.

Cecilia cupped John's hand, leaning her cheek into his palm.

John was in trouble. I had to save him. *Pronto.* I torpedoed Bunny's ball to her and hightailed my way back to John. I picked up my leash at his feet and ran off, refusing to look back, and I ignored his commands to return. My senses were in hyperdrive, and drool poured from my jowls.

My nose was sweating. All I could think was, *Must get home. Keep John safe.*

His voice grew louder as he chased me, and he was clearly annoyed with me, but I stayed on course and kept making my way home. I had a job to do, and it was to train him to not stray. He needed to heel. He was being a very bad boy.

I waited until we were a block away from the park to stop on the corner and let him catch up. A woman walking by said, "Look at the good dog holding his own leash."

Right, lady. If you only knew how capable I am.

"Damn it, Skip, what was that about? You've never run off before." John was huffing and puffing.

I wanted to say, "Well, you haven't either until now," but I couldn't, so instead, I dropped my leash to the ground and stared him in the eyes: *I saw you.* I had no intention of blinking before he did. Dogs don't stare their alpha down for nothing. Eye contact is serious business and not to be ignored.

He looked away. I was sure I had made my point. He leaned over and picked up my leash, and I let him snap it to my collar. Then he ran his palm across my crown.

"You're right," he said. "What am I doing? The grass isn't always greener."

I love green grass. I sighed and stood to all fours. I wanted to pretend he was talking about the dog park and the field, but I'm a dog. I get it. We're all animals. It's biology. We want as many chances as we can get with our female counterparts. I mean, I had to give him a break. He still has testicles. I can't be a hypocrite. I can't even begin to imagine how I'd be in the world today if I had mine. It's bad enough sometimes I still get a phantom surge of, I don't

know, something, and still mount up. Humans call it testosterone, but I call it *life*; I do things to pillows that make
everyone uncomfortable. Kind of how I jumped on Bunny
the first time I saw her. I'm not proud. I'm honest. So how
could I expect John to stop if I can't even control myself at
times?

Males. We disgust me sometimes.

"We okay?" he asked me. "No more Cecilia. I get it."
He tested the leash, and at that point, I willingly moved with
him. Improved behavior deserved a reward, even if it was
just taking a walk together.

Yeah, we're okay, but I'll be watching you.

That Friday night when Lucy came home from her shift
at the hospital, she asked John about his day. He didn't say
anything about our walk or which park we'd gone to, but
when she suggested we could all go to the new park on her
day off, John told her he preferred our neighborhood park.
They talked about his week working from home and
whether he was ready to go back to the office on Monday,
and he said, "Yeah, it was a good week, but time to go back
to reality."

I laid my head on his leg. *Good boy, John. Good boy.*

The last time I saw Cecilia was several weeks ago when
John and I accidentally, or so I thought, stumbled upon her
new dog biscuit bakery.

We were walking back from my annual checkup with
the vet when John said, "I'm taking you somewhere
special."

And boy was it. I could smell the dozen or so dogs
socializing at the sidewalk café a mile away.

"It's a café, just for dogs, Skip," John said.

Say what? Dog-damn brilliant. I thought I was in dog heaven just until I smelled her. Bunny. *Oh, oh.* No matter how cool the place, John and I had to get out of there. Stat! I tugged on the leash, but I was too slow. At about the same time that Bunny stopped beside me, a woman, you know who, asked, "John? Is that you?"

Now John, as I remember it, was totally cool. I mean cool like bored cool. His shoulders didn't roll back. His chest didn't puff up. He kept me by his side as he greeted Cecilia. I followed them around as she offered to give him a tour of the joint. She gave me a few extra biscuits. One was peanut butter. One was cheesy. Both were delicious.

In a nutshell, they behaved, so I wasn't worried. Unfortunately, I must have missed something because even though I never saw Cecilia again, a few weeks later, her biscuit scent was all over John. That's when everything began to change.

John grew quieter and started taking walks without me. As far as I'm concerned, that's canine treason. One afternoon he came home from his office and changed into a fresh set of work clothes just before Lucy got home from the hospital. These weren't home clothes, like usual. Then he moved his clothes hamper to our small laundry room. Later, I tipped over the basket to sniff out my suspicions. I smelled what I was looking for just before Lucy came in and chastised me.

"No, Skip. What are you looking for? Your ball is in the living room." She shook out John's clothes, and I almost fainted as John's and Cecilia's comingled scents exploded into the room, but Lucy just tossed the clothes in the wash, unfazed.

Remember that I told you humans smell last? Sometimes I think they ignore smell altogether. I'd like to say Cecilia reeks, but she doesn't. She smells like the peanut butter treats she makes at her bakery and like Bunny. And she's been right under Lucy's nose for weeks now.

4

SKIP

THE HOOD

ONCE MY BARKING forces John to abort his confession and leave, Lucy nosedives into a fresh tsunami of tears. I let her have a few wails and nose-blows and then pester her to take me out. She needs this walk as much as I do. There are too many reminders at home of what we've lost.

She slips on her boots and fleece. She pulls a hat low over her forehead and grabs her large Hollywood sunglasses. I guess she's trying to hide her swollen eyes because it's no sunnier outside than it is in this dismal place.

Distracted, Lucy breaks one of our safety rules: *always make sure that Manny's front door is closed before exiting.* His door is straight across from ours, so we not only share the back exit, but also the internal landing, stairs, foyer, and entrance. Manny and his Mastiff, Tank, always growl when they see me. Or it's more likely that their snarls are for John and Lucy over the hoarding complaints, but I'd rather not find out I'm wrong and have a *Come to Cesar Millan* moment.

It's pure luck that Manny and Tank aren't around. *Crisis avoided.*

Now, I've been trained to wait for permission to leave our apartment and follow behind John or Lucy, but obviously, Lucy's in no condition to adhere to formalities. Without the leash attached to my collar, I run ahead of her and tear down the flights of stairs to the foyer. I stand at the glass door until she catches up. She stops next to John's bike. He's been meaning to fix that flat. I used to run alongside him when he rode it. He'll probably ride it with Bunny someday. The image makes me whimper.

"I wonder why he left his bike?" she asks.

Okay, call me crazy, but Lucy's eyes light up a bit, like his bike with a flat tire is some sort of sign that he hasn't left us for good. Like he intends to come back to us someday so there's no need to take his bike. Don't get me wrong, I want her to be right, but alas, let's not forget his greener grass. *But what if? What if, after some time, Lucy becomes the greener grass for John again?*

Lucy clips my leash on. At least she isn't so distracted that she is going to let me run wild on the streets.

We live in the Richmond District of very expensive San Francisco. The sky is usually gray and foggy, and the area is a little cooler than Fisherman's Wharf and South Beach, where the ballpark is, but we love our neighborhood. There are beautiful houses here. Many have a yard, which is uncommon in the city. We have a routine walk that takes us from our front door, through our neighborhood, and to Lands End, where we walk the dirt path that is always damp and rich with the smell of mud and earth. The path runs parallel to the cliffs, and the mist of the ocean floats in the air. At any given time, we can see parts of the Golden Gate

Bridge poking through the marine layer. The view never gets old.

Lucy loves the mansions in our hood. She always says we'll never be able to afford one, and that's why we rent our apartment in the area instead. She says, "We have to get as close as we can to our dream." I've always hoped that someday we'll have one of these houses regardless of the "jacked up" prices that John reminds Lucy about. Correction: *reminded* Lucy about.

I know Lucy's favorite one. Every time we reach it, she stops and stands still with a secret smile on her face. I like it too because there's a bush shaped like a big dinosaur, a bronto-something she once explained, just inside the yard, and its long topiary neck hangs over the tall pink stucco wall surrounding the house. Lucy usually looks up at a solitary window at the highest point of the house. One time Lucy told me, "We were going to name you Garp, after the actor Robin Williams, who lives here, but you reminded me of a wolf from the zoo that Aunt Eve took me to when I was little, so I named you after him instead."

I'm glad they didn't name me Garp. Skip suits my gentle and breezy personality. Besides, the dog owners of San Francisco are a little out of control and pretentious when it comes to naming their dogs. *Dog Snobs*, that's what John and Lucy call them, and they'd be snobs too with a dog named after a character played by a resident actor. If I had a biscuit for every time I've met a dog with a stupid name, I'd be twenty pounds overweight.

I've met dozens of dogs with names that start with Sir or Princess. One time, Lucy said, "Sir Charles's and Princess Daisy's poo doesn't stink any less than yours, Skip." If I'd had the ability to chuckle, I would have, but I settled on sticking out my tongue and giving Lucy a big smile. I've met a Corded Puli named Whoopi Goldberg, a Shih Tzu named Zach Galifianakis, and a Greyhound called Bradley Cooper. There's Lumiere the French Poodle, and Simba the Chow Chow. Let's not forget the cliché names such as Pepe the Chihuahua, or my neighbor's massive Mastiff-mix named Tank. *Sigh.* The only dog with a clever name in our dog park belongs to a Chinese Crested dog named *Dee-Oh-Gee.*

I take my time walking us. There's no hurry to return to our apartment and start the crying all over. Besides, who knows when I'll get out again.

Lucy keeps taking deep breaths, but more for fortitude than air, methinks. I can tell by the way she keeps looking over her shoulder that she's thinking about aborting our walk and going back to the apartment.

Uh-uh. Not going to happen, Lucy.

I take our usual path and tug on my leash. It's not hard to make her follow since I'm easily three-quarters of her body weight. Sometimes Lucy walks me, but today I'll be walking Lucy. She needs this leash more than I do.

I cross Lake Street and continue to Sea Cliff and toward Garp's house to lift her spirits, but when we reach it, Lucy doesn't even notice. I stop, but she keeps walking. I bark, "Stop." She isn't listening. *Naughty Lucy.*

When she reaches the end of the leash, her arm jerks back, and she turns, startled. I'd say she smiled at me, but I don't know what to call those twisted sad lips.

She looks up at the window and moves to stand beside me. "He's dead. Didn't I tell you? The world's funniest man is gone." Her tears begin anew.

Where she keeps finding the tears, I just don't know. *No,*

you didn't. I'm trying hard to take care of you right now. If I'd known this would make you sadder, I'd have kept walking.

We continue my walk and Lucy's foot-dragging and turn right on El Camino Del Mar, slowly making our way to our hike at Lands End, where the sidewalk turns to dirt. Lucy removes my leash, but it's okay because I don't have to worry she is off-leash on this path. It's a safe and clear trail. Even little humans run freely here.

After my last few sedentary days, I lunge forward, the long strides stretching my muscles. The breeze smells like salt and fish, and my nails and paws sink into the soft dark mud as I dig in and run. I glance back at Lucy. She's falling behind, so I slow my pace. The trail has lots of ups and downs, and our breathing reflects our efforts. Lucy always says, "Uphill never gets easier," but she doesn't say so today. Instead, she pauses to stare across the bay at the Golden Gate Bridge, and says, "Lands End. This trail is up and down, just like my life right now. Maybe we should call this Relationships End or Couples End. Listen to the foghorn saying, 'Alone. Alone.'"

She's being more dramatic than usual, but at least she's venting instead of sobbing. Still, I beg to differ. I think the foghorn is saying, "Walk. Walk."

The fog is getting heavier, and Lucy groans. "My life doesn't work without him."

I whine, relating. Her loneliness is sinking into my bone marrow in ways I wish I could forget. But I remember when I lost my mom and siblings, how scared I was, certain it meant I'd die alone. I mean, come on! Soft Voice gave us all up once Strong Voice was gone. For the first time, it hits me that this could happen again. I always assumed "on to greener pastures" meant Strong Voice went to the Rainbow Bridge, that place where humans say dogs go to play after they die. But what if he also met a Cecilia and left Soft Voice? Could history repeat itself? Is Lucy strong enough to keep me?

I lean against her legs to smother my fears and try to convey my support. *We'll be okay, I promise. We'll figure this out together. You saved me once, and now I'll save you.*

My only chance to stay with Lucy and prove my love and commitment is to protect her now that John is gone. I remember the promise he'd asked of me when they rescued me at the pound: "What do you say, boy? Will you help me protect our lady?" He's left me alone to protect our lady.

A light rain pulls me from my reflections. Lucy seems unaware that she is getting wet, and now's not the time for her to get sick. She's weak already, and she starts her dream job tomorrow, even if she isn't as excited about her new job as she was this time last week when John was still with us. It's now my job to make sure she's healthy as a horse for her first day. I start to bark and nibble my leash hanging from her hand. *Let's get you home.*

She re-clips our leash, and I walk ahead and pull her along with me. *Good girl, Lucy.*

5

LUCY

CHERRY CHIP CAKE

LUCY FOLLOWED SKIP HOME, trying to make sense of her life and how it had fallen apart. Where had she and John gone wrong?

Four nights ago, they'd broken up over her Cherry Chip Cake. Literally, over her cake. Lucy had been standing on one side of the table, John on the other, when he'd said those earth-shattering words, "I want to be alone."

She had so many happy memories and birthdays tied to her annual Cherry Chip Cake. How could it now be linked to five such devastating words?

She had turned thirty-two three weeks ago. But she'd had a cold, so they decided to celebrate her birthday once she was feeling better. So on Wednesday night, she came home after a hectic evening at San Francisco General, overrun with flu victims in the emergency room, and was welcomed by the smell of the warm Betty Crocker Cherry Chip Cake. The sight of Skip salivating and John putting on the frosting made her heart melt. *He did this for me*. Like he had every year they'd been together because he knew the real story behind the cake.

Ditching her coat and purse, she did a happy dance into the kitchen, where John surprised her by saying, "I made it different this year."

"What? Why?" *Something is wrong.*

When she was ten years old, her life changed forever when her mom greeted her after school with her first ever Cherry Chip Cake. The real gift had been Mom's clear, gentle smile on her birthday. Usually, it was Aunt Eve, and not Mom, who made her feel special on her birthday. She would also receive a birthday card from her dad, a long-haul truck driver, postmarked from somewhere on the road. His card always started with, "Happy Birthday from somewhere in . . ."

But all her life, off and on in what seemed like two-week intervals, her mom refused to leave her dark bedroom, where she either slept or sobbed while listening to the same sad songs over and over. This was nothing new, the sobbing over her latest breakup or her "messed up life." Neither was the mania that often dragged her out of her sad cocoon.

But on that tenth year, Mom had asked her, "You know what today is?"

A trick question for sure. She'd been afraid to answer. Her mom's calm smile and mellow energy threw her off.

"Where is Aunt Eve?" she asked her mom. Aunt Eve always knew what to say and how to manage Mom's feelings. Lucy's birthday was not something her mom had celebrated up to that point.

Without Aunt Eve's help, Lucy whispered, "My birthday." She wasn't sure what her mom was going to say and was ready to run to her bedroom and hide until Aunt Eve came home. She wasn't afraid of her mom hurting her. She was afraid of making her mom sad again.

Too many times on Lucy's birthday, her mom had said, "I ruined my life because of a stupid one-night stand." Or on the years she'd been manic, she always said, "The sparks flew, and an egg was fertilized when I was a waitress at Boomtown Casino in Northern Nevada."

But that year was different. After setting the first ever Cherry Chip Cake on the table and kneeling, her mom had said, "Today is the day we celebrate you being you for the rest of our lives. Okay? I'm sorry I'm late to the party."

Party? Lucy had never had a birthday party before. "You mean I get a real birthday party?" She crossed her fingers, hoping she hadn't said the wrong thing. If she got this wrong, Mom's unexpected happiness would disappear.

"When Eve comes home, we will blow out candles, have cake, and open your present."

Lucy could hardly breathe. *A present?*

They'd had presents before, mostly on Christmas, but not consistently. Each holiday was different, driven by resources and rotating friends, and sometimes even her mother's rotating boyfriends. The only constants in the first ten years of her life had been Aunt Eve's love of Harlequin Romances and her dad's postcards and child support checks.

But on that day long ago, Mom had followed through on her promise. When Aunt Eve got home, the three of them took turns blowing out candles and making wishes. Lucy had wished to never celebrate another birthday without a Cherry Chip Cake. She couldn't even remember what her present had been, but she would always remember the cake. Later that night, her aunt told her that her mom had a new doctor and that everything would be better from then on.

Lucy had wrapped up all her mom's changes, and how much better life had been after that, into the delicious Cherry Chip Cake her mom baked every year until Lucy left home for college. It was their one and only tradition. The cake was exactly as Betty Crocker intended it to be made year after year. Perfect expectations in a box.

When she had first confided in John about her history and the cake, he had said, "Honey, you can count on me to make you a Cherry Chip Cake every year."

The day John broke up with her, she had thought her horoscope was about her career change. *Taurus: Changes are difficult for you, but be open. Sometimes the sweetest rewards begin as bittersweet change.*

She had thought the reference to "bittersweet change" was about leaving her coworkers behind or turning another year older. She would never have guessed her horoscope was about her cake, or that her cake was about her relationship.

Why? Why after ten years of care, had John put jam in her cake? For a moment, the nervous fear she'd had as a child when her mom had been sick resurfaced. Her gut whispered, *The cake is different because John is different.*

John had been out of sorts for several weeks, but she'd chalked his moodiness up to stress about his promotion and his new responsibilities at the law firm. But he was breaking tradition, and that was unlike him.

Bits of cake and jam stuck to the knife as she pulled it from the cake. She stared carefully at him.

John looked uncharacteristically smug, a challenging glint in his eyes.

"Are you okay, honey?" she asked.

"What's that supposed to mean?"

"I don't know. You've never messed with my cake before." She didn't know how else to explain that the cake, all of a sudden, felt like a bad omen.

"And that means something's wrong with me?"

"No. I mean, yes. The past several weeks you've seemed stressed, and every time I've tried to talk to you about it, you've changed the subject. And," she looked help-lessly at the cake, "you said you would always make my Cherry Chip Cake," she said. She'd hated feeling ten years old again.

"And I did," he said.

"But, John, it's not the same. You know it's important to me," she said.

"What's the big deal?" he asked. "It's just a stupid Cherry Chip Cake."

"'What's the big deal?'" she repeated. "Are you serious right now?"

John glared at her.

Skip slunk out of the room, tail tucked between his legs as if he'd been the one to put the jam in the cake.

"Even Skip knows not to mess with my cake," she said.

John snapped. "God, why do you always cry as soon as you don't get your way?"

Lucy had always prided herself on being a generous and patient person, especially with the man she loved. He'd wanted to wait until he was a partner with the firm before getting married. Okay, she had waited. They couldn't afford her transfer from trauma to lower-paid geriatrics until he was partner. She'd waited again. She never asked for anything. She never even pestered him about his long hours at the office.

"Why can't you ever try something new? This stupid

cake! If you want someone to make you a cake every year, you damn well should let *them* try something new and not keep eating this boring cake over and over. And you shouldn't complain when someone does something for you. Be grateful. Jesus."

John picked up the entire thing and dropped it in the garbage can.

So this is definitely not about my cake.

It seemed that John had turned the cake into a tool, a weapon, some message for her. She wasn't sure how change came into it. They'd made their plans together, hadn't they? They were both planners; they wanted the same things and had been focused on their careers. And she was the last person who needed to be told to be grateful. Everything she did and worked for, everything she'd planned for, was out of gratitude for their life together.

"I shouldn't complain?" She stood to her too-short five-foot-one-inch height and glared up at him. "When it's my cake and I only have it once a year, I can! I don't need you to use my cake to teach me something. My birthday cake *is* about *me*. You changing it? *That's* about *you*!"

John wiped his hands on a towel and sighed. "I'm sorry. You're right."

But she'd been so stupid. His capitulation should have been a warning sign. The lawyer in him was usually determined to be right. In fact, he often pushed until the other person admitted they were wrong.

All of a sudden, he looked so sad, so unlike the man who had been by her side for ten years, so she had retreated and said, "I guess there's always next year." And she had meant it because they would finally be getting married in five months, October, and going to Australia. Only an hour earlier, their smoker-voiced seventy-year-old travel agent had left a message using the worst faux Australian accent ever, "G'day, mate! Crikey, only one hundred and fifty-two days before you leave for your honeymoon walkabout!"

But John shook his head. He leaned over the table and caressed her cheek. He dropped his hand and said, "I'm sorry. I can't do this anymore."

Fighting over her cake was picking at the memory scabs of tiptoeing around Mom's depression from days of yore. "Me neither. I hate it when we fight. Let's take Skip for a walk and start the night over." And when the tension eased and tradition and cake didn't confuse the issue, she would ask him again what was bothering him.

Except John had something else in mind.

"No. I mean I can't do this," he pointed from his chest to hers then back to his own. "I can't believe I'm going to say this, but I need to be alone."

Skip returned to the kitchen and stood close to John, staring up at him and whining. John pushed Skip aside, rushed into the hallway, grabbed his keys, and left the apartment without looking back.

She and Skip stood in the hall staring at the closed door.

"What just happened?" she asked Skip and the room at large.

She looked down at Skip, but he refused to meet her eyes.

John was gone for hours. He ignored her calls and texts. Lucy tried to wait up for him but finally fell asleep before he got home, and when she got up for work the next day, he was sound asleep on the couch. All these years, they'd never slept apart. She hoped he'd had the time alone he needed. She couldn't wait to talk to him and find out what was bothering him, but she left him to rest. Next to laughter, sleep was the best medicine.

She should never have left, but it had been her last day at the hospital so she could hardly call in. He didn't call her that day, and when she saw him on Thursday night after work, he made it clear that he needed much more than a few hours to himself: *he was leaving her.* Leaving. Her. He'd found an apartment that day, he said.

An apartment?

"What? What do you mean you found an apartment? We have one *together!*"

He only said, "I want to be alone."

"You're seriously leaving me? Without even telling me what's gone wrong?!" she asked. "You're throwing us away?"

"I need to be alone," he said again.

And just like that, he left, saying he'd be back to get his stuff and return the keys by Monday.

Except for his bike, he'd removed all his belongings. So far he hadn't returned his keys, but maybe he had intended to do so tonight before Skip went bonkers and barked him out of the apartment. Between her teeter-tottering feelings of defiance that she didn't need John, anger that he would be back and this heartache would have been for nothing, and despair that he eventually might return his keys proving he was truly breaking up and didn't love her, Lucy racked her brain trying to figure out where they had gone wrong.

How could a Cherry Chip Cake undo us?

6

SKIP

LOOK BOTH WAYS

AS WE RETRACE our steps toward home and reach our first street corner, Lucy steps right into the road without looking. In front of a car! I yelp and jump back, using the leash and my body weight to yank her off her feet and onto the sidewalk. She lands hard on her ass and cries out. But we are alive. *Thank Dog!*

That's the second rule down the tubes: *Always look both ways before you cross the street.* This heartbreak is going to kill us.

The driver, who had swerved to miss us, stops several feet ahead in the middle of the road. A lady about Lucy's age jumps out and runs toward us.

"Oh my God! Are you okay?" The woman squats next to Lucy and fusses over her, but Lucy puts her hand out to stop the other woman's actions.

"I'm fine. I'm a nurse," Lucy says.

I guess she thinks that should make us all back off, but it just sounds odd to tell some stranger her profession. It's not like we're mingling at the dog park and making general conversation. We were almost roadkill!

"I'm so sorry. I didn't expect you to step out into the street."

Lucy snaps at her. "I get it. I wasn't paying attention. Don't rub it in." Her rudeness makes me cringe because even though we've never seen this lady around and the circumstances aren't the best, I can tell by her voice and flushed cheeks that she is truly concerned about our well-being. Besides, she smells like the warm chicken soup that John and Lucy used to make each other when they were sick. I already like this gal.

The woman straightens and frowns at Lucy. I don't blame her.

"I wasn't rubbing . . ."

Maybe Lucy is following my lead and can now sense the woman's warm-chicken-soup nature because she blushes and closes her eyes for a second before saying, "I'm sorry. I'm not myself. It's not your fault. It's my adrenaline. Don't pay attention to me. I'm fine. Really." She rises to her feet and dusts off her rump. Her movements tug on my leash, making me nod like a string puppet.

The woman tilts her head, and her eyes narrow in a thoughtful way. I bet she's noticing Lucy's red face and swollen eyes for the first time. "You appear to be having a bad day, and I haven't helped. What can I do?"

Shaking her head and avoiding the woman's eyes, Lucy says, "Nothing. Thanks for stopping to check on us. We'll be fine."

A dog avoids another dog's eyes out of respect or to avoid confrontation. Lucy's doing it to avoid more questions, and I wonder if, like me, the lady picks up on Lucy's flimsy tone and the flagging determination behind that claim. She must because she nods, smiles kindly, and says in a reassuring tone, "Yes, you will." She knows more than we told her.

Yep, definitely feel-good-warm-chicken-soup material. I'm a little sad to see her go as she returns to her car and drives off. If you ask me, Lucy could use a friend like her.

Lucy looks down at me. "You saved me, Skip."

I sure did. That's my job. Now, I just need to continue to keep you safe. I couldn't bear to lose you. You're the only family I've got left.

By the way she's looking at me, totally blank-like, I can tell she doesn't know what to do next. It's like she fell on her head instead of her butt. As we both catch our breath and calm down, my mind wanders. Lucy can't even walk herself. I start to obsess about her finding out about Cecilia, kicking me out, and getting herself killed crossing a street, or me having to live on the streets like that smelly cat, breaking into people's yards and scrounging for food. I'll be alone. Starving.

Seriously, I need to get back in the bow-now.

I'm obsessing about the dissolution of my life the same way I do when someone starts to throw a ball for me. I don't know when to stop. I can't stop. I just want to play more catch. And despite what the casual thrower or observer thinks, obsessing about the ball is not fun for me. I can't quit it. I'll chase that f-ing ball until my hips ache and my legs give out. It's an addiction.

So now you know what my mind looks like while Lucy and I stand on the corner and I worry about losing her. She's my ball. What can I do so I never lose her? *Aaaargh! I don't know what to do!*

Then the first inkling of a solution comes to me: the better I take care of Lucy, the more she'll have to keep me in her life once she finds out that I was John's wingman. Or wing-dog. Or traitor. *Whatever.* But if I'm her alpha, if she needs me like she needs John, she'll have to keep me! She needs help not getting hit by cars? Fine, I can do that. I'm her man. *Er, her dog.* You know what I mean.

I can do this. I can be her alpha and run our tiny pack of two. I have to, for both of us.

All for one and one for all. I look both ways before I pull on the leash and safely walk us across the street.

7

SKIP

LOST AND FOUND

I'll never forget the day John and Lucy entered my life. I was close to twelve weeks old by the time they rescued me from that dogforsaken place. I was alone, stripped of my furlicious, huggable siblings and my mother. Our eyes had barely opened before we were taken with Mama to the pound. Within weeks, I'd lost them all. Yes, Mama too. I try not to think of those days that I sat in the corner, resting my head against the concrete, at a loss to understand how my life had turned so cold so fast.

The caretaker had done the best he could. I was too naïve at the time to appreciate he had tried to prepare me. Heck, I was just a puppy.

"Poor little guy," he'd said as he held me. "People won't be able to resist the soft round features of the rest of the litter, but you look like your mom, so the two of you are going to have to wait for very special people." Mama had curled her lips back and growled until he told her everything would be okay and gave me back to her.

But everything hadn't been okay. One by one my

siblings that resembled our Labrador dad, who'd gotten to stay with Soft Voice, were picked out of our pen until only Mama and I were left behind. And then one day, I woke up and Mama's special person must have come while I was dozing because she was being pulled from our bed. Her eyes were rolling back into her head. She was frantic, trying to stay with me. Her anal glands were leaking, instinctively leaving me a trail to find her later. But her yelps warned me that this was it: *our goodbye.* Our pack was decimated. I howled and cried, waiting for her to respond and tell me where to find her. But I never heard her or saw her again.

Dogs came and went, handpicked by humans. At first, I always caught the little humans' attention if I smiled and wagged my tail—not too high to appear aggressive and not too low to appear skittish—and I did my best to get picked by one, hoping they were my special person. The kids would say, "Want that one." But their parents always ushered them to the cage next door, mumbling concerns about my wolfish appearance and saying, "But look at this cutie over here!"

Dumb a-*dolts.* They had been consumed with my looks rather than the truth of my personality: I am a family dog. I'd like to say it was their loss, but I was the one alone in the cage all those weeks. For twenty minutes a day, the caretaker who looked like a goofy Saint Bernard, tried to give me love and reminded me there was someone special out there for me, but over time, I had a hard time believing him. After all, *he* wasn't even taking me home. How special could I be? I started to give up and kept my head down, ignoring the families filing past looking for a pet. Why bother? The longer I was there, the bigger I got, and the less chance I had of finding a family. I wondered, what's the point of my life without a pack?

But then Lucy and John happened. I smelled them before I heard them. Their warmth and sunshine danced above the disinfectant-drenched concrete and wafted all the way down the hall and across my cold nose. They smelled like my mom used to when we lived with Soft Voice. A few times a day, Mama would leave us alone and go outside for a while. She'd get tired of my brothers and sisters climbing all over her, gnawing on her teats, and sucking her dry, and she constantly had to lick us clean. So she'd take a break, but she always came back calm and smelling like fresh grass and sunshine. Her fur was always nice and toasty from the sunlight. I missed Mama.

My interest was piqued for the first time in days. I lifted my head to track the warm-smelling pair's progress as they stopped at each cage to greet each dog.

I could smell-tell a lot about Lucy from my first whiff of her. The nose knows.

I could smell her sweet, pleasant hope and sour disappointment as she moved down the aisle of kennels. She was so focused, like a Pointer, but tiny in stature like a Chihuahua. A blond Chihuahua. John was much taller than her; he stood back and watched her closely, protectively. If he were a dog, I'd say he had German Shepherd in him. *Oh, what it would feel like to have his protective leadership.* And I was pulled to Lucy like she was my mama's milk. I inched toward the front of my pen. My head high. My ears pointed, not in alarm but in interest. I couldn't take my eyes off her.

She wanted something specific in a dog. I could tell by

the way she stared and took her time with each hopeful mutt. *But what? What did she want?*

The other dogs liked her energy too; they all had happy barks and gravitated toward her. They wagged their tails, if someone hadn't snipped theirs off. An older Terrier-mix was so desperate for her attention he started chasing his tail until she laughed.

Show-off.

Then she was in front of me. I didn't know what to do. And all of a sudden I felt like it was a life-or-death moment. If I lost her, I'd die. But then we made eye contact, and I'm not kidding, I felt a tingle all the way from my whiskers to the tip of my tail. Lucy grabbed John's forearm so hard he yelped like one of the newcomers getting a shot.

She said, "I have goose bumps. He looks just like Skip."

I had no idea who Skip was, but John wrapped his arm around Lucy's shoulders, pulled her to him, and kissed the top of her head.

I liked those kisses. Mama had given them to me all the time, so I liked him right then and there.

"Who's Skip?" John asked.

"The wolf that Aunt Eve and I used to visit all the time at the zoo when I was little." She leaned toward me. "You're perfect."

Perrrrrfect. Each letter's sound was carried to my nose by the force of her breath, which was sugary sweet, warm, and welcoming. *Bow wow!* At the time, I didn't understand what had come over me, but I leaned on my hind haunches, threw my head back, and howled my heart out. I couldn't stop myself. No kidding. I was howling the joint down. Pretty soon, all the dogs joined in.

John chuckled and said, "Looks like someone just imprinted on you like Jacob in *Twilight*."

Lucy tossed her head back and mimicked my howl. With her small stature, she sounded less like me and more like the yippy lapdog two gates down, but I didn't care. I'd fallen in love with her, novice howl and all.

"I don't know," John said. "He must be twenty pounds already."

I will never forget how they stared at each other for a long while, and it was the first time I ever saw two people talk without saying anything. And I don't mean body language either. We dogs are pretty good about reading body language from a young age; I'm awesome at translating now. But they'd been speaking with their eyes. At the time, I didn't know humans had the talent. Dogs, yes. Humans? No. Sure, I know, at the time my experience had been limited to the families adopting dogs, but I'd learned a lot while observing people during those desperate days.

Except John and Lucy had turned away. I arched my back and tucked my tail, stunned and uncertain. After our connection, they were walking away? What had I missed? What had I done wrong? I looked around to see if any of the other dogs were shocked for me. If John and Lucy weren't going to take me, no one was going to take me.

But then John waved to the caretaker and pointed at my cage. *My cage*. And he said, "We've found our guy."

I weep whenever I think back to that moment, when his strong authoritative finger pointed directly at my cage. When I was the chosen one. When I was enough. The hurt of Soft Voice giving up my family had started to float away under his unwavering strong finger.

The caretaker unlocked the kennel and picked me up.

"He's been alone more than a month. I was beginning to worry about him," he said and glanced at Lucy. "You sure? He's gonna get big. Big as you. And stronger."

Lucy smiled and nodded. "Positive."

He handed me to John. "Meet your special people, little guy."

People don't think dogs cry, but we do. The moment John's arms wrapped around me, what started as a whimper turned to a full-fledged wail of relief, and I was consumed by immediate, unconditional love for them. I remember the way he kissed my head and pulled me close. His breath tickled my ears as he said, "We're your family now. What do you say, boy? Will you help me protect our lady?"

I cried even more against his neck because one human word I knew for sure was "lady." It's what Soft Voice and Strong Voice called Mama.

John chuckled and said, "Family hug!" and all of a sudden I was sandwiched and squirming between John and Lucy, even though Lucy was much shorter than John. They felt like home, and it had been a long time since I had a pack to snuggle. Her face was buried in my back, and she mumbled, "Puppy smell."

"Oh God, you *are* in love, aren't you?" John laughed. "More like pound smell. What should we name him?" John asked. "Stinky?"

Lucy leaned back. "Skip, of course. Now, let's get him home."

Home.

"Skip it is," John said and smiled.

After a few shots and some paperwork, the three of us left that miserable pound as a pack. Then and there, I bow vowed I'd never lose my family again.

8

SKIP

MANIC MONDAY

IF I SEARCH hard for a silver lining, there is one pro to John leaving us: Lucy let me sleep in bed with her for the first time ever. The con, though, is that separation anxiety haunted my dreams. Yeah, dogs dream, and they aren't always filled with treats, balls, sticks, dogs, and sweeping landscapes with luscious green grass. John and Lucy have laughed before, after waking me up, saying my legs were running in my sleep. I have never remembered my dreams. But last night, I dreamt about Soft Voice and losing Mama and my siblings.

Lucy and I lie in bed, eyes wide open, waiting for the alarm to go off. We could get up early, but the sooner we do, the sooner we both have to deal with reality again, and to be honest, I'm already freaking out because a little bit ago I realized that today I'm going to be home alone. Just like that poor little boy at Christmas in the movies. I've been so busy taking care of Lucy, I forgot about what all of this means for me and my daily routine.

I've never liked Monday mornings. What dog would when he's had his masters home with him all weekend? But today? Today? This is going to be my worst Monday morning ever. Sadly, I don't think John or Lucy have even considered what's going to happen to me now.

John won't be coming home to have lunch with me like he used to Monday through Friday. I'm going to be left to my own resources. And Lucy, sweet Lucy, is going out into the world today without me to watch out for her. How many streets will she cross to get to her new job? What if she gets hurt and no one comes to check on me ever again and I die of starvation!

My nose starts to sweat. *Oh Dog, take me now.*

Even though we are both waiting for it, the alarm clock startles us.

Lucy groans as she turns on the lamp.

Dang! I take one look at her and yelp. All the cater-wauling hasn't been kind to her. Her eyes are narrow slits, and the skin under her eyes and on her cheeks has taken on a purplish hue. She can't go out into the world like that. She's gonna scare more people than *I* usually do. First impressions are practically irreversible in both human and canine society.

As Lucy climbs out of bed and moves away from me, I am overwhelmed by a sense of loss, a deep-rooted belief that the end is near. Like when Mama was taken. Lucy's going to leave me, and I don't know her exit cues. I don't know which steps lead to the next and which is the final sign that she is leaving me for the day. I had only ever paid attention to John's morning routine because he was always the last one out the door. I knew when Lucy was leaving only because she kissed John on her way out. With no John, how will I know? John's final cue was settling his leather shoulder bag across his chest. Lucy could be leaving within seconds after my walk or in over an hour. I can't even prepare myself or psych myself up properly.

Are those my teeth chattering? My tongue curls inward, and I have a hard time swallowing, so I gag. *What's happening to me?* My instincts tell me that I'll never see Lucy again if we don't stick together today. My legs tremble as I jump to the floor and follow her every move as she throws on her sweats and slips on her boots.

You can't leave me.

"Skip, honey, move." Her voice is hoarse. She scrounges in the freezer for an ice cube, wrapping half in a paper towel to protect her fingers, and she pushes the exposed portion against her eyes. "Let's go," she says and points toward the door.

I grab my leash. Just like yesterday, she takes it but doesn't use it. And, once again, she doesn't bother to see if Manny and Tank might be about: proof to me that she's still not paying attention to our safety.

I hesitate, trying to sniff and see if the coast is clear for us, but she snarls at me, "Go."

I'm too obsessed with the pitfalls of our day to feel the sting in her bark.

We are lucky. Manny and Tank aren't about. When we step out into the cool air, I take huge breaths and gain some clarity.

Okay. I know what I need to do. I need to make Lucy stay home with me. It's too soon. All of this is too new. I know she needs to work and her new job is important to her, but staying alive has to be our priority. She just can't leave me today. When we get home, I'm not going to eat any of my food. She'll know something's wrong with me because I never ever pass up food unless I'm sick, and she'll have to stay home and take care of me. Where she'll be safe. Where I will be sick but not anxious. And I don't even need to pretend because I feel like dog crap.

9

LUCY
JUST LUCY

WHEN SHE WAS LITTLE, Lucy set a goal to have two things in life. First on the list was true love. That's how several years of Aunt Eve's bedtime stories, aka "censored read-alouds for little princesses" of her Harlequin Romances, had influenced Lucy. True love would materialize in the form of an insanely rich Parisian businessman with *savoir faire* or perhaps as an Australian cattle rancher. But by the time Lucy was twelve, she gave up on the idea of marrying both a monsieur and an Australian once she realized how far he'd take her from Mom and Aunt Eve. And when she met John at the age of twenty-two while researching materials in the law library for her college social work paper, her French and Aussie-forfeiture were solidified. John was the one for her.

Second, she had sworn she would have a pet wolf one day (or at least a look-alike). She and Aunt Eve kept a weekly date with the wolves at the local zoo. They'd pack a peanut butter and jelly sandwich into her *Care Bears* lunch pail and a romance novel in Aunt Eve's purse and spend three hours every Sunday morning reading about love and watching the playful antics of the monogamous wolves. Some families went to church on Sunday morning, but they went to the zoo while Mom usually stayed home for some quiet time. Of course, as Lucy matured she stopped banking on such childhood dreams, so as far as she was concerned, it had been serendipitous when she and John found Skip on their third anniversary. Her little girl dreams had come true. Or so she thought.

Now she was a thirty-two-year-old woman navigating the ins and outs of the Broken Hearts Club, an experience most of her friends had battled and survived in high school or college. She had been a late bloomer and never dated in high school. But she should have at least *tried* to date. That way she might have had some personal exposure to heartbreak. She could have succumbed to hysterics, slept all day, spilled her guts via poetry in college ruled notebooks, and eventually learned that a broken heart wouldn't truly kill her.

I'm dying inside. When will I stop crying?

How does a responsible adult behave after having her heart torn out and dreams crushed? If she were younger, would she feel more resilient? Thinking back on the friendships that had dropped off over the years, she realized she had been such a stupid friend. She, the one with zero experience with heartache, had told so many bereft friends to "show your ex the hand," and to move on, or that, "he isn't your soul mate. Cut him loose." How many times had she preached and quoted *He's Just Not That Into You* by Greg Behrendt to friends or "gifted" them the book, saying, "Read this," whenever their relationships went down the tubes? When friends took their jerks back, Lucy wasn't always surprised, but she'd thought they were being a little pathetic. What an arrogant twit she'd been, assuming she and John were the exception.

Who was being pathetic now? She was.

Because if John walked in the door right now and said he'd made a huge mistake, she wouldn't hesitate to take him back.

They had invested so much time in their relationship. They'd shared so many good things. Sometimes relationships took work, and that was what they needed to do, the work. After all, John had been *into* her for a decade.

Take that Greg Behrendt!

There would be a wedding and a honeymoon to cancel, though, if he wouldn't do the work with her.

Technically, the wedding would be easy to cancel. *Or reschedule.* They'd made arrangements to get married at the courthouse, followed by a picnic at Golden Gate Park. The invitations, all thirty of them, were addressed but hadn't been mailed yet, and they were now shoved in a drawer of the entertainment center where she didn't have to look at them.

He just has to come around in a few days, realize he was anxious for no reason, and there will be no need to cancel their entire future. No need to tell friends he left her. No need to tell Mom, who'd always questioned John's sincerity because Mom questioned all men's sincerity. No need for a chorus of *I-told-you-so's.*

But what if he doesn't?

How long could she wait for him to come to his senses? She'd wait forever. *Yep. Pathetic.*

The honeymoon was another matter. To save money, they'd prepaid for a walkabout in Australia with a hiking tour group. It cost a lot of money, but they'd "only get married once," they'd said. *Puke.* That was what the idea of calling the agent about the cancellation policy made her want to do. Puke with an Australian accent.

The only upside was she could use the money because John hadn't said anything about paying his share of the rent or bills, and she'd been too shocked to challenge him about the lease. She'd taken a pay cut moving from the hospital to Golden Years, the private assisted living center. So much for swearing she'd never be financially strained like her mom and Aunt Eve had been.

Not having enough money and resources to be independent scared the snot out of her. She was going to break out in hives. *Right now.* If there had ever been a time she could use a winning lottery ticket, it was today.

She couldn't sleep last night, so she had lain awake all night and considered her choices. Actually, her choice. Singular. The only way to get John back would be to give him the time and space he thought he needed. She knew him better than anyone, didn't she? He'd be back. They loved each other.

Skip followed her to the bathroom and took the entire floor as he plopped down at her feet, looking up at her with his big sad eyes.

If dogs could talk, what would Skip say right now?

Lucy closed her eyes and leaned against the sink. Her bare foot sank into Skip's fur-covered belly as she rubbed gently. He'd been underfoot all morning. He hadn't touched his food, and his stomach gurgled. From time to time, he would open his mouth wide to gag.

Poor Skip. She was a horrible mom. She would be leaving him alone all day. A big dog in a small apartment was not a good idea. That had never been a problem when John was checking in during the day. But what could she do? When she and John had first brought him home years ago, it had taken a few months to assure him they'd never abandon him. He hadn't had separation anxiety in years. Would his abandonment issues resurface? As a puppy, Skip had howled non-stop whenever they left. How would his fears manifest as an adult dog?

If she could wait a week to start her new job, she would. In fact, she'd happily crawl into bed with Skip, cry all day, and flip ahead three hundred and sixty-five pages in *The Year of Lucy & John* to read the last page, just like Aunt Eve had taught her to do with the romance novels.

Aunt Eve used to say, "You always need to know from page one who the heroine is going to end up with. It makes the story better."

If she could just know they would end up together, she could take his absence one day at a time, and she could simply miss him rather than mourn the loss of their relationship and her frigging identity.

She was Lucy of John-and-Lucy. Not "Just Lucy."

Braving the mirror, she remembered too late that mirrors don't lie. *Talk about adding insult to injury.* Her skin was beyond blotchy from the flood of tears she'd been mopping off her face. Though she didn't want her mom to suspect any problems, she was the only person Lucy knew who understood colors so well. She texted her.

Mom, what color offsets purple?

Mom: *As in paint or skin?*

Just in general.

Mom: *Why?*

A friend is asking.

Mom: *At 7 a.m.?*

Never mind.

Mom: *Browns, tans. If face, friend should show cleavage. Distracts men from face.*

Normally, her mother's rampant generalizations about the male population annoyed her, but desperate needs called for desperate measures. In this case, she could swallow the generalization. Lucy lifted and squeezed her smaller-than-she'd-prefer-but-she-never-used-to-care-because-John-liked-them boobs together. Nurse scrubs didn't allow for cleavage, and *Booby Lucy* wasn't the first impression she wanted to strike with her new patients and coworkers anyway. Not that looking like Barney the dinosaur was going to help. She hoped that none of the senior citizens, who possessed years of life experience and wisdom, would point and shout, "I know that look! Brokenhearted woman walking!"

She looked at Skip. "Please tell me I didn't look this bad when your dad was here last night."

He sighed.

"So I did. Just wonderful." She caked on foundation and powder. No blush needed today, but waterproof mascara was a must.

Lucy and John had met at the college law library while doing some research for her minor, and it had been love at first sight. They'd been inseparable, and she'd thought she'd never be alone again. At the time, John was just ending a long-distance relationship with his high school girlfriend, whom he hadn't seen in several months.

When Lucy had told her mom how she met John, her mom said, "Typical Tarzan."

"Tarzan?" Lucy had asked.

"Men never let go of one vine until they've grabbed hold of another."

"I'm not a vine!" Lucy had shouted, sick of her mom's cynicism toward men. "He's not like that. Our relationship isn't like that." She wasn't like her mom. John was not like her mom's men.

Quantity did not an expert make. Her mom, who'd had too many boyfriends to count, believed she had all men figured out. Lucy had spent her childhood with Mama Man-Hater and Aunt Hopeless Romantic, and she'd always hoped for a TV-perfect family like the Keatons or the Seavers.

Aunt Eve had jumped in to defend Lucy. "Ignore your mother. True love is everlasting."

"Thank you, Aunt Eve."

Her mom had rolled her eyes. "You'll see. Nothing is everlasting."

Lucy had shouted back, "No! You'll see!"

Thoughts of the vine convo were freaking her out. *Am I a vine now?* No. Impossible. She would have known if John had met someone else. John was not a Tarzan!

Skip whimpered at her feet.

Lucy looked toward the ceiling. *Universe, please bring John back to us. I'll do anything. I won't fall asleep on the couch when we're watching a movie. I'll wear more lingerie and makeup. I'll exercise and finally lose my back fat. I'll learn to cook. I'll start running with him. I'll shave my legs every day. I'll make an effort to make more friends and be more social. I'll give him more time alone at home. I won't throw a fit over a cake. Just bring him back to us, and I will change.*

Not that John had ever asked for any of those things.

Well, except the cake thing.

Skip followed her to the bedroom, where she scrounged through her nursing scrubs. *Voila!* She pulled out a tan sct.

He climbed up on the bed as she changed. When her head cleared the tan shirt, he was staring her in the eyes.

As if she didn't feel bad enough. "Please don't stare at mc likc that," shc said.

Skip didn't budge.

"Good dogs don't stare. Go eat your food."

He ignored her and only plopped down on the bed and looked up at her with big brown pitiful eyes.

"Please? Please go and eat. I can't stay home with you today, as much as I wish to death I could. And I can't worry about you right now. I have to pretend to have my crap together today." She wished she were going to her old job. If it were her old job, she could do it blindfolded and escape into the routine.

Skip took his time getting off the bed and ambled away from her.

"Good dog," she said, but he didn't turn toward his food in the kitchen as she expected. Instead, he lay down against the front door, blocking it. As if to say, *You're not leaving this house.*

She couldn't blame him for not wanting to be alone any more than she did. Seriously, who in their right mind wanted to be alone? *Oh, John.*

Last night before Skip went barking nuts, John had said, "I don't want to be like my parents."

What did his parents' relationship have to do with them? They were absolutely nothing like his parents. *Not even close.* His dad had an affair when John was a senior in high school.

His dad. Tarzan.

With that one small connection, Lucy's world tipped.

Skip darted back to her side.

She leaned on him and lowered herself to the bed.

His ears stood straight up, and he was panting and drooling all over her scrubs.

"Is John having an affair?" she asked Skip.

Skip looked away but buried his snout between her knees.

Something clicked into place, and she could only hear Judge Judy's warning: *If something doesn't make sense, it's not true.* Lucy's anger almost gave way to relief. Anger doesn't feel as helpless as grief. *Had he cheated on her? Is that what this is all about?*

It made no sense that John wanted to be alone. It made no sense, after all this time, to compare their relationship to that of his parents for *no* reason.

Hands shaking, she texted John: *Why did you bring up your parents last night? Did you cheat on me?*

Teeth chattering, she prayed she was wrong. She couldn't believe that he'd ever cheat. Cheating would change everything because then he wouldn't be the man she thought he was. Cheaters played with other people's lives. He better not ignore her, leaving her to go mad all day with this horrible suspicion.

He responded within seconds: *No.*

Lucy fell back on her bed.

"Thank God. Skip, he didn't cheat." She held up her phone to the room as if Skip and the universe could read it. Her anger evaporated. *Oh my God. I just accused John of cheating.* Shame and guilt settled in. Where was her confidence? How could she stoop so low as to vilify him for wanting time alone. It had taken John years to forgive his dad for the affair, and he and his father still didn't talk about it. Just because she didn't understand why he wanted to be alone didn't give her the right to turn into a paranoid jealous shrew and compare him to a man he didn't respect. *Real attractive.*

Her phone beeped. A text.

John: *What about Skip today?*

What a relief. She hadn't offended him too much if he was still texting her, and at least he was worried about Skip, if not her. She acted on her earlier promise to the universe. Instead of asking him for help with Skip, she lied: *I've made arrangements.*

If John needed time alone, she needed to give him time alone. What choice did she have?

She lowered her nose to Skip's. "I'm going to leave the back door to the yard open for you. I'll tell the neighbors that John is away on business. And I'll check on you during lunch."

Lucy texted John: *I'm sorry. I know you're nothing like your dad.*

No reply.

Lucy finished getting ready for work, and just as she grabbed her purse, her cell phone dinged twice. She recognized the tone as calendar reminders. She didn't want to look. She knew from the tailored ringtones that they'd be about her wedding or honeymoon.

But it was worse than she thought. Yes, one was a reminder that she had five months to confirm seats for their flights to Australia, and "Woo hoo!" was typed next to it. *Yeah, right.* At the time, she'd had so much fun adding it to her calendar. She hadn't realized how

annoying it would be to see *woo hoo* when she was posi-
tively boo hoo.

But the second reminder was terrifying: Aunt Eve was
supposed to visit Friday and stay for the weekend to see the
wedding dresses Lucy liked.

Oh God!

She couldn't deal with Aunt Eve's visit right now. She
was on the verge of being late for her new job.

"Skip, try not to trip over Manny's junk and kill yourself
on the way outside. And I'll be back at lunch."

But Skip had resumed his barricade at the door.

"Up," she said.

He didn't budge.

Lucy knew how stubborn he could be, so she grabbed
his front paws and pulled him, sliding him across the wood
floors and down the hallway. "Don't look so innocent while
I drag you, buddy," Lucy said, breathing heavily. It took all
her strength to move him, and she was sweating by the time
she made enough room to open the door.

"I don't have a choice! I have to go! Who's going to pay
the bills? Huh?"

He just groaned and looked at her as if saying, *Dog
hater.*

Lucy sighed. "I hate this more than you do."

He howled once but stopped as she pulled the front door
closed behind her.

And to think earlier she was wondering what he'd say if
he could talk. Hmph. It would probably break her heart if he
could.

Welcome to single dog-motherhood.

She walked across the hall and knocked on Manny's
door, something she had never thought she'd do voluntarily.

Manny opened his door, raised his eyebrows, and mumbled around his toothbrush. "What do you want?"

They'd never been friendly, so no point in starting now. Though she could use a little kindness right now.

"John's away on business, and I have to leave Skip for the day. I left the back door open for him. You should know in case you want to let Tank out."

He paused, and if she knew him better, she might think his look was one of disbelief. Had he seen John leaving with his suitcases? His boxes? *Don't blush. Not in front of him.*

But he only said, "Okay." He closed the door in her face.

She really didn't like the man. No matter how "nice" he was to look at. She'd leave him to other women to ogle and let them think he was something special. Like the young women she often saw leaving his apartment in the mornings. They could have him. Besides, his apartment was probably piled high with junk.

She walked down one flight of stairs. Mrs. Brighton's teenage son, Thomas, opened the door when she knocked. She thought he was on the autism spectrum, but she'd never asked, and despite being a nurse, she tried not to diagnose people. Well, except the womanizing and hoarding Manny; he deserved it. She and John had always kept to themselves and didn't have relationships with the neighbors. But during the school year, Thomas always hopped on a private bus that stopped in front of the apartment building. He had never talked to Lucy or John, but he always said hi to Skip when he saw him.

Even now, he was staring at the floor as he shouted, "Mom! The crying woman upstairs is here."

Could the floor just swallow her up already? An epic

earthquake would be welcome.

Mrs. Brighton rushed down the hall to her door, turning Thomas around by his shoulders and ushering him to the living room. "Lucy, I'm so sorry. He can't help himself. He has good hearing, and—"

Lucy interrupted out of self-preservation. "It's okay." Her current composure was hard won. As she began her lie about John being away for work, she paused because all of a sudden tears were a-coming again.

Mrs. Brighton reached out and squeezed her wrist. "No need to explain. We saw him moving out."

No need to explain. Everyone seemed fine with no explanation except Lucy. John certainly wasn't explaining anything. Lucy swallowed and squared her shoulders. She had no interest in confiding in her neighbor anyway. *Pull yourself together. You have a job to do.* "I've left the back door open for Skip. Just for today."

Mrs. Brighton ignored her false bravado and said, "You'll meet someone new."

And there it was. The idea that someone was replaceable. She or John, it didn't matter which one. Lucy knew Mrs. Brighton meant well, but she was so angry at the woman's arrogance and intrusion into her fears that she snapped. "You don't know what you're talking about." She marched out of her building.

Why? Why tell someone who is clearly heartbroken that they will meet someone new?

She'd show Mrs. Brighton. *She* didn't need to "meet someone new." John would be back.

Instead of a new someone, she had a new mantra: *If you love someone, set him free. If he comes back, it's meant to be.*

10

SKIP

HOME ALONE REMEDIES

TO QUOTE THE GREAT DANE, Scooby: *Ruh-roh.* Lucy has left me to my own devices. I could just die.

After everything I've done for her this weekend! Not once did I leave her side, and I chose her over John. I chose *her*. But the second I'm the one who's sick and afraid to be alone, *poof*, she's gone.

Sure, she left the back door open like she said she would. But so what? I can urinate outside, great. That's not the point. I'm a grown dog who can hold his water. Heck, I can hold it all day if necessary. I could give a camel a run for his money if I wanted. The point is that I hate to be alone all day. Let's face it, I'm more loyal than Lucy and John put together. Well, except for the other woman thingy. That's a big flaw on the canine loyalty spectrum.

Sigh. Am I being melodramatic?

Maybe it's not fair of me to expect her to stay home from her first day of work and ensure the safety of both our lives. Someone has to put food in my bowl and a roof over my head.

When she asked me if John had cheated on her and started punching away on her phone (I hate that stupid noise of her nail against the screen, by the way), I thought I was going to die of a heart attack. Did you know that a dog's heart can beat twice as fast as a human's when *nothing* is stressing us out? This is it, I thought, the time of reckoning. But it wasn't. John didn't cave. *Whew!*

Lucy's voice carries as she speaks to Manny and then Mrs. Brighton downstairs. I try to resist the pull of the front window, where I normally sit on the ottoman and watch the sidewalk below, but you can't teach an old dog new tricks, and being stubborn and pouting doesn't work without an audience, so I trot to my post. Besides, what else am I going to do all morning?

My spot at the window is my favorite at home because I can see Lucy (and John, before) off to work, and I know everything that's happening on my avenue. I've neglected my post the last few days for obvious reasons.

Wait, where is my ottoman? My seat isn't in position beneath the window. John always used to push the furniture against the window for me to sit on before heading off to work. I need it so I can sit comfortably and high while on guard duty. *Surprise, surprise.* Lucy didn't hook me up. Fine, I'll push it to the window myself. But I can't find it when I walk around the room. My ottoman is gone. John took my favorite seat! Did he take it for Bunny to use?

Damn you, John! The ottoman was mine. Mine! Is nothing sacred? Have I earned no respect?

By the time I get back to the window, I've missed Lucy's exit from the building. Unbelievable. How many disruptions can I take? I'm only canine, people.

What about my responsibilities as a member of the neighborhood watch? I can't be expected to be on my feet all day. Just because John is gone, and he won't be taking me to the monthly meeting, it doesn't mean that I want to shirk my duties. Sure, we live in a nice neighborhood, and Lucy always remarks how we live on the safest street because nothing criminal ever happens. But let's be honest, *I* have something to do with that. If a stranger walks down my street, I make sure they hear me and see me from my perch, safely from behind my window. I'm already big, but with the additional height of my ottoman, I bet I look like the Abominable Snowman in that Christmas movie with the reindeer. A simple bark or howl sends strangers a message: *I see you. No crime on my watch!*

I'm a tall dog and can see out the window without the ottoman, but I'd rather not stand all day. I like to be comfortable while I look around. But now, without my seat, I have to brace my front paws on the windowsill, which Lucy hates, especially if I've just come back from a walk or it's raining outside and I get my paw prints on the white paint. In the standing position, I have to lean close to the window, and my breath fogs it up so I have to lick it clean so I can see. Lucy will be annoyed with me for getting spit on the windows. Last time it happened, she grimaced and said, "Your spit is like liquid shellac, Skip." *Whatever.* That's what she gets for leaving me today.

Yeah, I know. I've been alone before, but this is different. I'm not convinced she'll come home for lunch. When she promised, her voice had that lilt to it where her sentence sounded wide and slow at first but grew narrow and fast toward the end. She also lifted her eyebrows high on her forehead, and that's always a bad sign, an "I'm not positive" sign. This has happened every time Lucy and John have taken a vacation without me, leaving me at Aunt Eve's. They've smiled, lifted their brows, and said, "We'll be right back. Be good." *Right back my ass.* They were gone forever. Every time.

Lucy and I both know she isn't sure she will come home for lunch, at least not at lunchtime as I know it. I hope she comes home again period; there are streets to cross without my assistance. My routine has gone to hell. And this isn't easy for dogs. We have a very sophisticated body clock if I do say so myself. So much better than a human's. But if she loves me, Lucy will put her foot down and train her new boss that she must get home every lunch to be with the (almost) best dog in the world. Like John trained his boss. John never missed lunch. Not once.

I'm obsessing again.

I try to calm myself the heck down by getting to work. I watch the usual happenings outdoors. The routines give me comfort. The old Asian couple across the street take their morning walk. The large family (John doesn't understand "how the parents can afford all those children in this expensive city") climbs into their minivan and takes off. Manny leaves and comes back with Tank, a tall coffee, and a white pastry bag as usual. A few regulars don't show up, but I don't know if I missed them somehow or if they are messing with my routine too.

I just want my old life back. It was a good reliable daily life.

Thomas's bus has arrived to pick him up for school. What a relief. As the doors swing open, he runs and jumps on the first step, and turns to wave at me. I bark back. We do this every school day.

He's a nice young man. Different and better than most people I come into contact with, even at the dog park. I haven't quite put my paw on what makes him different because I haven't spent enough time with him. I only see him in passing in the hallways, and he moves fast because I don't think he likes people. But he likes routine as much as I do. I know because his bus returns the same time every day, after I've had my lunch and walk with John and have taken my afternoon nap. I always wake up when I hear his bus coming down the street. It has squeaky brakes, and the driver starts braking three houses down. I always go to the window, watch for Thomas to get off the bus, and wait for him to wave at me. I always bark back. Then he goes to his apartment, where he rings his own doorbell three times before he goes inside. The ringing used to drive me bonkers, but now I look forward to the noise. Soon after the three rings, he always cooks a grilled cheese sandwich. Sometimes it's toasted pizza, but usually grilled cheese. Both smell delicious. Next he plays a video game until his mom comes home. The frequency is just right, and I can hear the *pings* and *zooms* through the floor. And at that point, I used to expect John home shortly thereafter for the night. Lucy always arrived later, but I don't know about her new hours yet.

Thomas just left for the day, so I have a lot of time on my paws. Time is dragging. *Hum dee dum.*

Manny came back with coffee and breakfast. Check.

Thomas is off to school. Check.

Thomas's mom has left. Check.

Now it's waiting-for-Lucy time. My hind legs and back

are tired from leaning on the sill. I drop to all fours and look around our small apartment. Maybe standing on one of the couch pillows will help. I drag one off the couch. I've never touched it before. *Oooh, this is nice.* The leather is so soft and malleable. I like the sensation of the fabric encasing my bicuspids. It tastes like John and Lucy smell. I close my jaw a bit more, and my teeth sink into it.

Oh man, the sensation is so gratifying, my fur stands up like the goose bumps Lucy gets sometimes when John is rubbing her shoulders or lightly brushing her back with his fingertips. I dig my teeth in, and there is a satisfying *crunch* and a *puff* of air in my mouth that tickles and almost makes me sneeze. I open my mouth and bite again. *Crunch. Puff.* This is addictive. Before I know it, the entire pillow is punctured. But I feel so relaxed, just like when John or Lucy brush my fur or rub my stomach.

I am reminded of the times Lucy has received a package wrapped in that plastic with lots of little air bubbles. The sound of her popping them makes me and John want to climb out of our skins, but she always says, "But it feels so satisfying. Like cheap therapy."

Now I get it. I grab another pillow for some cheap therapy.

Crunch. Puff. Crunch. Puff. Aaaaaaaah. Turns out pillow chewing helps me get in the Now, but not in the scary I'm-all-alone Now. I'm in the I-couldn't-chew-on-this-if-I-wasn't-alone Now.

I wonder what little humans who aren't in school do alone all day when their parents go to work. I bet when they're sick, their parents don't desert them.

Crunch. Puff. Crunch. Puff.

As I lie on the floor and go through the pillows, air

puffing in my mouth and across my ears, I miss the noise of the mailman entering the building and climbing the stairs to our apartment. I jump with fright when he starts shoving the mail through my door's mail slot. I hate surprises, and my anxiety takes flight again. How dare he destroy my peace? I was so happy, so zen with my pillows! I rush to the mail flap and claw at it, tearing some paper from his grip. Some of the door paint is chipping away and shooting this way and that under my ferocious activity, but I don't stop. A dog's got to do what a dog's got to do.

"Whoa! What's gotten into you, fella?" the mailman asks through the door. "Do that again, and I'm giving your owners an orange warning card. They won't be happy with you if I stop delivering their mail."

The hair rises on my neck. *Are you threatening me? Lucy? Come in and deliver the warning card right now. I dare you.*

He shoves in more paper, so I grab it with my teeth. I swivel my head from side to side. Saliva and mail go flying. All the kinks in my neck loosen up. I drop my mail and glare at the flap for more, but he has finished invading my territory. I showed him. He's moved on to Manny's. He gets no problems from Tank, but why would he? Manny is there to protect them.

I stare at the paper carnage around me. Maybe I got a little carried away. Lucy's going to be mad because she likes getting mail. Thumbing through the envelopes and catalogs is the first thing she does when she gets home.

I use my snout to push the mail into one pile. It's worse for the wear. A white tip is poking out from underneath the hallway chest, but when I try to retrieve it with my paw and then my tongue, I sneeze from the dust, and the mail disappears under the chest. Hope it isn't important.

The mail has worn me out. Drained, I cuddle up with the scraps of leather and foam and close my eyes. I hope I wake up to Lucy's face.

11

LUCY

NEW THRESHOLD

"You coming in, Lucy, or have you changed your mind?" Dr. Doug Ryan smiled at Lucy through her car window.

Lucy stared for a second at her new boss before having the common sense to start moving and opening her door. She'd waited years for this job. Now that she was here, she'd give anything for her former confidence at her former job in her former life.

She got out and plastered on a professional smile. "Good morning," she said with excitement she didn't feel. She removed her sunglasses.

Dr. Ryan stepped back. "Whoa. What happened to you?"

"Strawberry allergy." She shouldn't lie to her boss on her first day, but telling him that she'd been sobbing uncontrollably for days because her fiancé left her didn't seem smart either. Who wanted an unstable new employee?

"Allergy to strawberries? Okay," he said, "I'll take that for now."

She wouldn't be changing her story. She had no intention of telling him about John. Lucy had known Dr. Ryan for several years. He used to be the chief doctor in trauma at San Francisco General, and she had gotten to know him on both a professional and personal level. She knew his wife and his two young children. He knew John from holiday parties. So she was delighted when he'd called her four months ago about the opportunity to work for the privately run assisted living center. She'd always liked how Dr. Ryan was straight and to the point, but she was relieved when he let her red, puffy face go.

Although Lucy was familiar with the property after multiple interviews, she was still nervous as the doors slid open and they walked in together. What if she couldn't do a great job? Dr. Ryan reintroduced her to the front desk staff, Sheila and Derek. They took a second look at her face but were polite enough not to ask what had happened. She pointed to her cheeks to control any speculation. "Strawberry allergy."

As she and Dr. Ryan walked down the hall, Lucy felt a twinge of hope. This was all new, nothing to do with John, and everything to do with her career performance. *All hers*. And while she might not have the confidence she'd had in her former position, she'd be distracted by her new responsibilities in all the right ways: learning the ropes, generating ideas, fixing things. Yes, this was going to be a reprieve from the mess of her life. She could compartmentalize her life: *Do great at work. Suck at home.*

"Let me show you your office; then we can get started," Dr. Ryan said.

As they reached her office, a man in his sixties with a buzz cut, clad in a T-shirt, overalls, and cowboy boots stepped into the hall, carrying old fluorescent light tubes.

His "don't mess with me" expression and the gigantic buzzard and naked woman tattooed on his forearm made Lucy want to take a step back, but she didn't.

Are they hiring ex-cons here? Because that's what he looked like.

"Hey, Walter," Dr. Ryan said.

Walter lifted up the old lights and nodded toward the office behind him. "Last switch to LED."

"Thanks for spearheading the savings, Walter," Dr. Ryan said.

An ex-con who cares about the planet and energy efficiency?

"This is Lucy Bell, our new Wellness Director. Lucy, Walter is our handyman extraordinaire."

"You look like hell," Walter said and continued down the hall.

Lucy normally liked coworkers who didn't beat around the bush, but she would happily avoid the "handyman extraordinaire" in the future.

"Don't worry, he grows on you," Dr. Ryan said and winked.

She doubted it.

"He's been working here for decades. The staff and residents love him."

She was ready to meet the residents. Ready to get busy.

Before she could step inside her new office, Dr. Ryan stopped her. "It's great to have you on the team again. This morning you'll be in orientation for human resources purposes. Then, assuming you can stay for lunch, we've planned a Resident Town Hall to introduce you to the staff and the residents. I hope you like lasagna. It's a favorite around here."

Shoot. She needed to walk Skip at lunch, but she didn't want to explain her situation or be problematic on her first day. Getting the job had been so important to her, and she'd only get this one chance to make a first impression with her new team and the clients.

But Skip . . . The two of them would have to figure out life together and how to make their new situation work. For now, there was nothing she could do. Thank goodness she'd left the back door open for him.

She could run home after lunch real quick. Should she text John to see what time he normally went home for lunch to walk Skip in the past? No. She needed to leave him alone. Not reach for excuses to contact him. The sooner he was done being alone, the sooner she and Skip could be done being alone too. Plus, she'd already told John she had Skip covered.

Dr. Ryan waved Lucy forward. "So here's your office. Ready to cross the threshold?"

With her back to him, she smiled. A bittersweet moment for sure, but still her moment. She'd waited so long for this career move, and though it was a threshold she'd meant to share with John, she was resolved to rock this new opportunity. She was an excellent nurse. She had earned this job on her own. No one could take this experience away from her except herself. *You've got this*. She crossed the threshold.

12

SKIP

LIFE STINKS

A NOISE AWAKENS ME. My internal clock tells me it's too soon for lunch with Lucy, though the sooner I see her the better.

A sound again.

Someone is nearby, maybe in my house. Snapping out of my daze, I rush to the front door and sniff the air. No one. But whoever is causing the ruckus that woke me stinks to "high heaven" as I've heard Mrs. Brighton say from time to time through the floorboards. I am reminded of the skunk I met when I was two years old. John had taken me for a long walk at the nearby golf course after hours, and when the skunk crossed the green, I was off leash, and John's warning came too late. Too late for all of us.

People who've never had a loved one sprayed by a skunk can't appreciate how the assault is a family affair.

John and I had rushed home. He and Lucy tried everything to clean me up: tomato juice, vinegar, and even John's shaving soap. I had more baths in one week than I'd had in a lifetime, and I still smelled like *L'Eau de Skunk Stink*: a contradictory blend of marijuana (like the old man in Apartment Number Two smokes "for medicinal reasons" according to Nurse Lucy), roofing tar prominently used in the Bay Area, fetid mud, and toilet bowl cleaner (which I once drank when Lucy forgot to flush the toilet after cleaning it. That was not a good day for me).

Apartment Number Two must be tainting my olfactory skills because even though the municipal golf course is nearby, a skunk's never been near our apartment.

There! Again, the noise.

The sound is coming from the back door landing. I freeze with ears pointed straight up, hackles raised, and tail high and prominent; it's a warning flag to all who dare approach me. I hope it's that rotten stinking stray cat. Maybe he tiptoed up the stairs, unaware that for the first time ever, my door is open.

Lucy calls him Tom. She says he's homeless and that his territorial spray is as foul as a lion she used to visit at the zoo, only the lion could spray up to ten feet. Ten feet! Lucy said there had even been a warning sign for visitors to stand back.

Can you imagine? Ten feet? I'd love to be able to mark my territory from ten feet away. I'd own prime pooch real estate in San Francisco. I'd be known as *Ten Foot Skip*, and believe me, in a neighborhood where there are dogs who are known for being scared of their own farts, eating poop, vomiting in their master's lap, or ingesting their owner's undies, I'd like to be known for something more significant.

My predatory proclivities kick into high gear. I'd love to finally catch that rank stupid cat. John has never let me chase him. He blames Manny for the cat coming around because "he might as well be hoarding litter boxes with those dead plants and pots" and so "it serves him right." But Lucy has said, "If you get a chance, Skip, scare him off. I won't tell." Maybe she's been joking because she likes animals so much, but *maybe* she *hasn't*. There might be one speck of happiness about being deserted today after all: *I can finally get that cat.*

I creep through the kitchen, taking my time so I can hear the interloper's progress. *Amateur.* He's growing louder with confidence. Though I've never hunted like my ancestors, my instincts tell me that overconfidence is my prey's rookie move.

My dog food is now being looted. We've always kept the bag on the landing. I would recognize the crackling of that bag and the rumble of those kibbles anywhere. John and Lucy have never once had to call me for mealtime. The shift of the bag and a sliding measuring cup are all I need to hear, and I'm at my bowl waiting for them.

Now I wait for the perfect moment to pounce into the doorway and surprise my quarry. I lunge out the door. Tom's faster than Cheetah, the Dalmatian at the dog park, and I only have enough time to glimpse black and white. Then I only see red. *How dare you enter my domain? How dare you touch my food?*

I wish Lucy could see me now. I must look amazing whipping down the four flights of narrow stairs, jumping over Manny's piles, and gaining on the burglar. The door to the yard is ajar enough for him to squeeze through without stopping, the same way he must have entered. I don't hesitate. I slam the door wide open, and I catch up to the culprit at the fence corner.

Busted! Now what are you going to do, you stupid cat?

But I stare into the eyes of no cat. No face either. The

white stripe against the black with the rising tail do not penetrate my thick skull quickly enough. It's a frigging skunk! The horror. The funk. There's nothing medicinal about the vile odor one foot from my face.

Time all but stops as I wait for what I don't have time to turn tail and escape. The hunter has become the hunted. One of the great ironies of being a dog is that I will go out of my way to sniff butts of every other living creature, and the one animal that loves to share its ass freely is a skunk. Mother Nature has a sense of humor, and Mother Nature's evil spawn lets me have it.

EEEEOOOOWWWW!

My eyes are going to pop out of my head. My nose is on fire. I gag as if I'm being forced to drink scalding roof tar. I crash to the concrete patio, rolling frantically, trying to wipe away the killer juice, but it just spreads like oil.

It's eating me alive! Alive!

The miscreant is probably watching me writhe in pain, pleased with himself for having such a superpower. My eyes and nose deluged with his chemical warfare, I have no way of knowing if he has left or if he's going to attack again.

I must get out of here. I stumble like a drunk to the building, unable to nose my way there. I labor back up the stairs, and into my apartment. I need hands. These paws are useless under duress. I need to be human in order to wipe this poison off and turn on the shower. *I need you, Lucy!* I jump on her bed that usually smacks of manufactured lavender and roll around until her down comforter wraps around me. I wiggle and shimmy. Some relief! I can open my eyes now.

I'm not permanently blind. I roll and roll, saving the parts of me I can. My snout and head took the brunt of it. I think. I panic and sniff between my legs, but I can't tell if it's just my nose or if my junk reeks too. If both, the dogs at the park aren't going to recognize me for days. My markings will be all messed up. I'm scarred by this smell. I bury my face in Lucy's pillows.

I did this to myself. *Why, oh why, did I rush into the chase?*

The taste in my mouth is the worst thing I've ever eaten, even worse than the medicine Lucy made me take when I had a tapeworm. Water. I must get to water. I just want to douse my tongue in it. I jump off the bed and rush into the kitchen for a drink from my water bowl, but just as I get there, Manny steps out of his back door onto our shared landing. And, oh man, if looks can kill, I'm a goner.

13

SKIP

THE TRUTH HURTS

MANNY POINTS DOWNSTAIRS. "OUT!"

No way, I'm not going back out there. *Are you nuts? The skunk may have gotten his stinky-ass friends. There could be a skunk posse out there. I'm defenseless. If you and Tank have been wanting a piece of me, now's your chance.*

Just then, Tank pokes his head out the door but shakes his head as if trying to dislodge the stink in the air and returns to the safe recesses of his home, which I imagine smells pleasant.

No threat from him.

Manny bends over and inspects the food bag where the skunk had dug in. Despite my excellent hearing, either Manny is an expert mumbler or the skunk has destroyed my sense of hearing. I can't understand what he says.

"Skip," Manny says loud and clear.

I'm sick to my stomach and desperate for water. I ignore Manny and take a drink of water and immediately regret it. The water has triplicated the skunk spray in my nose and mouth. I gag and gag.

Manny! Call 911!

"You bonehead," Manny says. "I'm trying to help you. Come."

What else can I do but follow him downstairs? He's all I've got right now. I'm pissed when he tricks me and locks me in the backyard. I start to cry. *Nobody loves me. I'll be known as Stinky Skip.*

"Quiet," Manny yells from the stairs. "I'll be right back."

Sure you will. I don't even want to be around me right now.

But he returns with a large white bucket, a bottle of dish soap, that brown bottle of fizzy stuff that Lucy is always putting on scratches (thankfully none of mine), and a small box of baking soda.

Based on my limited experience with being sprayed, I run to the hose even though I'm afraid the water will burn my mouth again, but Manny commands me to stay still.

"Never water first," he says. "Multiplies the thiols in the skunk's spray."

Thiols, what? And John always hoses me down first.

Like he can read my mind, Manny continues. "Thiols are a sulfur atom. The other atom in the spray is hydrogen. You need to oxidize the spray to get rid of it. Not throw water at it."

Dude, now is not the time for a chemistry lesson. Save it for John if he comes back. Save me now.

Manny pulls a black garage bag over his head, pushing his head through the seam. He's taller than John, and the plastic covers him down to the crotch of his jeans. He yanks on long yellow plastic gloves and mixes his three ingredients in the industrial-size bucket.

"Sit."

I sit.

His arm disappears into the bucket, and he pulls out a handful of foaming slop.

Oh no. You're not putting that on me. Where's the tomato juice? I shy away from the chemicals and his descending hand, but he uses his free hand to grab my collar.

"Stay." He rubs the cold gooey concoction into the dry fur on my head. The mixture seeps into my eyes, and they begin to sting anew, but not as bad as the skunk thiols. I hear a trillion *pop, pop, pops*. I reflexively lick my upper jaw, and the bitter paste makes me shudder, but the more Manny lathers my dry coat, the more the skunk fades away. And then, as Count von Count from *Sesame Street* would say: *à la Peanut Butter and Jelly Sandwiches*, the smell disappears into thin air. Like magic.

How did he do that? What is this magic elixir? *Manny, you're brilliant. A hero!*

He doesn't stop with my head. After every inch of my fur is frothing, he steps back. I'm pretty sure he's given me a Mohawk hairdo and is laughing at me, but I don't care. *Make me look silly. Go for it. I no longer stink.* I'll take looking like a cockatoo over reeking any day.

He tosses the containers into the now empty bucket, lifts it high by the metal handles, and shakes it until I look up at him. The sun is above him, and while I can't see his face, I can see his halo. My angel.

"See?" he asks. "The 'crap I don't throw out' is the reason I could help you."

Touché, Manny. Touché.

He puts the bucket aside and walks to the hose. "Now it's time for water."

I bark. Happy for the first time in hours.

As he turns to spray me, he pauses and says, "You're both better off without him, you know?"

I know he's talking about John, and I feel a bit defensive. How would he know if we'll be better off without John? I love John, and I'm mostly a loyal dog. But Manny is here. John isn't. *That's that.* I'm feeling back in the Now.

As the rivulets of water wash over me, I am overcome by a sense of well-being, like everything is going to be okay because it dawns on me that I've protected Lucy from the fierce super-skunk. What if the skunk had taken over our home? Lucy's and my sanctuary? Sprayed or not, I protected our territory today. Lucy could have been skunked. She'll be so proud of me, and she'll see how much she needs me. This is the first time since John left us that I'm confident Lucy will recognize my commitment to her. I can hardly wait for her to come home for lunch and find out.

And then there is the way my muscles flexed and my blood surged as I pursued the skunk. I was full of verve and vigor. I can now intuit why my undomesticated ancestors were thrilled by the hunt. Is verve and vigor what drives Tom to be a street cat? His drive to be free to prowl and chase mice? I find myself respecting him, even though less than an hour ago, I wanted to kill him. You know, sometimes you have to hit bottom to see the light. This Skunktastrophe has made me stronger, wiser. Now I know not to rush into a battle but to take my time to scope out the situation. I am a better canine because of this, a better pack member. I can be a better leader to Lucy.

I think Manny is wrong, we aren't better off without John, but we don't have to be worse off either. Lucy and I are still a pack. A micro one right now, but we can make friends. Like Manny.

I smile at him as much as I'm able. Less than an hour ago, he was my enemy, but now he's my friend. Actually, right this second he is my best friend. If John were here, none of this would have happened, and I wouldn't be getting to know the real Manny. I'd been looking at Manny through John's eyes, not my own. Lucy is looking through John's eyes too.

"Shake," Manny says and takes a few steps back. I know he doesn't mean his hand, even though I'm prepared to make the exception for him, and that he wants me to rid my fur of water.

Starting from my snout and moving to the tip of my tail, I jerk and whirl like our washing machine. I don't stop until every drop has splattered the concrete in a five-foot radius.

Manny rinses off the concrete patio then takes off his plastic poncho. He grabs the towel he brought down with him and starts to dry me.

He spreads the towel on our small patch of grass and takes a seat in a plastic lawn chair.

I lie down on the towel and look at him. I pour my heart into my eyes and meet his. *Thank you, Manny.*

"No prob," he says. "Cleanest you'll ever be."

I lick my fur to get rid of the loose hairs. He's right! My fur hasn't been this soft and fluffy since I was a puppy.

"I keep Tank's food out there too. I was just about to get him some. You took the skunk for me and Tank, Skip. Thanks."

Manny digs into his jeans pocket. He pulls out a dried

cow hoof and tosses it at me. I'm in heaven. I never get these sorts of treats because John and Lucy think they stink.

I'm flattered when Manny hangs out with me for some time, his face turned up to the sun. I wonder if Tank will be jealous and if he's watching us from the upstairs window.

I would be. From the top floor, their apartment faces the backyard. Our apartment faces the street. I might be jealous if Lucy were hanging out with another dog like this. My thoughts stray to John, and my stomach hurts a little thinking about him and Bunny.

After a time of silent companionship, Manny stands and stares down at me. "Stay out here until you're dry." But he doesn't leave. He hesitates. His shoulders drop and he frowns, his eyebrows meeting in the center of his forehead. He starts to say something but pauses. After a few more seconds, he says, "Tank's dying."

I stop chewing on the hoof and focus on him. I've never met Tank, but I have a feeling I'd like him now. Not because he's dying. But because of Manny. I've seen Manny's true colors.

I can smell Manny's tears brewing. I'm surprised because he doesn't seem the crying type. Then I immediately feel bad because I hate it when people think a big dog like me can't cry. Lucy has always said, "Manny's a player and makes women cry," because from time to time she has seen pretty women leaving his apartment, faces puffy and red. But maybe we're wrong. Maybe he's a softie. Just like me.

His tears smell like wet tortilla chips. No words of comfort to offer, I stand up and lick his hand hanging at his side.

He turns his hand and lets me lick his palm and wrist. A

sign of trust. "Thanks for understanding, buddy." He sighs and walks off.

Poor Manny. Poor Tank. I get a lump in my throat thinking about Tank dying and leaving Manny alone.

I want to help them, but I don't know how. Maybe it will help to invite them both into our pack. Then when Tank goes to the Rainbow Bridge, Manny will still have me and Lucy.

I lie in the sun, and after a while I fall asleep, confident I'll hear Lucy's cheers when she comes home. She'll be as grateful for Manny's help as I am.

When I wake up, I'm drooling all over my towel and what's left of my cow hoof. The sun is high, and I'm warm and dry. And I'm hungry. I grab the hoof and take it upstairs to share my reward with Lucy. Sure, she thinks they stink, but it's the only way I can tell her Manny is our friend now. She'll know Manny gave me the hoof, and she'll put two and two together.

I climb the back stairs, each step growing stinkier and stinkier. In my clean state, I'd forgotten that Manny hadn't worked his magic in my apartment. His back door is closed, but where my dog food bag used to be, there is a larger bin with a lid. Tank's and my food storage receptacles are now sitting side by side. Only a human will be touching my food from now on.

That Manny. So thoughtful, even while worried about Tank.

I go inside the apartment, and as I walk by the bedroom door, the skunk fumes about blow me over. To think I once smelled like that. Lucy is so lucky it wasn't her who got sprayed. Heck, John's lucky it wasn't Lucy who got sprayed. I don't think he'd like to see Manny spreading his magic paste all over Lucy and rinsing her off.

I'm super duper anxious for her to come home and see how we can expand our pack. I'm still imagining her proud face when I hear the bus's brakes announcing Thomas's return.

Wait a minute. No. But this can't be.

I run to the window. Sure enough, Thomas is jumping off the bus. He waves at me, but I don't bark back. I'm beside myself. Lucy forgot me.

14

LUCY
NEW BEGINNINGS

Lucy met seventy of Golden Years' residents at the town hall. Folks were happy to meet her, but they were mostly jazzed about an excuse to gather and eat lasagna. "It's lasagna day," she heard over and over.

Okay, so not every resident was thrilled. Enid Gray, the self-appointed resident Chairman of the Board for the Satisfaction Committee, was on a mission. The woman barreled toward Lucy as soon as Dr. Ryan finished the introductions. She dragged her silent companion, June Lloyd, along for the ride.

"First things first. You've got to fix the food, Lucy. Lasagna is the only good-tasting thing we get here," Enid complained. "We're not getting any younger. *What else* do we have to look forward to but our meals? Tell her, June."

June just nodded.

Identifying the "what else" was one of Lucy's first goals.

"This is a private institution, and we're using our retirement money to live in style, not to eat cardboard," Enid said.

No surprises here. So often meals suffered in health care institutions in order to avoid putting residents into a diabetic coma or clogging their arteries. And few establishments, if any, could afford to tailor meals for each individual. It would be her responsibility to make sure they wouldn't put a patient's health at risk by ignoring their dietary restrictions but also provide meals that would suit the majority.

And, seriously, eating shouldn't be the thing they looked forward to the most. But it needn't be dreaded either. People had such an emotional tie with food. Look at her attachment to Cherry Chip Cake.

Lucy couldn't wait to implement some new programs to enhance the dignity of her residents' lives. She had so many ideas for partnering with schools, day care centers, animal services, art programs, and more. Dr. Ryan had hired her for her experience and ideas, and she intended to deliver.

"Mrs. Gray and Mrs. Lloyd, may I call you Enid and June?"

"Of course," Enid answered for both of them.

"Enid and June, may I attend your next Satisfaction Committee to collect additional feedback?" Lucy asked, opening her iPad to update her calendar.

"Why, yes. Yes, of course. It's every Thursday after breakfast," Enid said.

June smiled and nodded.

"Excellent. Count me in for next Thursday."

Enid tried to look over Lucy's shoulder. Lucy was petite, but the elderly lady was even shorter. "Fancy gadget there," she said, trying to get a better look at the iPad. Enid pointed to the cell phone hanging from a lanyard around her neck. "All I have is this large you're-blind-as-a-bat flip phone. Doesn't even let me text my grandkids." Enid sighed.

Lucy took more notes: *Potential computer center for Skype? Computer classes?* Changes wouldn't happen overnight, but planning was her strength.

June whispered in Enid's ear.

Enid rolled her eyes and asked Lucy, "That gadget have music on it?"

Not yet, but it could. "What type of music are you interested in?"

June elbowed Enid.

Enid shook her head. "Oh no. You want to hear *that* kind of music, you'll have to tell Lucy yourself. I want none of it."

June's voice was so soft, Lucy barely heard her say, "Backstreet Boys."

Was June blushing? Did seventy-something June have a crush on the Backstreet Boys? Lucy didn't have any of their music, but for that sweet face, she'd download their top hits as soon as possible.

Enid hooked her arm through June's. "We've got to go. It's collage time. June and I have a vision board we're using to plan our pilgrimage on the Camino de Santiago together."

Lucy tilted her head. *Hmm. Isn't the Camino de Santiago in Spain, France, and Portugal?*

She made a note to find out more about this impossible trip abroad. Lucy knew from her interviews that the Golden Years residents were there to stay and normally had health or financial constraints that prohibited travel. So much for *golden years*. Lucy wondered if she could add some sort of travel or documentary event to the activities schedule.

As June and Enid shuffled away, Dr. Ryan came up beside Lucy. "Well done. You've clearly won over Enid. Come with me. I'd like to introduce you to our newest resident, Martha Knight. She's been here less than a month. Her husband of sixty-five years passed away, and her children moved her here the following week. The adjustment has been difficult."

Lucy's chest constricted, both humbled and embarrassed about her own private pity party because John wanted to be alone. At least he was alive! Mrs. Knight had lived and breathed with someone for sixty-five years, and he was gone forever. No chance for a reunion in this lifetime.

A few times over the past days, she'd thought it would be easier if John were dead. At least then she wouldn't have to constantly replay his rejection and obsess over the idea of him ending up with someone else. His death seemed less painful. Seriously, that was just gross thinking, and she wasn't proud of it. At least she'd been honest with herself. She'd watched an interview with Michelle Obama recently and remembered her saying something like, "Most of our initial thoughts shouldn't see the light of day." She wondered if other people going through a big breakup or a divorce had thoughts like hers but just never spoke them aloud.

Mrs. Knight was eighty-something, thin, and composed. She wore her hair pulled into a tidy bun, and her small frame was all but swallowed up by the empty table before her. Yet, somehow she looked strong and confident. For a brief moment, Lucy was jealous seeing how poised and confident the woman looked even while sitting alone. Lucy had always hated to be alone, whether playing alone as a child, eating alone in public places, or hanging out alone at any social gathering. After Dr. Ryan introduced them and left, Lucy asked Mrs. Knight if she could join her for lunch.

"Please don't take this personally," Mrs. Knight said, "but, just for today. I'd prefer to be alone."

Alone. Lucy was coming to hate the word.

"Oh, okay," Lucy said. Nothing like being rejected right out of the gate. "Can I get you anything from the kitchen?"

Mrs. Knight shook her head.

Despite feeling like an unwelcome lunch guest, Lucy returned a few minutes later with a plate of dried-out lasagna. After a few moments of silence, Lucy found the guts to ask, "Why just for today?"

Mrs. Knight sipped her tea. "I'm not fit company for anyone."

"I don't know about that. You might be surprised."

"I'm in mourning, and I'm not rushing the process." Mrs. Knight fiddled with her wedding ring. "And the last thing anyone around here wants to do is be reminded of loss and death. I certainly don't blame them."

Lucy nodded. After all, she was procrastinating telling anyone about the big breakup because not only would it make it final, it would make the other people feel like crap too. Misery doesn't always love company. Her mom and Aunt Eve loved John. They'd be devastated for her, and depending on her mother's state when she found out, it might trigger her mom's depression. Or worse. If manic, her mother would be protective and trash talk John. Lucy wasn't in a rush to be on the receiving end of either reaction. Medicine helped bipolar disorder, but it didn't cure it.

Maybe grief was all Martha Knight had left of her husband to hold on to.

The old widow nodded at Lucy's engagement ring.

"Your happiness is just beginning. You don't need to hear about my suffering."

Lucy spread the fingers on her left hand wide against the Formica tabletop, her ring scratching the surface with a metallic whisper: *fraud.*

She surprised herself by asking, "Can you keep a secret?"

Mrs. Knight nodded.

"My fiancé left me last week. I haven't told anyone."

Mrs. Knight reached her left hand across the table to set it atop Lucy's. But she said nothing.

Once she could find her voice, Lucy said, "Thank you for not telling me I'll meet someone else."

"And thank you," Mrs. Knight said, "for not saying I was lucky to have my husband for sixty-five years."

"Thank you for not telling me I have my whole life ahead of me," Lucy said.

"And thank you for not saying life is short, and he'd want me to be happy."

They smiled at each other and settled into quiet companionship. Lucy tried the lasagna. This was the best meal? She'd have to reserve judgment because she wasn't sure if it truly tasted bad or if she still had zero appetite. When Lucy stood up to leave, Mrs. Knight said, "Lucy, you're welcome to join me anytime you're not in the mood for pleasantries."

"Thank you, Mrs. Knight." Lucy could guarantee she'd have those moments as long as John was gone.

"And, please, call me Martha."

If Lucy could pat herself on her back, she would. She'd made a difference in someone's life today, and it hadn't required stitches, casts, heart scans, drugs, or enemas. This was what she'd been missing in trauma: the chance to build meaningful relationships with patients.

After lunch with Martha, the first thing Lucy did was block 11:30 a.m. to 12:30 p.m. on her office calendar for the next few months. Golden Years was fifteen minutes from her apartment. From now on, five days a week, Skip and she would have a half-hour lunch date. They were going to be okay until John could realize his mistake and come back. His lease was short-term, only six months, he'd said. She told herself this was the longest he'd be gone.

We can do this. We will do this. She recited her adapted mantra (something she'd come up with thanks to Martha): *If you love him, set him free. He'll come back because it's meant to be.*

LUCY
FALSE STARTS

Lucy smiled while she parked her car. Her first day had been every bit as rewarding as she'd always hoped. Sure, her salary was lower, and she had no idea how she'd pay her bills now that her rent had just doubled, but her career satisfaction and work-life balance had done an about-face in a single day. No more twelve-hour shifts. No more blurs of faces coming and going, denying her the satisfaction of witnessing her contribution to patients' recovery. No more addicts coming off the streets, faking symptoms for pain pills, and her feeling helpless as they walked back out the doors to sell the meds. Nope. She was going to make a difference.

Now she could build relationships with patients like Martha Knight, June Lloyd, and Enid Gray. Most caretakers were afraid to do that, given that the elderly eventually died. She wanted to do everything possible to make their last days, months, or years the happiest and most comfortable and dignified they could be.

She grabbed her bag, tapped her car door closed with her heel, and rushed down the sidewalk toward her building. Today's only fail had been her complete abandonment of Skip. But they had survived. Or at least she assumed they had. Skip might disagree.

Her phone beeped. A text from John! Her heart quickened, ready to gobble up anything he had to offer.

John: *How was your first day?*

See? Despite his need to be alone, he knew her better than anyone and recognized how important the day was to her. Granted, she thought, he'd left her during this important time, but he still cared!

She weighed what to say. *Keep it simple and sweet. Give him the space he says he wants. Be confident. Secure.*

She texted him back: *Fantastic.*

John: *That makes me happy. I'll try to call later.*

A little positivity on her part equaled a call from him later. *Progress.*

Lucy opened the apartment building door and was slapped in the face with an awful stench. As she climbed the stairs, the smell worsened and so did her concern. On the top landing, she noticed two things at once. First, there was an orange slip taped to her door, and second, an old plastic milk gallon filled with something thick was sitting on the floor.

What in the world? She started with the orange note. A warning from her mailman. Next, she nudged the gallon of who-knew-what with the toe of her Danskin work shoes. The attached note said: *Skip skunked. Soak sheets in this. No H2O for 10 mins. P.S. Dogs hate being left alone. P.P.S. Skunk gone.*

Irritation burned. She was pissed at herself for assuming Skip would be okay, and pissed at Manny for the unsolicited guilt. Panic quickly followed. *Skunked!* "Skip," she spoke through the door as she sorted her keys, "I'm coming, honey. I'm coming."

He barked and barked. She could hear his nails clicking against the hardwood floors as he ran around. Something hard and heavy banged against the walls. Had the fumes made him sick and dizzy? Was that him falling about?

She scrambled to unlock the deadbolt. The thrashing and crashing grew louder and louder. *Boom, boom, boom.* Skip sounded drunk.

Lucy heard Manny's door open behind her. Great. That was all she needed. She didn't like talking to him on a good day, much less one where he'd already left her a note saying she sucked as a dog owner.

The deadbolt slid. Without turning around, she grabbed the jug of whatever, rushed inside, and leaned against the door until it slammed shut, almost falling to the floor after slipping on her scattered and torn mail.

The stench in her apartment nauseated her within seconds.

Skip was running up and down the hall with one of her shoes hanging from his mouth by a shoestring. It slammed against the walls, leaving scuff marks everywhere on the white paint. She grabbed for him as he ran past, but her hand just skimmed his soft fur. He stopped at the end of the hall, and she could swear he was grinning at her despite the shoe hanging from his mouth. He looked like he did whenever he got a stick or ball and wanted to play chase. He was clearly proud and playful and saying: *You can't catch me.*

The smell in her apartment was no game.

She chased him into a corner and grabbed his collar, expecting to drag him and lock him outside so she could run to the store for tomato juice, but he didn't stink. In fact, he didn't even smell like a dog.

Which meant only one thing. Her apartment stank.

Eek! Had the skunk sprayed inside her apartment?

Skip trotted away to play more tag.

"Stop it, Skip."

But Skip just kept wagging his tail and giving her a goofy grin.

"What's the matter with you?" she asked him. "What kind of dog lets a skunk in his house?"

Skip tossed his head in a carefree way as if he were in a shampoo commercial. Maybe she should have talked to Manny. It was his fault with all of his crap piled up, perfect spots for strays and wild critters to hide and nest in. She'd kill him.

Her bedroom smelled the worst. Skip's work was written all over her messy bed. She lifted one corner of the quilt, and the skunkiness infused the air around her like one big assault of nature.

So Skip had been sprayed, and he'd gotten on her bed. She dropped the quilt, holding her hand far from her person as she retrieved the bottle Manny had left. "Deskunker" was written on the side with a permanent marker. She walked with it to the kitchen, where the back door was now closed. When she opened it, there was an old blue fifteen-gallon plastic container with another note from Manny taped to the lid: *Skunks like dog food.*

So the skunk had gotten into Skip's dog food, and Skip had chased it. Better him than her. Of course, if she had been there, he wouldn't have chased it. She set the jug on her counter and walked back to her room.

Her closet's sliding door was wide open, and every shoe she owned was pulled out and chewed. A tip of a pump here, the sole of a boot there. Skip had terrorized her belongings. He'd ruined every shoe she owned.

"Why did you do this, Skip? Just because I didn't come home one frigging day!" He didn't respond or come running. A good thing. Her hand was itching to spank him. This was so not like her.

She dropped her head back and held her breath as she gathered her bedding and carried it to the bathtub. She walked back to the living room, where the couch pillows were shredded into slobber-drenched scraps.

Meanwhile, Skip was running around, pleased as could be with himself. The maniac.

"Bad boy!" she yelled. Then she started crying and looked at Skip through blinding tears.

He stopped and lowered his head.

How stupid she'd been to think they could do this alone. That Skip could be alone all day. Her dog was acting like a wild animal, and she had a neighbor who thought she was the worst dog owner in the world. Even the mailman was pissed at her.

Psycho Skip stopped near her, and she screamed at him, "What are you so happy about? We suck!" She ripped the shoe from his mouth and threw it to the floor. Skip dropped to the ground on his back, tucked his tail, and looked away.

"Don't act like I'm a monster. Like I'm the meanest mom in the world. John's the one who left us! This isn't my fault!"

And it wasn't Skip's fault. John should be there to help.

She decided Skip's behavior constituted an emergency and a good excuse to contact John. Not pathetic, but necessary. Forget being strong and letting him be free; she needed John.

She grabbed her phone and dialed his number. In the past, he'd always answered after the first ring, but this time she went to voice mail. Fine, she'd leave him a message, and he'd call her right back. She knew he would. "John, I know I shouldn't bother you, but I really need you right now. Skip got sprayed by a skunk, and he tore up the apartment, and I just, I just need a hug or someone who understands, or something. Call me as soon as you can."

But he didn't call back, and despite John's earlier message that he would call later, he texted: *Something's come up. Sorry. Have a good night.*

Lucy dropped to the floor among the destroyed couch pillows and cried, cried, cried. Her relationship was ruined. Her apartment was ruined. Just everything was ruined.

Skip scooted toward her on his belly until his head rested on her thigh. He sighed and looked up at her like she was as hopeless as she felt.

Lucy was ready to cry all night, but she knew she had to do something about the smell if she wanted to get any sleep, and she'd have to figure out what to do with Skip tomorrow. She made her way to the bathroom and emptied Manny's deskunker all over her sheets and the mattress pad she'd dropped in the tub. She followed his chicken-scratch instructions and lathered them up without any water and was stunned and relieved when the smell evaporated within minutes.

What is this stuff?

Skip was watching from the bathroom doorway. He looked as impressed as she was with the white goo.

Lucy left the saturated sheets in the bathroom and shoved her non-washable and unsalvageable bed pillows into a trash bag.

John's pillow couldn't be her surrogate-John anymore. She wouldn't be cuddling it tonight, and the fact brought on tears of frustration. She had no choice but to get new pillows. Not only had the bed been deskunked, it had been de-Johned. At this rate, pretty soon, it would be like John had never even been there.

When she returned from taking the bag down to the trash outside, the skunk smell was almost gone. She had Manny to thank for that. Not John.

Life was becoming so strange. The person she thought she knew better than anyone, she didn't know at all, and the person she didn't know had surprised her with his helpfulness (even if it included a dose of judgment).

Skip waited by the tub, wagging his tail. He had a half-gnawed pig or cow hoof on the floor. "Manny give you that for being a bad dog?"

He tilted his head to one side as if confused. He barked.

"Figures."

She turned on the water and flicked her fingers at him.

He snapped at the droplets like she'd started a new game.

He yipped happily. She knew that yip. Mothers often said they knew what their baby's cries meant. She knew what her dog's yips meant. His "Skip Yips."

"What am I going to do about you? Hmm?" she asked.

He licked her elbow.

She sighed. "I guess if I want the details, I have to talk to your new pal, Manny, don't I?"

Skip barked.

"I'll think about it," she told him. "Let's walk to the store. Time to bake that Cherry Chip Cake I never got. With no jam."

And she'd eat the whole damn thing if she wanted to.

16

SKIP
DOGTV

KILL ME NOW. Someone. Anyone.

To demonstrate her approval for my skunk-homeland-security, Lucy bought me some rewards last night. Unfortunately, she totally f-ing missed the memo on what I consider treats.

First case-in-point: a subscription to DOGTV.

Who thought up this absolute crap? I'm serious, who? I want to bite their head off. I'm going to go fur-raising crazy if I have to watch and listen to this nonsense all day.

Lucy had said, quite proudly, "I know it's not much. It's what I can afford right now."

In the past, I've liked it when John and Lucy have left the tube on for me. Lucy turned this new DOGTV on just before she left for work this morning, and I didn't pay the show any attention until after I finished my morning watchdog duties, and, well, what in the hell was she thinking?

Does she know me at all?

Why would she think I'd enjoy watching a bunch of

dogs running around outside, rolling in grass, playing together, and sniffing each other's asses? Look around me. Do you see any dogs? Last time I checked, I was alone in our tiny apartment. She might as well have locked me in a car with all the windows rolled up parked right outside our dog park. Like a sad *Look But Don't Live* promo.

Wait. It gets worse.

In addition to a bunch of dogs cavorting, frolicking, and leaping together, they get to chase balls.

Balls!

Lucy knows how I feel about balls. Irresistible fluorescent green tennis balls. I'm utterly tormented by my inability to participate, and yet, I can't look away either. I'm obsessing that I can't retrieve them, that I can't race other dogs to the catch! And what really pisses me off about the people who created this station and who take advantage of gullible distracted owners like Lucy is they think I'm so stupid that I don't get that a *human* is throwing the balls.

I don't have a human right now, you buttheads.

To rub more loneliness in my isolation, every now and then a clip comes on with dogs getting cozy with one another, sometimes on a dog bed stationed in front of a window under a beam of sunlight, and sometimes on a nice rug before a crackling fire.

I love to cuddle. Who am I suppose to cuddle? This stupid purple stuffed monkey Lucy bought me last night? This is a total head game.

No human.

No dogs.

No ball.

No canine *carpe diem* for me. Just some stupid show reminding me of how empty my life has become.

Here's an idea. How about I stop the insanity by knocking over the television? *Oh, that sounds so satisfying right now.* The only reason I hesitate is because of the black cord between the wall and TV. When I was one year old, I chewed on a lamp cord. I got zapped. My tongue was uncoordinated and floppy for a few days. I drooled everywhere. *Not pretty.*

Another option for ending this media pain would be to hide in the bedroom, where I would still hear the obnoxious show due to my stellar hearing, but at least I wouldn't have to see it. But guess what? I can't go into the bedroom because not only did Lucy remove all of the remaining cushions from the couch and chair and put them in the bedroom, she locked me out of *our* bedroom.

My environment has shrunk to the living room, hallway, and kitchen. I can't self-soothe with my newly discovered pillow and shoe-chewing therapy. And forget going out to the backyard; Lucy decided to keep the door closed in case the skunk came back.

Last night, Lucy finally had an appetite. I'd thought, *Good on me. My invigorating day drove her to eat.* We walked to the corner store and saw Mr. Ghafoor. He always greets us with "Lady Lucy and Sir Skip." I like his wife because a long time ago, she discovered my favorite petting spot, the area between my eyes, but she wasn't there.

Mr. Ghafoor said, "She went home to visit our family, but with the travel ban going back and forth, she can't return just now."

Lucy gasped, placed her hand over her heart, and apologized. I wasn't sure what she had to do with Mrs. Ghafoor's absence. Neither did Mr. Ghafoor because he said, "It's not your fault, and it will work out. This is America, my friend."

I must have missed something because Lucy looked unconvinced. She frowned and looked away, ashamed.

The Ghafoors have a small aisle of pet supplies, and Lucy bought me a bunch of squeaky toys that are now lying around the room; they're the only things she left out in the open. I've never been a dog-toy chewer. She did pick up some cow hooves, but she put them up on the fridge. I'd like one. It makes me crazy to smell them in the apartment. But maybe, just maybe, she is going to pay Manny back with them. I can't wait to see them become friends over cow hooves, just as I planned.

Before we left Mr. Ghafoor's last night, Lucy requested her lottery ticket. "I'd like to buy the winning ticket this week."

Mr. Ghafoor smiled and said, "Sure thing. Winning ticket coming up."

She then bought some of his deli salads and stuff for her special cake, and I was happy when later at home she sat down on the kitchen floor with me and we ate our dinners while the cake baked. Then she said we needed to talk. She told me she'd be here for lunch from now on but maybe not always right on time and that I need to "keep it together."

What does she think I've been doing? I saved her from the skunk, didn't I? *Keep it together. Right.*

She went on to explain why she couldn't afford a dog walker or dog camp. She said, "I can't afford to take care of you like you deserve."

My nerves stretched thin, and my whiskers started twitching. Lucy saying stuff like that reminds me of Soft Voice's weakness and losing my first family. And then Lucy asked, "Did I do the wrong thing? Telling John he couldn't have you?"

Whoa!

John asked for me? He wanted to keep me? This was news to me. Big news. Gigantic news. Somehow I missed this conversation. On the one hand, it means Lucy wants me because she didn't let him take me, and if that's true then I might be okay even if she finds out I introduced John to Cecilia. No pound. On the other hand, she's admitting she can't take care of me the way I deserve, like Soft Voice.

Inside, my heart was saying, *John wants me. John wants me.* He didn't just desert me. I have a Plan B. If I can't prove my worth to Lucy, she can give me to John. I want to stay with Lucy more than anyone because I love her, and I owe her, but if she gives up on me, John will take me. I was feeling some in-the-Now relief.

But then she pointed out, "Of course, if he had really wanted you, he wouldn't have gotten a place that doesn't allow pets."

A crushing update. Dashed hopes. Either Project Lucy works or I'm going to the pound if she finds out my secret or can't handle me.

"But," she continued around small bites, "maybe he took that lease because it's short-term and in his heart he knows he will return to us both."

What a roller coaster we are riding together. And I don't know of any dogs that like roller coasters.

After that, we were silent. Lucy ate a lot of cake. I even had a bite. Too sweet for me, but I enjoyed watching her lick her fork and plate like I would do if it were a plate of meat.

Before I fell asleep last night, curled up beside Lucy in bed, she asked, "What am I going to do with you?"

Keep me would be the obvious answer. Hadn't I proved that I could take care of our home for her, and that I could make new friends for us, like Manny?

We took a long walk this morning, and she let me take the lead: a sign of relaxed confidence in my blossoming leadership. I kept my eye on her and made sure she didn't jump in front of any cars. When we got back, she stayed in the kitchen while I ate my breakfast, and instead of yelling at me for following her around the apartment like she did yesterday morning, she kept pausing to hug me and say, "You're a good dog."

I thought she meant it, but if she had, she wouldn't have chosen DOGTV or these stupid toys she bought me. I thought, okay, she knows she needs me, and if she ever finds out about Cecilia, she'll still keep me. I'm becoming indispensable. But now I think she said it as false praise, a way to manipulate me into being her idea of a "good dog" today. So what does *good dog* mean to Lucy? So far, I've stuck by her side sans John. I've saved her from being puréed by a car. And I took a skunk for her. What would it take for her to recognize my value permanently? When is "good" good enough?

When will *I* be enough?

I sniff the new orange plastic squirrel that squeaks when I bite it, but there's no *pop pop pop*. No *crunch*. It's not the same as the pillows. It's not enough. It's just an annoying squeaker that hurts my ears. Forget chewing on the purple monkey like a pillow because the fake fur just comes out in my mouth and gets stuck in my throat. I had a coughing fit earlier to prove it. Dog Bless Lucy's innocence, but she also bought me a braided rope. Maybe she didn't realize it's for playing tug of war with a human. I imagine John pulling it from the other end, the way we used to with a hand towel or one of his knotted up socks, and I just want to weep. Depressed, I push it under the couch where I won't have to look at it anymore.

She also bought a hard black rubber toy shaped like a snowman I saw once in Tahoe that bounces all over the place, but in unpredictable directions. "This will engage your mind and reflexes," she had read from the package, but with a small living room, what's the point? There's nowhere for it to bounce in this four-corner solitary confinement. Still, I give it a try and toss it with my jaws. It does its spastic bounce and ends up hitting me in the face. "Engage my mind" my butt. It could've poked my eye out.

And most important of all is that none of these toys smell like Lucy or John. They are empty gifts. Meaningless rewards. *Snort.*

I stare longingly out the window, missing my ottoman, missing watching John walk down the sidewalk to be with me. I wonder what he's doing right now. Right about now, he'd take me for my post-breakfast walk before leaving for his office. Is he walking Bunny instead?

I lie down on the floor and sigh. *I miss you, buddy. Even though you cheated on us.*

Cruelly, DOGTV switches to two snuggling Golden Retriever puppies.

Something comes over me, something dormant, an instinct that's so natural it's like a part of my being, my blood. I stand and toss back my head. I howl a new howl. Not my watchdog duty howl. I put my heart and soul into this call. I recall the sound of my mother's voice when they took her away from me at the pound, loud and permeating. Even after they took her through a door, I heard and felt her. For the first time since I lost her, I feel my mother's spirit racing through me and saying, "*Howl until your pack comes home.*"

My fur stands up. I bellow and howl. "*Mama! Lucy! John!*" Again and again.

From a distance and in my neighborhood, I hear other dogs join my calls.

They are spreading the word. I can do it. I can get this message to Lucy and John.

And my howls gain support closer to home. Tank joins the cacophony despite his illness. Shortly after, Thomas, who started summer vacation today (my nose knows because his bus never came, but Mrs. Brighton still went to work, and Thomas made pancakes, which is his summer breakfast), starts to bang on the ceiling and yells, "Too loud! Too loud! Too loud!"

Usually, I'd stop for Thomas because I can sense his fragility, but my mother's blood pushes me on. I just keep going. Inspired. Encouraged. *I can never be "too loud" if it means my pack will hear my calls.*

Through my cries, I feel and hear Thomas's door open and the pounding force of his steps as he runs up the stairs. He flips open my mail plate, and says, "Skip. Too loud. Too loud. Too loud."

My howling works. Maybe I wasn't calling for Thomas, but he's human, and he's at my door. Right now. Within seconds of my calls. I stop howling and run to him. He slides his fingers through the slot, and I lick them. I have to give him credit; he's never been scared of me. He replaces his fingers with a rolled-up piece of paper that keeps the small flap ajar. I can see his flannel shirt and smell the fresh maple syrup smeared on his sleeve.

I follow Thomas's movements with my ears and limited view as he slides down to the floor and rests his back against the wall adjacent to the door. I hear the whisper of turning paper, and Thomas begins to read to me. His man-boy voice vibrates against the wood door and floor and dances through the mail slot. He starts to share a story of a boy whose parents were brutally murdered by an evil serial killer, leaving him to be raised by his aunt and uncle, who lock him in a cupboard under the stairs. The boy's name is Harry, and his loneliness touches something inside of me. I wish I could jump all over Thomas and lick his face to show him how much I appreciate him, not only for comforting me, but also for choosing *this* story.

He gets me. Someone gets me.

I don't have to be strong with Thomas. I don't need to lead him. I just need to listen and let him be my friend. He never has friends come over, at least none that I've smelled, heard, or seen, so maybe I can be his friend. Maybe he's lonely when he isn't in school and his mom leaves him all day because, like Lucy, she's single. She's a widow and making ends meet. Other than sharing a gratification for a strict routine, I never thought about what else we have in common. I wonder if his mom tells him to "keep it together" too?

My howls brought Thomas to me. My mother's love soared through my blood and guided me to make another friend. Thomas and I are peers in the pecking order of life.

Without my leadership, the neighborhood dogs and Tank stop howling. I lie down, separated from Thomas by an inch of wood, and relish the hum of his steady and calm voice. If

DOGTV could see us now, they'd probably steal this idea to tease a dog that doesn't have a human to read to him. But I do. *So there, DOGTV. You can't tease me anymore today.*

I doze off. When I wake up, Thomas is still reading to me. He's so engrossed in the story he doesn't hear what I hear: Lucy has just let herself in the building. She is home for lunch.

17

LUCY

DAY TO DAY

LUCY WALKED into work with a sugar hangover to beat all sugar hangovers. What had she been thinking? She shouldn't have eaten her whole Cherry Chip Cake. Sugar sabotage at its very best. She'd woken up in her bed hours later drenched in sweat. If she were any older, she'd worry she was premenopausal.

But her cake had been so good, at least going down.

Prevention had been Lucy's game plan with Skip this morning. She'd dog-proofed the house by moving every chewable thing imaginable into her bedroom and closing the door. She littered the living room with new chew toys. Last night she'd made sure he slept in the bed with her in case he got sick in the middle of the night. Had he ingested any of the leather, feathers, or stuffing from the pillows? One of her shoes was missing a shoestring, and she'd been unable to find it. After a long walk this morning where Skip took care of his business, Lucy slipped her hand into a Pooper Scooper bag and poked around in said pile of business.

The joys of motherhood.

As a nurse, she'd had her share of analyzing crap. Most people couldn't check out of the hospital without having a healthy bowel movement. Being a nurse required as much humor as fortitude. She'd kept a running tally of enemas she'd given since she'd become a nurse. *Keep your defibrillator close and your enemas closer.* That had been her motto. So when she didn't find any remnants of a shoestring or further evidence in Skip's waste, she figured his physical condition was healthy enough for her to go to work. His mental health was another issue. She was putting her last penny on DOGTV to save his sanity and ease her guilt.

Hopefully Skip's morning would be uneventful until she could check on him this afternoon. If he made too much trouble or noise, could he get them evicted? Mrs. Brighton didn't seem the complaining type. But Manny might enjoy a bit of revenge. She couldn't afford to move right now. Her annual lease should protect her for the time being. Rents had skyrocketed in the area over the past year, and finding a place that would take a dog, especially Skip's size, was almost unheard of. But she needed to find some money. She could ask John, but it made her feel so needy and non-resourceful. *And besides, he should have offered*, a little voice niggled its way into her thoughts. *He's on the lease too.*

The night nurse, Sheila, greeted Lucy as soon as she walked into Golden Years. Sheila was a tall woman in her fifties who had a booming laugh that echoed off the walls. She was quick to smile but had a no-nonsense attitude, and if two days was enough of an indication, she only wore scrubs with Disney character prints. Today she wore Mickey Mouse. From what Lucy had witnessed at the end of her workday yesterday, the residents were fond of Sheila.

Seventy-eight-year-old Mr. DeWitt had raised his chatty brows at her and said, "Hubba-hubba."

Playing along, Sheila had covered her cheeks. "Why, Mr. DeWitt, you're making me blush."

And he'd said, "That'll be the day."

"Lucy," Sheila waved her over, "a true first happened this morning. We've always had to press Martha Knight to get up for breakfast. But this morning she was sitting up in bed, waiting for me, and she asked, 'What time does Lucy get here?'"

Martha had asked for her? Her? After only one day of work? This was just what Lucy needed. This confirmation that she mattered and that she could help someone in their final years. That she had always been great at her job. That she'd built this career and had not just fallen into it.

Sheila squeezed Lucy's shoulder. "She's in the cafeteria working on a crossword puzzle."

After opening her office and checking email for any last-minute schedule changes, Lucy started walking through the facility to check on all of the residents. She smiled at the extra bounce in her step. She passed by Walter the janitor, who only grunted in response to her hello. But at least he'd initiated the grunt. He'd see. He'd end up liking her in time. Everyone who had ever worked with her had liked her, or at least respected her work ethics and productivity.

She was determined to give each person her undivided attention, use her morning rounds to build relationships, and find out what needed to be done to improve Golden Years. She'd start with Martha in the cafeteria.

The room was bright and large. The long tables made it a great space for group crafts and games. June and Enid were currently waving at her from a table where they were working on their vision board for the Camino de Santiago.

Yesterday afternoon, June had spoken a full sentence, something she apparently normally left Enid to do for her. She'd said, "The Camino is for letting go."

Lucy asked, "What do you need to let go?"

June shook her head, obviously not ready to divulge her secrets. Even Enid didn't try to spill the beans. And Lucy didn't push because if there was anything she was learning right now, it was how hard it was to let go.

She spotted Martha sitting alone a few tables away.

"Good morning, Martha."

Martha looked up from her crossword puzzle. "Good morning." She waved at the chair across from her, and Lucy joined her.

"I understand you had a more energetic morning than usual." Lucy felt a little shy saying so, knowing she was fishing for praise and eager for a little more confirmation that she was important to someone, all the while feeling ashamed. Was she so desperate for praise that she would claim a little old lady's progress for her own? *Apparently.*

Martha nodded. "Up until I moved here a few weeks ago, I had a reason to get up every morning."

"Your husband." Lucy assumed but was surprised when Martha shook her head.

"No, a good cup of tea," Martha said.

Humor too! True progress. Lucy laughed, and Martha joined her. After talking about Martha's favorite chai tea with almond milk, which Lucy intended to arrange with the kitchen staff, Martha got serious.

"My home was in Half Moon Bay, and my Charlie built me the most wonderful crates so I could plant a vegetable and fruit garden as well as flowers. Each morning after my tea, I'd go outside and tend to my garden. She dabbed her eyes. "Sometimes I miss my routine more than I miss Charlie." She looked around the room at the other residents then flicked the crossword puzzle book. "Maybe I just need a new routine."

Lucy took a deep breath and reached over and squeezed Martha's hand because what Martha said poked holes in a resolution Lucy had made earlier that morning while reading her horoscope.

Taurus: You may not be looking forward to what you have to do, but if you approach it with the right mental attitude, it won't be so bad. Commit yourself to it, make a plan, apply it consistently and, above all, don't give up on it halfway through.

While reading it, she'd felt inspired and perplexed all at once. If she could commit to giving John the space he'd asked for, eventually he'd realize his mistake and come back for her: *If you love him, set him free. He'll come back because it's meant to be.* But how was she expected to plan for letting him go when all her energy had gone into planning *them* since the day they'd met? How could she plan for setting him free when her real motivation was to bring him back to her?

Plan. The word was overwhelming, even for her, someone who normally liked planning. Plans could take years, or even forever, to bear fruit.

She was putting words in Martha's mouth, but what if Martha was right, what if a new routine was part of healing when you had no other choice? Somehow, a routine seemed easier to manage than a plan. A routine was just a bunch of steps that added up to one day. Each step could be checked off. An accomplishment. Plans were big. Plans were for a lifetime. Routines were baby steps and practice.

Martha missed her routine right alongside missing her husband. Why wouldn't she? Her relationship and her routine had been together for sixty-five years. Lucy didn't know how to plan to be without John temporarily any more than Martha could plan the rest of her life without Charlie. But maybe finding a supplemental routine until John came back was doable.

It made sense. How many of her tears since John left had been about the changes to her daily routine that she hadn't realized were so important, such as the way John had taken care of Skip while she'd had wonky work hours at the hospital? Or how she spent her evenings curled up with John on the couch watching TV, and later, falling asleep listening to his breathing. She'd once read that the three most unsettling changes in a person's life were ending a relationship, changing jobs, and moving homes. So far she was two-for-three in the same week. *Time for a new routine.*

Lucy needed to figure out how she might be able to help Martha adjust to her new life at the center, but she didn't want to get Martha's hopes up or make any promises until she did some research. Strangely excited by her new determination, Lucy excused herself, but Martha asked, "Will you be joining me for lunch today?"

Having a routine meant going home and walking Skip. Clearly, she needed to establish a schedule for her and Skip if they were going to make it. But she also had a job to do. Being present for Martha was part of that job. "Can I join you for a half hour?" If she joined Martha from 11:30 a.m. to noon, she could make it home to walk Skip by 12:15 p.m., take him on a walk, and be back at work by 1:00 p.m.

Martha winked. "It's a date. My treat."

Lucy finished her rounds, which included listening to Enid vent about the food yet again.

"Lucy," Enid said, pulling June alongside her and waving a *Better Homes and Gardens* magazine. It was probably one that had been dissected for her vision board. "I can't tell you the last time I had a fresh strawberry or a plate of food that had any color on it besides tan and white. How hard can it be to serve decent food for the price we pay?" Enid tapped Lucy's iPad. "Put that note in your thinga-majigger."

"I've been noting all of your concerns, Enid." What Enid and June, who was standing quietly beside her, didn't know was that Lucy had a glimmer of a plan; a twofer plan that would make both Martha and Enid happy. But she would need Walter's help, and she needed to build up her nerve to talk to him about it. But she would.

18

LUCY

MOVE FORWARD OR GO UNDER

FINALLY HOME for her lunch date with Skip, Lucy looked up at her apartment window, expecting to see his wolf-like face, but he wasn't there. Looking out the window was one of his favorite pastimes. She crossed her fingers that he was MIA because he was consumed with DOGTV.

She raced upstairs and was startled when the Brightons' door slammed closed just before Lucy passed it on her way to her floor.

Skip barked and jumped on her as soon as she opened the door. On his hind legs, he was as tall as Lucy, and his weight threw her against the wall.

"Skip! Down!"

When he wouldn't listen, she gripped his forelegs and lowered him to the ground. "I missed you too, but you can't start jumping on people."

He wasn't paying attention to a word she was saying and started running around the apartment, his tail wagging.

"Somcone's happy."

She laughed when he barked as if saying, "Yes!" He

was doing something new, a chatty-type bark now. She could swear he was telling her a story, as if he were saying, "This happened. And then this happened. And then I said . . ."

She played along, and replied, "Uh-huh. Oh," as she picked up the mail. Though wrinkled and covered with fur as if Skip had been lying on the pile, the letters were still intact. No shredding. No additional warning card from the mailman.

So far, so good. DOGTV must be helping.

He ran back to her and shoved his nose between her legs.

"Whoa." She pushed his snout away and walked into the living room. "I don't need to return to work with your slobber all over my crotch. That would get Enid gossiping."

His new toys lay where she'd left them except for the braided rope, which stuck out from under the couch. DOGTV played in the background, and when she couldn't find any damage to home or property, she called, "Good dog!"

Skip stopped in front of her, and she scratched his ears. They were going to be okay.

"I knew you'd like DOGTV. See? I told you the show would help. Doesn't feel like you're alone anymore, does it?"

Skip tilted his head to the side and whined, plopping to the ground and burying his snout in his paws.

What an odd reaction. *Oh, but of course.* "You must be dying for a walk. Let's go."

As soon as she said "walk," Skip jumped up and rushed for his leash.

It felt good to stretch her legs with Skip and get some

fresh air. All in all, a quick walk was a welcome break in her busy schedule.

When they returned home, she grabbed one of the cow hooves she'd put on top of the fridge.

Skip started to salivate, tiny spirals of slime hitting her hardwood floor.

"Gross." She grabbed a paper towel and wiped it up, pointless given she planned to leave him with the treat. "I'm going back to work now." She used the cow hoof to point toward the now open bedroom door and the living room.

His eyes followed the cow hoof, and his tongue hung from his mouth in anticipation.

"Chew your toys and this hoof. Nothing else. Stay good." She tossed him the treat and promised to see him after work.

He whined, despite his mouth being full of cow, as she grabbed her purse and opened the door. As soon as she shut it, he started to howl.

She cringed. Darn it. The guilt. She hoped once she was out of sight, she'd be out of mind and he'd stop howling. As she hurried downstairs, she could hear Thomas yelling from his apartment, "Too loud! Too loud! Too loud!" Maybe Thomas and Skip would drown out each other's cries. Must be summer break. *Beginning of June. Yes, it is summer break.*

Just as she passed his apartment, Thomas yanked open the door, froze when he saw her, and slammed the door shut. His avoidance was nothing new. *Hello to you, too, Thomas.* She'd have to ask Mrs. Brighton if it was better for Thomas if she ignored him or if she should start saying hello, then she shook her head because she'd never worried about Thomas's needs before. Her new job was making her more sensitive.

She let herself out of the building and looked up at her window. Skip was staring down, ears pointing straight up, and howling. *Ugh.* She decided to try something new. She stepped out of sight into a doorway one building down. Sure enough, within a minute, he stopped howling.

Yes! Out of sight, out of mind.

What a relief to know that he only cried when she first left. She imagined him turning to the TV and watching the dogs run and play. As she walked to her car, she sighed with relief. They'd figure this out. One day at a time. One decision at a time. Her phone rang. She sighed. Like taking Auntie's call.

She answered. "Hi, Aunt Eve."

"Hi, sweetie. Are you ready for my visit on Friday?"

Lucy hesitated. Of course she wasn't. How could she be? Aunt Eve would expect to see John, not Lucy now five pounds thinner. But was there a right time, and would she ever be ready?

"It's good you're coming. What time will you get here?"

"Around seven o'clock. Tell John not to worry about me. I'm taking a bus from the BART station."

How easy it would be to stall and pretend life was life as usual and call John and beg him to act like they were together for her aunt's visit, but she knew that would be stupid. They couldn't pretend everything was okay. That was the opposite of what she was trying to commit to: respecting John's need for space. Routines started with small steps, items on a list. Setting him free, telling the truth . . . all needed to become part of her life and routine *today*.

Like it or not, her life was different today and would

still be different on Friday whether Aunt Eve came or not. She recalled a BBC movie she'd seen about a housewife during WWII, *Housewife 49*, where the heroine was advised during her depression, "Move forward or go under."

Summoning the words brought tears to Lucy's eyes. "Aunt Eve, about John," she swallowed hard, "he, um, he won't be here."

"Where's my handsome future N-I-L going to be?" Aunt Eve had been calling John her nephew-in-law for years, long before he and Lucy had gotten engaged. When Aunt Eve first met him, she'd hugged Lucy and whispered in her ear, "He's *the one*, isn't he?"

Lucy got in her car and rested her forehead against the steering wheel. *Just say it.* Her throat began to swell up.

"Lucy, honey, are you okay?"

She and Skip were hanging on by a few chew toys, a subscription to DOGTV, and her job. Was she okay?

"He left me." How could three stupid words gut her so?

Aunt Eve didn't say anything except to make soothing noises while Lucy pulled herself together.

"Please don't tell Mom yet."

"I'll leave that to you, honey. Just hang in there until I get there."

"I will," Lucy said. "I have to go now. New job."

"Real quick," Aunt Eve said, "what about Skip?"

Of all the things her aunt could ask such as why John left, what happened, or something about the new job, her aunt's first question had been, "What about Skip?"

"I have him," Lucy said and jumped as Aunt Eve shouted.

"Oh, thank Dog!"

"Thank Dog?"

"Skip's your soul mate, darling," her aunt said in a tone that brooked no argument.

Lucy couldn't help but laugh through her tears. Aunt Eve had that way about her. Her aunt had spoken of true love and soul mates as long as Lucy could remember, but in all her life, she could never remember Aunt Eve saying a person's soul mate could be a dog. Lucy had to ask, "If Skip's my soul mate, what does that make John?"

"Blind," Aunt Eve said softly, leaving Lucy with more tears to wipe away and smile through.

"I love you, Aunt Eve."

As Lucy drove back to work, it began to rain. Whenever it rained, she and John had a standing date to have pizza delivered and watch a movie. *Well, that won't be happening tonight.*

Her phone dinged as she pulled into the parking lot at Golden Years.

John was texting her: *Can't help but think about you right now. I know this isn't fair of me. Sorry.*

Her heart rate quickened. *He's thinking of our rainy night dates too.*

Her fingers twitched as she began to type and then paused. She wanted to respond so badly. To connect to him. Just some small texted indication that they were still an "us." She backspaced until the screen was blank and shoved the phone in her purse.

Her horoscope had said to be consistent and not to be Miss Halfway. Free is free, she coached herself. Alone is alone.

Her rainy nights required a new routine. After work, she'd grab an umbrella, walk Skip to Mr. Ghafoor's deli, pick up her favorite salads, and start watching *Sex and the*

City. It was the one series John had never wanted to watch. There were six seasons, and they should hold her over for a while.

New Rainy Night Routine. Check! *Move forward or go under.*

19

SKIP

SEX AND THE CITY

IT'S OFFICIAL. The only thing more maddening than DOGTV is *Sex and the City*. This is our third night watching it and trying our new rainy night tradition. When we were all cuddled up at first, I was thrilled. At one point, I even climbed up on her lap like a lapdog, but I was squishing her, and she couldn't see the screen, so I had to settle down next to her. I like being a big dog, but sometimes I'm jealous of the little guys.

I like how the women stick together in this show. I like their pack and how they meet every Sunday for food. My problem is I don't like this Big guy. I think the only thing that's big about him is that he's a big selfish jerk.

Lucy is obsessed with Carrie and Big and hopes they end up together. She has actually said out loud, "John is my Big."

Um, hello, Lucy. John's nothing like Big.

I'm not sure how many episodes we've watched or in what order, but I can tell you this: Carrie could do better than Big. Believe me, dogs are better judges of humans any day. She's not Big's first choice. He marries someone else for Dog's sake. And whenever he gets bored, jealous, or lonely, he calls Carrie. He totally sucks.

John left us for Cecilia, but he's not like Big. He's not a game player. He's not rubbing Cecilia in Lucy's face. He's not showing up here unannounced and throwing us a bone here and there to keep us wanting more.

If I could talk (and I was smaller), I'd sit on Lucy's lap, stare into her eyes to show her how serious I am, and explain that the real moral of *Sex and the City* is not to fixate on one man but to surround yourself with a supportive pack. She's overcomplicating everything.

But it's so simple. Pack = Happiness.

I'm pretty sure Lucy is the only woman in this world who thinks the point of the story is about Carrie and Big ending up together, that people can't fight true love. *Barfola.*

Lucy doesn't need a Big. And honestly, as much as it pains me to say it, she doesn't need a John either. She needs some good friends. And me, of course. And on that note, in my humble opinion, I think Carrie would have a dog if her apartment wasn't so small. Then the series could be *Dogs and the City.*

Crazy part is, for the first episode the other night, Lucy was getting the promise of a pack. She was rallying her spirit. Episode 1 opened with the challenges of male-to-female ratios, aging, and gender income levels, and Lucy had sided with her gender. Her breaths had grown shorter, and she'd crossed her arms. She had begun to glare at the television. Her anger had smelled like singed hair and burnt toast or like the time she was boiling milk in a pot and it boiled over on the electric burner. It had taken a week of open windows to get rid of the angry stench.

With the ladies in the city on the screen before us, Lucy had even said with absolute conviction, "Maybe John hasn't cheated on me, but I bet he left me to have sex with other women. As soon as he became partner at the firm, he ditched me. *Be alone* my butt."

You know what certainty sounds like? Like freedom. Like a long run across a grass field freshly mowed. No doubt, no questions. There's one direction across that field. Run and don't look back.

Lucy's announcement filled me with pride for her. She seemed stronger than even an hour before, and certainly more than a week ago. She radiated independence. Resilience.

She continued, "I deserve to know the truth. Because if John upended my life just to sleep around, then this is over, and I won't welcome him back. Ever." With that kind of conviction, she would be strong enough to take the lead and charge ahead with our lives without John. And something else. If Lucy won't ever take John back, they'd never talk again, and Lucy would never find out I know Cecilia. I wanted to run around the apartment and do a four-legged happy dance.

Then she turned to me and said, "The only male you can trust is your dog."

Okay, that had made me feel like an impostor, at least 50 percent impostor; let's not forget I'm not entirely innocent in the annihilation of our pack. But overall, her response was very good! Lucy knows she can trust me and that I'll never leave her. She knows she needs me.

Yeah, baby! Success! Concerns about the pound faded, and I stopped paying attention to the show so much.

But now during tonight's episodes, her shoulders drop, her breaths deepen, and she keeps grabbing the Kleenex. Soon, she's crying steadier than the rain falling outside.

"If John is my Big, and I've already lost him, I'm doomed. You only get one chance at true love. I can't even begin to try to date in the environment this show is talking about. I've only ever slept with John. And the idea of him being with anyone else, having sex with them . . . oh my God. And what about a family? I'll never be able to have children at this rate."

I growl. She's all over the place now. Spiraling downward faster than a flushing toilet. I want to warn Lucy that she's lost the crucial point. Damn. She was so close to getting it right. I want to remind her of how she felt before and that *Sex and the City* is supposed to be about friendship. It's about support. It's about building a pack.

But thanks to Carrie and Big's toxic relationship, Lucy has taken a step backward and is romanticizing what it means to wait for John.

Lucy blows her nose some more, and I roll my eyes. I can't take any more tonight, so I get up and walk to the window. My heart drops. John is staring up at me from the road, leaning against his car.

Oh, John. What are you doing here? I yawn and whine at once. It's something I do when I feel overwhelmed.

Behind me Lucy sniffs and asks, "What do you see out there?"

She's not moving, so I'm not worried she will join me and see what I'm seeing. What I can't believe I'm seeing. He climbs into his car. My ears and eyes follow the hum of

John's vehicle and his blinker as he reaches the end of the street and turns. I walk over to Lucy and curl up at her side, my heart heavy.

John isn't letting us let go. John really is our Big. Our big selfish jerk. Just when I was starting to move on, John has pulled me back in. Seeing him gives me hope he wants to come back. Hope is a powerful drug. And I'm afraid again about the pound, because if John is just keeping his foot in our door like Big, he's keeping his foot in Cecilia's door too.

20

LUCY

HOLDING OUT AND HOLDING ON

LUCY COULD HARDLY BELIEVE it was Friday. Last night was the first time in eight days that she hadn't woken up crying in the middle of the night when she stared at John's empty side of the bed. Progress was in the small things.

Skip was adjusting to their new life. He hadn't torn anything else up. So far, there hadn't been any further complaints from the mailman, and her neighbors hadn't pounded on her door at night saying Skip barked and howled all day. Sometimes he barked when she was watching *Sex and the City* and wouldn't stop until she turned the television off. Maybe he was getting spoiled with the dog channel because last night instead of turning the television off when he barked, she switched it to DOGTV. Skip immediately stopped barking and left the room.

She guessed it was pretty funny that Skip had dog shows and she had *Sex and the City*. She found strength in the show about the challenges women face in today's dating world, mostly because the show made her laugh or made her angry at men. Though, like all women, she knew Big and Carrie were meant for each other. She hadn't finished watching the series, but she knew how it ended because the show had been over for years, and there'd been two movies in theaters since. Big was the prize.

It was silly to rely on fictional love stories as guidance. She partly blamed Aunt Eve for all the years of romance books. But show or book, like Aunt Eve always said, "Listen, someone out there wrote from experience, right? That makes it real in my book. No pun intended, honey." From that point of view, *SATC* looked pretty good. It was an Emmy award-winning show for goodness' sake. The practical side of her told her she shouldn't buy into it all, but it helped the nights go by. And as far as therapy went, it fit her budget.

As Lucy locked the door to head to work, Manny opened his door across the hall, and he and Tank walked out. At least Manny did. Tank just stared up at Manny. She had a bag of cow hooves in her hand that she'd intended to leave outside Manny's door, so his timing was good. She owed him her thanks.

Tank looked a little worse for wear, though. Like he'd been hit by a car, was sore, and slow to move. She'd paid just enough attention to him in the past to think him mean, but now he looked thin, weary, and old.

She and Manny rarely acknowledged each other, but she was grateful to him for helping Skip, and she hadn't found the energy to knock on his door and thank him. Not that she cared what he thought about her social etiquette.

Okay, maybe I do.

Pride, she supposed. It was a good sign she still had scraps of pride left. Right?

She'd never been certain what his hours were, if he

worked from home or where he worked. Truth was, she didn't know anything about Manny except that he had a dog, collected pots and dead plants, and was popular with the ladies.

Over the past four years, she'd heard him coming in late, often with a gorgeous woman in tow; not that she was spying on him or anything. Sometimes she'd been awakened by a woman knocking on his door. She and John used to remark about his steady flow of visitors. Often these women, who looked younger than him by a good five years or more, would leave the next morning with red faces and swollen eyes.

Snap judgment said he was a player and heartbreaker, but she did wonder what the women thought when they saw all of the pots stacked outside his door. She could only wonder what the inside of his apartment looked like. Though he was always clean cut. Well, neat for T-shirts and jeans. Well-worn jeans that fit him nicely . . .

While she and John had been annoyed with Manny, Lucy wasn't blind. Manny was good-looking. She wasn't surprised the ladies were around. One time John caught her glancing at Manny's ass as they followed him into the building, and he'd teased her all day. She had felt warmed by his silly misplaced jealousy, so she'd smiled and said, "Actually I was looking at his jeans." And John had pointed to his own ass and joked, "Eyes over here, missy."

"You're cute when you're jealous," she'd said, and they'd proceeded to tease each other until they fell into bed and made love.

Now Manny nodded at her as she walked toward him, swinging the bag of cow hooves in her hand.

"Good morning," she said.

Manny spared her a quick glance as he slid his hands on either side of Tank's hindquarters and gently swung his back legs over the threshold.

There was no pretending she hadn't noticed. "Is Tank okay?"

"He's fine." But then Tank laid down in the hall like he'd just walked for an hour.

Manny scratched his head and looked down at Tank. Then he looked back at Lucy. "How's Skip?"

Okay, so he didn't want to talk about Tank. "He's cleaner than ever. I've been wanting to thank you."

"It was no problem."

"We've been going through some changes, and, well, you really helped."

"Good changes, I think. Like I told Skip, you're better off without him."

Who asked him?! "Can't you just say, 'You're welcome'?"

"You're welcome."

She had tried to be nice, hadn't she? "I'd like to reimburse you for whatever you cleaned him with, and the bin for the food."

"I don't need the money."

She extended her hand. "Here are some hooves for Tank. Skip enjoyed the one you gave him."

Manny took them and tossed them from hand to hand. Tank followed the treat with his head, but otherwise didn't move.

"Are you sure he's okay?" she asked, nodding toward Tank.

"Worry about your own dog," Manny said.

"What's that supposed to mean? I know we had the skunk problem. But we're doing just fine together."

"Oh really?" Manny smirked.

"And what's that supposed to mean?" She put her hands on her hips to avoid slapping the smug look off his face.

"Just suggesting you might not be doing all this on your own like you think."

The nerve. He had helped her with one thing! "You know what? Every time I try to be nice to you, you just piss me off. Can't you see I'm trying to extend an olive branch here?"

Lucy stormed down the stairs. Skip began to howl, and she was so frustrated she wanted to cry. Her jaw clenched and her fists balled.

Once she got outside, she took a deep, long breath.

Don't let the jerk get under your skin. What does he know about you or your relationship?

She looked up, and sure enough, there was Skip, glaring down at her from their window. Well, he wasn't glaring, but she was defensive. She waved. *Skip, honey, are you okay?* Just when she thought they were doing all right, Manny made her doubt herself. Men sucked.

As she turned to walk away, she heard Skip howling as he'd done the past three mornings. She followed her new routine of stepping into the alcove two doors down and waited until he stopped crying before she carried on. She was always careful to peek and make sure he wasn't still standing guard at the window. He was gone. She could go.

But just then, Manny and Tank stepped out and started walking, or barely walking, in the opposite direction. Manny would take a few steps and then stop and wait for Tank.

Something was wrong with Tank, and no matter how surly his owner was, she felt a pang in her heart because if she lost Skip right now, it would be the final straw. She made a vow to avoid Manny in the future, but if she couldn't avoid him, she'd be patient and kinder to him. In fact, she'd be kinder to everyone as part of her new routine. She of all people should know that nobody's life was as it seemed. They all had bad days and problems. Look at Mr. Ghafoor. Look at Manny and Tank. Look at Martha Knight.

Manny sighed and leaned over to heave Tank into his arms. Tank dangled before him as Manny headed back to the apartment. He looked silly carrying the large dog.

Manny saw Lucy and stopped dead.

Compassion ruled the moment, because maybe just as Lucy hated telling people that John was gone because saying it made it real, Manny couldn't admit that Tank was sick.

She lifted her hand and gave a gentle wave. Indeed, she'd be kinder to Manny and more patient with him despite his bad attitude. Tank too. Tank and Manny weren't a threat to Skip anymore. Like John had once said, "Anyone who loves dogs has to be good, right?" Of course, she wasn't so sure his generous proclamation included Hoarding Manny.

21

SKIP

THE THOMAS ROUTINE

THOMAS and I have our routine down. Thomas makes his summer pancakes and fiddles around in his apartment until I tell him it's time to come and read to me.

As soon as Lucy leaves the apartment, I go to my lookout point at the window. When she exits the building, I howl. Sometimes she stops and looks up at me. I howl to tell her it's okay to leave me alone. I've picked up Thomas's habit of howling three times; that's the signal that it's safe for him to come and read to me. By the time Lucy disappears from sight and I stop howling, Thomas is propping open the mail slot with some paper and finding our place in the book.

I'm hooked on *Harry Potter*. So hooked that I've forfeited my watchdog duties these past mornings. I don't have the ottoman anyway, and Lucy still hasn't noticed it's gone. Plus, I didn't have Thomas reading to me before. I'm not a slacker; I'm an opportunist. I figure my neighborhood watch duties can go on hold for summer vacation.

I hope we finish Harry's first book today. Thomas told

me there are seven! Harry's story could be *my* story. He Who Must Not Be Named has become symbolic of the person who will ruin my life if she ever comes out into the open: Cecilia.

Harry has the best and fastest-growing pack ever, even if he doesn't appreciate them yet. I'm listening and learning. My pack is growing too with Thomas, Manny, and Tank. And Thomas likes Manny. He doesn't jump or stop reading when Manny comes out of his apartment. Manny only says hi and keeps going where he's going. Probably to get his coffee and donut with Tank, when Tank's up for it.

Sometimes I fall asleep while Thomas is reading, but I'm pretty good at catching the drift of the story when I come to.

We always take a break for lunch. Thomas goes away to make a sandwich. Lucy has walked me the same time the last two days. Thomas has a pretty good internal clock (like me!). His stomach starts to growl around the same time each day. Then after lunch, Thomas and I follow the same routine. I howl thrice, and Thomas answers my summons. It all works like wizardry and Hogwarts.

22

LUCY
TURN THE PAGE

Lucy had to take an early lunch. She wanted to talk to Walter in the afternoon about her idea to add gardening crates to the outdoor space. Dr. Ryan had supported her idea and said Walter should have the final say because he handled the landscaping and they'd need his help with the crates. She'd need to leave at five o'clock on the dot to meet up with Aunt Eve. Plus, she was still peeved about Manny's comment, hinting that she wasn't taking care of Skip. So, she let herself into the building quietly and tiptoed up the stairs, wanting to surprise Skip for lunch.

She didn't register the steady thrum of Thomas's voice until she reached the upper landing. When she caught sight of him through the bannister sitting on the floor at her door, it was so out of context and unexpected that she frowned and asked, "What are you doing?"

Thomas jumped. "You're early! You're early! You're early!" He dropped his book and all but tripped over his feet as he rushed past her and downstairs, where he crashed into his apartment and slammed the door.

By now, Skip was barking. It was his curious bark. Lucy reached over to pick up *Harry Potter and the Sorcerer's Stone*. What in the world?

She unlocked the door and sat the book on the entry table, not quite sure what to make of what was happening, ignoring Skip bumping against her legs.

And then it hit her.

Dammit. This was why Manny had been laughing at her this morning. He knew Thomas was reading to Skip. Skip couldn't be alone. Thomas had rescued him.

Deflated, she looked at Skip and his calm but happy-to-see-her expression. She hadn't been doing well at all. Skip had Thomas reading to him. For how long? All day? When had this started? Was this why he stopped howling when she left? Because Thomas was taking care of him? On Tuesday, she'd heard Thomas leaving as she left. So that was when it had started. Her gut told her so.

DOGTV wasn't the only reason he was happy at night and hadn't ransacked her apartment and hadn't mutilated her shoes again. Even her walking him at lunch wasn't the answer. Thomas had been the answer. Not leaving Skip alone all day had been the answer.

While on their walk, she peppered Skip with questions about Thomas. How had this all come together? Did he love Thomas more than her? She wished he could talk, but he was busy being a dog and sniffing here and peeing there. She wished she could learn more from Thomas, but she didn't want to scare him. She'd have to wait until Mrs. Brighton came home tonight.

Step up. Face it. If Thomas was helping Skip then she obviously needed Thomas's help. Was it so bad that she couldn't do it alone? What was so horrible about admitting it? And who knew, maybe Thomas needed Skip too. Maybe when she spoke to Mrs. Brighton, Mrs. Brighton would tell her that Thomas had been happier the past few days. Now that would be a sweet turn of events.

But had she permanently scared Thomas off? In case he came back, what could she do to show him it was okay that he read to Skip?

She'd start by making the area more comfortable and welcoming to Thomas. But she couldn't find an extra chair in the house to put in the hall for him. And for the first time, she noticed that John had taken Skip's ottoman. Who was worse? She for not noticing, or John for taking it? *Poor puppy.*

She took a cushion from the couch and set it in the hall, but it looked trashy and accentuated Manny's pot clutter. She moved the bedside table, John's bedside table, outside her door, and sat Thomas's book on the stand.

Maybe Manny had an extra chair? He certainly had a surplus of everything else. She could practice being nice to him and ask him what he knew. She really did want to know when this had all started.

She left her apartment door open and instructed Skip to sit and stay.

He froze inside the doorway, watching her with great interest.

When she knocked on Manny's door, Tank didn't bark. She looked over her shoulder at Skip and reminded him, "Stay." Manny either wasn't home, or Tank was getting worse and could care less.

But Manny opened up. "Wow, twice in one day."

Lucy pointed behind her. "Thomas reads to him, doesn't he? That's what you were insinuating this morning."

"Bingo."

"I didn't know."

"I gathered."

"I was wondering," she looked around and eyed the stacked pots in the corner of the common hall and wished his chest wasn't so wide that she couldn't peek around him and into his apartment, "do you have an extra chair, bean-bag, or something I can borrow to set out here for Thomas to be comfortable? Or I can pay for it."

Manny's brows slammed together. "Why would I have a beanbag? Do they even make them anymore?"

Lucy blushed. "Well, you seem to have a lot of stuff—"

He scratched his chin and squinted at her. "Just because I have a few extra plant pots around, you think I have a beanbag?"

"A few extra pots . . . you have enough to open a nursery!"

He glared at her. "You know what I used to like about you?"

"That I'm observant?" she asked.

"You didn't use to be talkative."

"I usually like to mind my own business."

"What a joke. We both know that's not true," he said.

Right. The property manager. Of course he knew because she and John had complained constantly to the property manager, who always came back and offered to let them out of the lease, saying that the owner of the building understood their frustration but wasn't going to press Manny to get rid of his stuff.

"That was John," she said. *John isn't here. He can take the blame.*

"Birds of a feather . . ."

"Well, that's hardly the case now. No flocking happening." She couldn't believe she was admitting it. To Manny of all people.

"You need to flock someone new."

So arrogant! "Who I flock is my business, thank you. And you *do* keep crap everywhere. It's not like I'm reaching."

"So some pots make me a hoarder?"

"Some? Forget it." *What is it about him that gets me riled up so easily?* "I didn't come over here to talk about your stupid pots! I came to get a beanbag!"

Skip was whining like a toddler. He hadn't budged, but she could tell their bickering was stressing Skip out.

She took a breath and started again. "Listen, I'm sorry. I just wanted to encourage Thomas. He doesn't talk to me. I thought I'd leave signs that it's okay." She was sick of having to tilt her head all the way back to stare up at Manny. She turned away.

The sofa cushion would be better than nothing.

He sighed. "Hold on. I have something." He vanished into his apartment, closing the door behind him.

Lo and behold if he didn't return a few minutes later with a vintage green beanbag.

"Don't say a word," he growled.

Tank poked his head between the door and Manny's legs. It was nice to see him up and about.

She smiled and pretended to zip her lips as she stepped aside to let Manny pass. He dropped the beanbag next to the nightstand and *Harry Potter*.

"Are we done here?" he asked, crossing his arms.

Lucy nodded. "Thank you. I'll return it."

"Don't bother. Have a dozen more like it," he said.

"You're kidding," she said.

"Yes, I'm kidding. I don't want it back because I'm not a hoarder. Would a hoarder say that?" He walked away.

"Probably, because it's going to good use," she said to his back.

Manny stalked back inside, mumbling something that sounded like *I'm no damn hoarder.*

Once everything was situated and she said goodbye to Skip, Lucy made extra noise stomping down the stairs to the foyer so Thomas would hear her leave. When Skip stopped howling and left the window, she snuck back to the building and quietly slid into the foyer, pressing herself against the wall. A few seconds later, Thomas's door opened.

She smiled as she heard him climb the steps, plop into the beanbag, and start reading. Skip had made a friend. And a few seconds later, just before she snuck out of the building, she heard Manny's door open, and he asked, "Hey, Thomas, can Tank listen too?"

23

SKIP

ACHES AND BREAKS

THOMAS READ to me all afternoon from the new beanbag but still ran off like a startled squirrel as soon as Lucy came home for the night.

What a day!

Harry defeated He Who Must Not Be Named in the first book, and it was amazing. *He* was in Quirrell's turban the entire time. There was a three-headed dog in the story that Harry, Ron, and Hermione had to get past. Three heads! Even if I have nightmares tonight, reading time is so worth it. And don't get me started on Quidditch. I know the Sorting Hat would have put me in Gryffindor, and I would have been the snitch catcher in Quidditch. It's a small ball, *duh*. Who's your snitch dog, Harry? This dog right here, man.

My afternoon flew by with all the excitement of the book. We've already started *Chamber of Secrets*, but Lucy doesn't work on Saturdays and Sundays, so I'll have to wait until Monday to find out what happens with Harry's pack.

For the next two days, I will frolic with Lucy and Aunt Eve.

I love Aunt Eve's visits. Even before, when we had John, she brought light with her. She always laughs, and she never cares if I sniff her between the legs. She never cares about my shedding, and she always slips me some of her dinner. Aunt Eve does whatever she wants and anything that makes her happy. And with Aunt Eve here to take care of Lucy, I can take a few days off.

When Lucy gets home, she says, "Before Aunt Eve arrives, I'm going to talk to Mrs. Brighton about your new best friend."

She opens the door but then hesitates. "Or should I not say anything and if he wants to do it, he wants to do it? Aaaah! I am overthinking everything, and I hate it."

I like how she is talking to me like I deserve the explanation. But she's right. She's overthinking this.

"All I can do is ask," she says to me. "If Mrs. Brighton says no, she says no."

I dart in front of her. Otherwise, she could take all night.

"Skip, get back here. I need to talk to her alone."

Not a chance. I'm going with you. This is about me.

"If you keep disobeying me, I'm going to get rid of DOGTV and get you a kennel."

Trust me, lady, the kennel would be less torture. Actually, that's kind of not true. I'm embarrassed to admit that I'm starting to enjoy a few of the dog shows. Not the ball-throwing ones. Those still piss me off.

Since I can't smell the dogs on the shows, at first I had a hard time recognizing them as repeat actors, but sound is my second strongest sense, and I'm starting to recognize their barks and am tracking a few. I'm using it for research and studying when they're all playing together so I can see how the alpha dog takes control so I can better manage Lucy while I have to. In the past, all the dogs at the park have had human alphas, so our pecking order started with humans and went down from there. But the shift to me having to manage the crowd as an equal to the human alphas? I'm not quite sure anymore how to approach dogs.

I don't know any of the dogs' names, so I've been nicknaming them myself and trying not to be as pretentious as the San Francisco dog owners. And you know what? Old dogs *can* learn new tricks. Where I thought naming was tiresome before, I have an appreciation for it now. Since I've never had to name dogs, I didn't get how hard it is to come up with an original name. Well, since I can't smell them, I decided to name them after what I think they'd smell like. Skunk, Rose, Biscuit, Mud, and then there's Peanut Nutter, whose name is punny because he's a nut.

I sit, head held high, as Lucy knocks on the Brightons' door. Presentation is everything. It's too late for first impressions since they've seen me for years. But I want Mrs. Brighton to know that mine and Thomas's book club is a good thing. That I'm not a bad influence, and that I'm alpha material.

"Oh hello, Lucy. Is everything okay?" Mrs. Brighton asks. She's tentative.

"Hi, Mrs. Brighton. Thomas has been a great help the last few days. Do you have a moment to talk?"

"Yes, please come in."

We follow her to the living room. The apartment is larger than ours, but just like our apartment, their living room is at the end of a hall, the bathroom halfway down on one side. Thomas is nowhere in sight, but I can smell him and hear him moving in another room. His nervous energy is tangible, and I wish I could talk to him alone. I don't think the Brightons have many visitors. And there's no Mr. Brighton.

"It's not often I hear someone say that something is better thanks to my boy," Mrs. Brighton says as she and Lucy take a seat.

I sit like a good dog at Lucy's feet.

"Oh, Skip and I owe him a great deal. I don't know if you know, but he has been reading to Skip through the door since Wednesday, and I know Skip really enjoys his company because he hasn't been tearing up anything."

Thomas cracks a door, but my instincts tell me to wait for him to invite my attention.

"He told me," Mrs. Brighton says. "Are you okay with him reading to Skip?"

"Absolutely, but only as long as you are and as long as Thomas wants to," Lucy says.

"He's always wanted a dog. His therapist has recommended a service or therapy dog, but we've never had the funds or space for one. And we'd need to walk him, and that won't happen. Thomas doesn't like to take walks anymore."

Huh? Who doesn't like to take walks?

I think back to a time when I remember Thomas taking walks every day. I'd watch him from my station. Sure, they were quick ones, probably just around the block, but Mrs. Brighton is right, he stopped taking walks dog years ago. Even if I lost all four legs, I'd want to take a walk. Have you seen those dogs with wheels for their back legs? That'd be me. Nothing would stop me. *Roll on, man.*

"I hope you don't mind my asking," Lucy said. "Is he autistic?"

I'm not expecting Mrs. Brighton's reaction any more than Lucy can have been, but she totally tenses up and rolls her shoulders back, lifting her chin. Her actions make her look three feet taller, like a mama bear on her hind legs in those nature shows on TV.

"Thomas isn't a label. He's a young man *with* autism."

Whatever message Mrs. Brighton is delivering, Lucy snatches it up by leaning forward in an interested and receptive manner.

"Oh, of course. That was stupid of me. I'm sorry, Mrs. Brighton. Diagnostics and labels are a bad habit of my nursing, but I am getting better."

Mama Bear releases a long breath and says, "I just hate the assumptions and, worse, the expectations that come with saying someone is this or that, rather than what they have. Do you know, he doesn't have a single friend?"

I face her. *He has me now, Mrs. Brighton.*

"I'm sorry," Lucy says. "It must be difficult as a mother when your child has no friends. Maybe he and Skip are friends? I've never researched autism before, and I didn't know service dogs were an option."

Me neither. Look at us canines representing. Damn, we're good.

"Yes, the service dogs especially help younger children with autism with sensory processing, social interactions, and reading. The dogs can also help keep them safe and calm. Thomas has come a long way and has learned to stay home alone, as you know, after school and during the summer. He has a routine that works for him. He reads for a large portion of the day to calm his thoughts and the world around him. I think it's wonderful how he transferred this coping tool to Skip's howling. I think it works well for him, but we can ask him."

"I'd be happy to pay Thomas. It wouldn't be much, but I could pay him ten dollars a week, and he wouldn't be obligated to do it when he doesn't feel like it."

Mrs. Brighton smiles. "I think that would be wonderful for his self-confidence. That he has taken the initiative to leave the apartment on his own has been a huge step for us. Granted, as a child this would have been scary, but he's fifteen now, and the more he improves his social skills, the better chances he will have as a functioning adult someday. And I won't always be here . . ." Mrs. Brighton waves her hand before her face and shakes her head as if to rid herself of her thoughts.

So it's sounding like Thomas and I have the A-OK and he will be reading to me from now on. Look what a little howling can do. Not only do I have Thomas, Thomas gets to build his confidence. Good work on my part if I do say so myself. I might have a little therapy dog in me. I lick my chops and raise my snout with pride. Dr. Skip is in the house!

"Skip," I hear Thomas call to me. As I jump to my feet and wag my tail, I glance at Mrs. Brighton to see if she's okay with me going to him. Her smile is a green light as far as I'm concerned. I trot to the cracked door of Thomas's room and tune out Lucy and Mrs. Brighton's conversation.

"Hi, Skip," Thomas says.

I know my barking up close bothers him, so I greet him by wagging my tail.

He's reading a piece of paper. He looks more stern than usual and says to me, "Sit."

Ah, I get it. He thinks he's teaching me something. But I like him, so I sit.

"Lay down."

Easy breezy. Okay. Done.

"Roll over."

I saw that one coming a mile away, buddy. Done.

"Speak."

I am surprised. *Ruf!* I only hope he won't ask me to shake because that's not going to happen.

"Good dog, Skip." And he lets me lick a handful of the most delicious, delectable pebbles of food I've ever had. They're so good, I begin to over-salivate. I hope Mrs. Brighton doesn't mind a little drool on her floors.

By now Lucy and Mrs. Brighton are standing in the doorway. His mom asks, "What are you feeding him?"

Thomas doesn't look up. "Bacon Bits. Dogs need treats to learn new tricks."

Lucy laughs. "I'd better get some Bacon Bits."

"Thomas," his mom says, "do you like reading to Skip when I'm at work?"

"I like it."

"Would you like to help Lucy and Skip and keep reading to him when Lucy's at work?"

"Help will always be given to those who ask for it."

Hee hee. Nice quote, Thomas Dumbledore.

Lucy doesn't get it, but Mrs. Brighton says, "Good one." And Thomas smiles at me.

"Lucy will give you ten dollars a week. What do you think of that?"

"I like it."

I look from Thomas's bowed head to Mrs. Brighton's and Lucy's smiling faces.

Sounds like Thomas might be an official member of our pack, and I like *that*.

"We'd better get going. My aunt is arriving soon," Lucy says.

"Lucy," Mrs. Brighton stops her, "I'm sorry about the other day and for pressing about John. That was none of my business."

"No, you didn't do anything wrong. I'm just having a hard time admitting what's happening." I'm not sure she's aware of it, but Lucy covers her heart with her hand.

Mrs. Brighton reaches out and squeezes Lucy's shoulder. "Just remember, you *have* heartache. You aren't heartbroken."

24

SKIP
PHAIUS TANCARVILLEAE

AUNT EVE HAS JUST ARRIVED and is talking a mile a minute. Lots of questions for Lucy about John, but I can tell by Lucy's hunched shoulders that she hears Eve but doesn't want to say too much about John. Plus, and I tried to tell her as soon as she got home, the toilet overflowed just as she rushed back to work after lunch. I stayed out of the bathroom all afternoon. Lucy is calling the property manager and mopping up the water with our towels.

I haven't even been walked yet, but she did open the back door so I could get out and relieve myself (being skunk-shy, I no longer rush out, but the smelly asshole hasn't been back, so I have that going for me). But I don't care. Auntie is here! At some point I'll get walked.

"I'm so embarrassed about the toilet," Lucy says. "Maybe we should find you a hotel."

"No worries, sweetie. I just want to spend time with you and Skip, and now a plumber. And you can tell me about John."

"Ugh, that's the last thing I want to talk about," Lucy

says and drops the wet towels into the washing machine. "Don't you have big news to tell me? Let's talk about you."

"We'll get to that, but in the meantime, don't worry about me. We can settle in, order pizza, and wait for the plumber."

Just then there's a knock, and I can smell Manny before Lucy opens the door.

"Oh, um, Manny, now's not a good time."

He lifts a plunger and a metal thing that looks like a snake. "So I heard."

"How did you know?" Lucy frowns.

"Property manager called me. I help them out when they can't find anyone fast enough. You just haven't needed my help in the past."

"I guess that's why you get special privileges?" Lucy lifts her brows. She is still annoyed with him about keeping mine and Thomas's book club from her.

"That's one reason," he says.

Lucy brushes a few wisps of hair away from her face. "I'm sorry. You've already helped me twice this week. The skunk, the beanbag . . . all the good things in life."

"Third time's a charm. Maybe I won't have to help you again."

Lucy's had a long and emotional week, but I'm still surprised when she says, "I don't need you to rescue me, you know."

"Good," Manny says, "because I'm not rescuing you. I'm rescuing your toilet, the wood floors, and Mrs. Brighton's ceiling."

"What skunk? And what is the story with his beanbag?" Aunt Eve glides over with a friendly smile. "I'm Eve, Lucy's aunt."

See? I wasn't kidding. Aunt Eve does whatever she wants. By the way Lucy's lips pinch and her eyes widen, I can tell she wishes Aunt Eve had stayed in the living room. But, if you ask me, Aunt Eve's a super tension breaker.

Manny must think so too because he smiles at her.

"Aunt Eve, my neighbor Manny," Lucy says.

Manny nods. "Can I get started?"

"Yes, of course. I'm sorry. I'm frazzled. I haven't walked Skip."

"I'll start on this while you walk him," Manny says. "I promise not to steal and hoard your things."

"Very funny," Lucy says and retrieves my leash.

I want to shout, *Wait!* I don't really want to go anywhere. I act like I don't need a walk, but Lucy isn't falling for it. I look at Aunt Eve, and I'm so jealous when she says, "I'm going to stay here and get to know Manny."

"I'd rather you come with us," Lucy says, straight-faced and staring hard at Aunt Eve.

"I'll be here when you get back," Aunt Eve says.

Normally, Aunt Eve loves to walk me, but I can tell she is like a dog with a bone, only Manny is the bone. She's always curious about other people. "What makes them tick?" she often asks. And she always tells people, "I'm a student of human behavior."

"Go ahead. We'll be fine." Aunt Eve ushers us out the door.

Lucy and I look at each other: me envious, her doubtful.

I can't tell you much about our walk because I walk and pee as fast as I possibly can, and Lucy seems as eager as me to get back to the apartment.

Who knows what Aunt Eve will be chatting to Manny about when we get home again. One time Lucy and I caught her talking to Mr. Ghafoor at the corner market about his parents. He was crying like a baby. "She's like Barbara Walters," Lucy once told John and me. "She gets people to confide, and in no time, they've cried through an entire tissue factory."

I imagine Manny doing the Barbara Walters Bawl in a fetal position as I run up our stairs, ignoring Lucy's cry to wait for her. What if Aunt Eve innocently asks Manny about Tank? I feel a sudden urge to protect him. Fortunately, the door is open, so I don't have to wait for Lucy to open it. Aunt Eve has pulled up a stool outside the bathroom, and Manny is pushing the strange metal hose down the toilet.

Aunt Eve says, "I used to take Lucy to the zoo when she was little. That's where she fell in love with wolves."

Manny chuckles. "I see."

"They mate for life," Aunt Eve says.

"Got it," Manny says.

"Do you have a partner?"

Lucy hears the question just as she enters. "Leave Manny alone so he can get back to his life."

"What?" Aunt Eve winks at me. "Manny is a grown man. A very grown and handsome man." Aunt Eve eyes his hindquarters and smiles at Lucy, who cringes. "He knows he doesn't have to answer if he doesn't want to."

"Feel free to ignore her, Manny. Since this space is too small, we will leave you alone. And wait in the kitchen. Skip. *Eve.*" Lucy never calls our aunt by her name alone. Aunt Eve is gonna be in trouble.

Lucy points aggressively at us and toward the kitchen.

What? And miss this convo? I plop down between Aunt Eve and Manny. Lucy glares at me, but I'm not moving. *No way, Jose.* The more I learn about Manny, the easier it will be to bring him into our pack.

"Come on, give him room," Lucy begs us.

She's about to throw a fit, so I know I need to forfeit my position if Aunt Eve is to keep playing detective. One of us has to give. *All for one and one for all.* I join Lucy down the hall, but I can still hear the discussion. Lucy was only pretending she didn't want to learn more anyway. Like me, she can't help but eavesdrop.

"And you have the Mastiff and live next door?" Aunt Eve asks.

Uh-oh.

"Yes."

"And what's his name again? Turf?"

"Tank. But I like Turf."

Aunt Eve sounds flirtatious when she asks, "That's a bit cliché, isn't it? A large dog named Tank."

I have a thing about dog names, so I love Aunt Eve all the more for asking Manny about Tank's name.

But all noise stops. Everything and everyone has stilled. Lucy looks down at me and raises her eyebrows.

Then Manny asks, "You get to the point, don't you?"

"At my age, there's no reason to beat around the bush."

"Tank is short for *Phaius Tancarvilleae.*"

Now that's a mouthful.

Lucy and I look at each other. I have no idea what *Pha-whatever* means, but that's one hell of a fancy name. Kind of sissy-la-la sounding for a Mastiff if you ask me.

"Latin for?" Aunt Eve asks.

"It's an endangered swamp orchid."

Lucy covers her mouth to hold back a snort.

Oh man, I want to laugh too. That husky and surly-looking dog is named after a flower?

"Oh, of course, you're the one with the pots. So you named your dog after an orchid. That's lovely."

The toilet flushes. Water runs, and I hear splashing. Manny must be washing his hands. "My younger sister named him."

Ah-ha. Now we are learning about Manny. He has a younger sister. Never seen her, not that I know of.

"That was generous of you to let her name him," she said.

"Tank was her dog first."

Whoa. Lucy and I look at each other with surprise then we jump as footsteps near the kitchen. I pretend to be contemplating my empty food bowl, and Lucy refolds a kitchen towel.

Aunt Eve stops with Manny in our front doorway adjacent to the kitchen. "She must like plants as much as you do."

Manny chuckles. "Making assumptions runs in the family, I see."

"With little information, what choice do we have?" Aunt Eve asks.

"The pots were hers. She was a botanist," Manny says.

Were? Was? We all glom on to the words. Even Aunt Eve knows better than to pry further.

"Eve, nice to meet you. Skip, try not to clog up the toilet again."

Hee hee. Poop jokes crack me up every time.

Lucy nods. "Thanks for your help. Sorry you had to mess with the toilet. I'll be sure to give the property manager some praise."

"That will be a first."

"And probably the last," she says.

"Lucy," Aunt Eve says in a "don't be rude" kind of voice.

"Don't worry, Eve. Lucy and I understand each other."

Not really, I want to say, but okay.

I sniff Manny all over while he pets my head. I like Lucy's energy around him. She gets so strong and bossy. He inspires strength in her. He is bona fide alpha material.

He leaves us, and I turn to look at the ladies.

"You're so nosy," Lucy swats at Aunt Eve, but she giggles for the first time in days.

"But he's so mysterious and irresistible."

"Trust me," Lucy says, "he's not one of the heroes in your romance novels. I'm beginning to think no man is."

Aunt Eve pulls Lucy into her arms. "That's one of the things I want to talk to you about."

25

LUCY

GOING TO THE CHAPEL

DUMBFOUNDED, Lucy needed a minute to digest what her aunt had just announced. *No way.*

"You're what?" Lucy had drunk a glass of wine with pizza, something she rarely did, but Aunt Eve had said, "We need to toast," which had seemed like such an odd thing for her to say. Especially after Lucy had just finished explaining how and why John had left her. Hardly the time to celebrate. Aunt Eve had even laughed, albeit apologetically, when Lucy recounted the demise of her relationship over her cherished Cherry Chip Cake.

So not funny.

"I'm engaged," her aunt repeated, swiveling her shoulders from side to side, sounding both excited and a little embarrassed to be sharing her news. Her smile was wide. "I would have waited to tell you, but our engagement won't be long."

Even Skip looked dizzy on his feet. He yipped, and if Lucy didn't know better, she'd think he was as shocked as she was and asking, "Did she say 'engaged'?"

"I don't understand," Lucy said because, honestly, she really didn't.

Aunt Eve took their plates to the kitchen and returned with full wineglasses. It probably wasn't the wisest decision, but Lucy took the glass and guzzled. *Bottle. She needed the bottle.*

Aunt Eve turned to face her on the couch and took her hand. "Sweetie, I know this is a bad time to tell you."

Lucy felt like a selfish twit for agreeing with her. "It's the worst possible time to tell me. John has only been gone for a week. I have wedding invitations stuffed in the cabinet less than five feet from where we're sitting because I can't look at them without crying."

"I'm sorry."

Lucy leaned across the cushions to hug her. "I don't know if I'm jealous of you or happy for you. Mostly I'm confused how it happened."

"I want to tell you about him, but only when you want to hear our story."

Our story. Lucy turned her cheek on Aunt Eve's shoulder, taking in her apartment sans John. Skip poked his big head into her stomach, through the core cavity between hers and her aunt's embrace, and rested his snout on Lucy's bent knee.

He always seemed to know what she needed and when she needed it.

She was having such a hard time not making Aunt Eve's engagement about herself. So far she was failing. Too bad she hadn't read her horoscope yet today. She imagined it said something like: "*You won't believe your ears today, but you have no choice but to try to take it all in.*"

She wanted to know how her aunt had met and was

marrying someone after all this time, and she *didn't* want to know. Aunt Eve was fifty-eight, and for Lucy's entire life, her aunt had been single and Lucy's constant companion on loving love. She'd sat on her aunt's lap in the theater as they watched *The Little Mermaid*, and she'd fallen asleep most every night listening to her aunt read a romance. Lucy had watched her aunt cry "happy tears," as her aunt called them, at the end of *You've Got Mail*, *Pretty Woman*, and throughout *Outlander,* which they'd binge-watched for three days together one rainy weekend last year. No one loved love like Aunt Eve.

And Lucy knew that no one, not even she, deserved true love more than her aunt. Aunt Eve's generous heart had been one of sacrifice. She'd been there for Lucy and her mom before and after her mom was diagnosed with bipolar disease. Lucy had figured out a long time ago that her mom and aunt had made raising her their priority, and no man would be good enough to be a male influence in her childhood. That didn't stop her mom from dating, but she never brought the rotating boyfriends around once diagnosed. But Aunt Eve? She never even dated. She was waiting for "the one that's right for all of us."

Their love and dedication had shaped Lucy, and she loved them to the moon and back for being who they were. Over time, the long-term consequences of each woman's sacrifice were different. Aunt Eve thrived on the idea of love, while Lucy's mom had eventually given up men altogether and now said they weren't worth the trouble. Now Aunt Eve was getting married. *Married!*

Lucy was determined to stop putting such a damper on her aunt's life-changing news. "I do love you, Aunt Eve."

Skip burrowed his head deeper between them. His

happy groan made a low vibration, like a purring cat. Lucy made a note to be more affectionate with him. They all needed more love, and thank goodness her aunt would be getting her share.

Lucy sat back. "Okay," with a single clap, she mustered some bravado, "tell me the most amazing love story you will ever tell me and the one only you deserve."

Aunt Eve blushed, her cherub cheeks and eyes oozing with adoration, and Lucy was struck by how she seemed to look ten years younger.

"Look at you, the blushing bride." She meant it. She hadn't even choked on the word "bride." Her aunt looked lovelier than ever. Lucy squeezed her aunt's hand.

"I met him at my fortieth high school reunion," Aunt Eve squealed like a teenager.

Yikes. Lucy was already having another immature moment, and she wanted to take back all of her newfound graciousness and challenge her aunt: *But that was only a month ago!* She bit her tongue. She was beginning to sound like her love-hating mother.

This isn't about me. This is Aunt Eve's story.

Skip rose from where he sat at their feet and started pacing, but she knew he didn't need another walk yet. He was getting antsy. Probably picking up on her confusing signals. *Happy. Not happy. Happy. Not happy.* She'd probably gotten him used to only being unhappy lately.

"Hold that thought," she stood, "and let me turn on DOGTV for Skip." But even with the channel playing, he kept pacing and watching them. "When did you get so nosy?" Lucy asked him.

He dropped his jaw and looked at her like she was an idiot.

"Did you see his look?" she asked her aunt.

"It's in Skip's DNA to be alert, especially when change is in the air," Aunt Eve said.

"We've had our share of changes," Lucy said.

Skip barked.

"No one asked you, Skip. Watch your show. Go lie down." He ignored her, but she didn't have the energy to make him obey. She turned to her aunt. "Enough about Skip. Continue."

"His name is George. I recognized him immediately. He looked the same as I remember. He said I looked the same too. We talked all night! And our first kiss was magical."

Her aunt kissing was TMI for Lucy.

"You might even remember me telling you a story about Skinny George."

Skinny George? "Skinny George!" Lucy shouted, too surprised to do otherwise.

Of course she knew the story about Skinny George. Skinny George had a crush on Eve all through high school. She'd had to chase him away, time and time again. "Poor lovesick puppy," was how her mom had always referred to him. And Aunt Eve would say, "The only man who has ever been head over heels for me is the one I'd never want."

"But you didn't want him." Love at first sight had been one of her aunt's preachings: *I'll know him when I first see him.* Lucy's fragile acceptance of her aunt's newfound love flew out the window.

"I know. I know. But I saw him, and he just swept me off my feet." She giggled.

An alien had abducted her aunt. Next, her mom would show up and say she was getting married too.

"What about your talk about wanting love at first sight?

You never liked him. You're telling me that after forty years of not seeing him, all of a sudden you're attracted to him? That you love him? That you're engaged to someone you tossed aside without a doubt before? And this all happened just weeks ago?"

"People change," Aunt Eve said, lifting her chin.

"Aren't you settling? You of all people, the person who has taught me, outside of John, almost every thing I know about love? You're telling me that you would be with someone who wants you and someone you never used to want, rather than be alone?"

"Oh honey, this isn't about being alone. I'm more than fine alone. I think I've proven that. It's about timing, and it's about falling in love. So it took us forty years, and it wasn't love at first sight. So what? I'm older and wiser. And maybe our attraction and love needed to percolate for four decades."

Lucy was being a bitch. She knew it. She wondered if she was the only thirty-two-year-old woman who felt so clueless about reality and love that someone had to explain it to her in a coffee metaphor.

"I hesitate to even ask this," Aunt Eve said, "but what if you and John are finished now, but the two of you run into each other in five years, twenty years, or forty years, and all of the experiences and changes in your life help you connect on a different and better level? Would you say it wasn't love? That you were settling?"

Lucy couldn't answer. Aunt Eve was being rhetorical, and these days Lucy was incapable of processing any wisdom outside of a television show's snappy tips. She defaulted to thinking about Carrie and Big. She might feel alone about her experience in love right now, but if millions of women could follow a series for six years and, like her, buy into Carrie and Big finally being together and it being meant to be, why couldn't she cut her own aunt some slack? Because, yes, if she were honest, she'd probably wait for John if she knew it would happen someday. Who was she kidding? She was already waiting.

And yet, she couldn't get past everything Aunt Eve had always believed in, had told her, and had read to her. She couldn't get over how much her aunt had truly influenced her own choices.

"The truth is, Lucy, love doesn't have to be a whirlwind. It can be about friendship and companionship. I wish you could have known your grandpa. Once, I asked him how he knew he was in love with your grandma. I was so excited to hear their story." Aunt Eve started to laugh. "And boy was I in for a surprise. You know what he said? He said, 'Well, I was actually in love with a woman named Belinda, but then I met your mom, and I knew she'd be a better wife and mother. So I proposed.'" Aunt Eve shook her head. "I was so appalled by what he said that I made a vow that I'd never do anything so unromantic and practical."

Maybe Lucy's mom had inherited some of her practical views on love from her own father, not just from her hands-on experience with male turnover.

And just as her own beliefs about love had been shaped by Aunt Eve, Aunt Eve's (and probably her mom's) had been shaped by their parents' relationship.

Her aunt continued, "I was young, hopeful, living through books that had no true basis in reality: millionaire city men falling in love with the virgin country girl. Just silly. I should not have filled your head with all that nonsense."

Lucy's breath caught. It was as if Aunt Eve had punched a hole in her chest. To hear her aunt refer to their history, some of her most cherished childhood memories that had given her something to dream about, as "nonsense" and in the same dismissive tone she'd expect from her mother, made Lucy feel like an idiot and an immature fool who had romanticized everything, even her relationship with Aunt Eve. Had Lucy believed everything in those books? No. But did she like how the books, full of love and endless possibilities, made her feel? Absolutely. That was the gift of her relationship with Aunt Eve. Or so she'd thought.

"It wasn't nonsense to me," Lucy said. "It was the foundation for most everything you and I did together. How many days did we spend at the zoo watching the wolves, the eagles, all the animals that mated for life? What was that about?"

Her aunt cringed, tilting her head to one side as her eyes filled with remorse. "Oh, Lucy, the influence I wielded without thought. I always loved zoos and those animals. At one point, I thought I would become a zoologist. Plus, the wolves were special to me, and I loved spending time with you."

"You wanted to be a zoologist?" *How had she never known this about her aunt who had helped raise her?*

"Yes, and I also did believe in fated love . . . then. And I had a huge crush on the zookeeper of those exhibits. I always thought it was a sign that he managed most of the creatures that tended to be monogamous. We went out a few times and had a lot of fun, but it fizzled, and we went our separate ways."

Lucy's heart broke into a million pieces as she put two and two together. "And that's when we stopped going to the zoo every week."

"Yes, probably," Aunt Eve said. "But more than our good memories came out of it, right? You have Skip, and you wanted him because of the zoo."

Lucy wasn't quite sure she could articulate how much her aunt and their zoo visits had influenced her life choices, but if she started writing a list, it would contain more than picking Skip. What else in Lucy's life had resulted from those discussions and misbeliefs that started on a zoo bench between bites of a peanut butter and jelly sandwich? Maybe she should get a therapist.

She was an idiot. A certifiable idiot. Unsophisticated. Like a thirty-two-year-old going on nine, packing around stupid love stories. John would probably meet someone with more experience in love, someone who had been in and out of love a few times and seemed more like a grown woman. More sophisticated. Not some buffoon running around trying to live a fairy tale.

Her aunt changed the subject from George to wolves.

"Did you know that the wolf pack is run by the lead male and female? And the pack is the parents and their offspring, but most wolves will leave their pack around two to three years old to find a new territory and a mate. Some might stay behind to fill a need in the pack or to help raise a new litter. And, as you know, they mate for life. I wonder if they fall in love or if it's more like my dad seeing my mom and knowing she'd be a good mate, and then the love comes later?"

Her aunt had Skip's full attention. Even he was susceptible to Aunt Eve's gift for storytelling. You'd think she was waving bacon in his face he was so enthralled.

Lucy welcomed the chatter. She was so hurt by Aunt Eve's revelations, she was afraid of saying something she'd regret, if she hadn't already.

26

SKIP

A DOG'S GOT TO DO WHAT A DOG'S GOT TO DO

As Aunt Eve preaches about my ancestors, things begin to click. Suddenly I understand why I've felt torn between leading Lucy and wishing I could still follow. Everything makes sense now!

My genetic makeup explains so much about my recent anxiety and spurts of aggression. It's the wolf in me! If I see a rift or need in the pack, I can't help but fill the need. But, I don't want to be in charge. So as long as Lucy doesn't have a mate, I have to be her mate. That's a lot of pressure on a dog like me. I need to find her a mate and go back to being a follower. Sure, I'm networking with Manny, Tank, and Thomas, but a pack isn't enough. We need a leader.

I think about Soft Voice and about losing Strong Voice. What if Mama had found Soft Voice a mate to help manage the pack? We would never have gone to the pound, that's what. I'm onto something. I can feel it in my bones.

So what would a good leader look like? What if I come up with a list of things that John did as our alpha? *Brilliant.*

But I can't. My mind has gone blank or, rather, it's all

over the place. I can't concentrate on the task at hand. It's like I'm chasing that damn green ball in my head, but I can only chase the idea, not create the list.

Must focus. Come up with criteria and a plan. Sometimes activity clears my mind. Though I'm best suited for simple problem solving, not reasoning. I once heard a "Chi" dog trainer at the park talking to John and Lucy. I was never taken with the Chi-ster dude, so I always ignored his attempts to be my whisperer, but I remember him telling John that the best time to train a dog is after "owners increase their dog's Chi and enhance the dog's mental capacity for learning."

John asked, "And the best place to start is?"

"Hiring me."

John and I just looked at each other. I stuck out my tongue like I wanted to cough up a hairball. John shot me a warning look, but I could tell he wanted to laugh by the way he bit his cheek. Then he asked, "What's the *second* best place to start?"

"With exercise, of course," Chi-ster said. "Burn off their excess energy. Then they can be more present and able to learn."

John said, "So you can teach an old dog new tricks, you just have to make sure they've had a good workout first." John turned to me, "Hear that, buddy? Next time we work on your 'shake,' I'll wear you out first."

Exercise leads to Chi, which leads to focus. I run around the room, chasing my Chi, but I bump into the floor lamp by accident.

"Skip!" Lucy jumps up. "Calm down."

Her voice sounds tired and lacks the assertion I need. Yep, I need her to get a mate.

Aunt Eve comes to my rescue just in time. "Skip. Sit," she commands.

I sit, but one eye starts to twitch, and my jaws spread wide in a nervous yawn. I'm losing control of my body. *Must exercise.*

Aunt Eve takes her thumb and index finger and rubs the spots behind my ears. Within seconds, I melt like ice cream on a warm summer day and drop to the floor. *Humm-mmmmmmmm.*

"How did you do that?" Lucy asks.

"I'll show you."

Lucy's massage isn't as smooth as Aunt Eve's, but my thoughts are clearer. Aunt Eve should show her technique to Chi-ster. I just needed to breathe. I miss living in the moment. I can't keep putting my paws in the past and future. Life gets too confusing. My Chi is overwhelmed by the time continuum.

I don't want to find territory of my own or a mate of my own like my genes dictate. I have domesticated genes too. I'm just trying to preserve the space I already live in and be a happy-go-lucky minion in the pack. And speaking of mates, we could get puppies. Some human puppies.

I get distracted by the idea of little Lucys petting and crawling all over me. I could give them my chew toys and let them win tug of war. Like my mom did, I can lick their fingers, bellies, and toes clean. And when they learn to walk and throw, they will take me to the park and play with me. I bet they'll be awesome cuddlers; I'll teach them how. I'm going to be a good big brother because I can help Lucy clean up after them by following the crumbs they drop all over the place. There I go again. *My head's in the future.*

Obviously, Lucy and I will need someone who likes dogs. I think about the men at the dog park. Chi-ster is out.

Maybe Manny knows someone who likes dogs. *Oh! Manny!* Of course! See? This is why I needed to find my Chi.

Manny is perfect and right under my nose. I always smell and sense the sparks between him and Lucy even if they don't know they are inhaling each other's pheromones, and with Tank being sick, Manny's going to need us more than ever. Lucy gets all bossy around Manny too. Good. Manny's got the right stuff.

The ladies have stopped fussing over me. I pretend to watch DOGTV and tune them out while I devise my plan to force Manny and Lucy together more often. My mind flashes to John. Forget him. I can't do anything about John, and he's left me to clean up his mess. A dog's got to do what a dog's got to do.

27

SKIP

DONUTS TELL ALL

MY INNATE SENSE of time tells me it's walk-for-coffee time for Manny and Tank.

Lucy and Aunt Eve are still asleep. Lucy's not used to drinking like she did last night. Our apartment smells a bit like the homeless guys we pass at the park. The fumes alone could make me drunk.

Just because Lucy doesn't have to work on Saturdays anymore doesn't mean we don't have work to do. *Chop chop.* I whine in her ear, my I-have-to-go-on-a-walk-and-relieve-myself whine. I need Aunt Eve to stay behind, so I save my alarm for Lucy's ears only. After a few attempts, Lucy gets up and drags on her sweats. But she is holding her head and moving *so* slow. I just heard Manny's door open. I run and scratch at the doormat to rush her.

Lucy shushes me. "You're going to wake people up," she whispers as she pulls on her sweat jacket.

Get a move on. Tank's dying and he moves faster than you.

Based on the creak of the stairs, I can tell Manny and

Tank are reaching the building door. If we don't shake a leg, we're going to miss them. I'll have to wait another twenty-four hours for an opportunity.

When Lucy opens the door, I don't hesitate. I dart ahead and run downstairs. I'm a little nervous Tank will misinterpret my speed as an attack, but sometimes a dog has to take a risk.

"Whoa, buddy," Manny warns me with his hand out and keeps the building door closed.

Perfect. I catch my breath.

Tank is glaring at me. I'm taller than him, and stronger now, but I let him take the lead as he sniffs me. I lower my head and avoid eye contact; that's canine speak for "you're the boss." If he stays protective, I'll have to roll over and expose my belly. But that turns out to be unnecessary. With a grunt, Tank's posture relaxes and the tension vanishes.

So far, so good.

"Sorry," Lucy says to Manny as she reaches us and clips on my leash. With one hand, she finger combs her bed head.

Excellent. Lucy's grooming herself at the sight of Manny.

"No problem," Manny says.

Outside, Manny and Tank turn right, and Lucy turns left as expected. Too bad for her I'm turning right and following the guys.

"Skip, this way." She tugs on the leash, but she is no match for me. I take another step after Manny. I start trotting and make her tag along.

"Skip!" She jerks hard on the leash.

Manny and Tank pause to look at us, and I don't stop until we are a few steps ahead of them.

"Having a little trouble there?" Manny asks.

"Obviously."

"Is this how your walks usually work because there are these people who train dogs, you know?"

"Thanks, Dog Whisperer," Lucy says. She's given up turning around and now is hell-bent on leaving Manny in our dust.

The leash is like a tight rope as Lucy marches on and tries to pull me along with her. *No go, Lucy. I have other ideas in mind.* I refuse to match her pace, and Manny and Tank gain on us. Tank doesn't seem to care. He's walking slower than usual, but he doesn't seem to mind that I'm trying to tag along.

Manny raises a brow and smirks. "I think Skip wants us all to walk together."

Bingo.

"Don't pretend to know my dog better than I do, thank you very much," Lucy says, staring forward.

"Someone's not a morning person," he says.

"And don't pretend to know me."

"Fair enough," he passes us, "Grumpy." Tank knows Manny is his leader and heels. I fall into position next to Tank, lagging only a few inches, and match his pace. Soon, Lucy has no choice but to heel to me, Tank, and Manny.

Now this is how a pack should walk!

Manny snickers.

Lucy blushes. "Crap. You *do* know my dog better than I do."

"I know dogs."

"And ladies too." Lucy says.

"Don't pretend to know *me*."

"Touché, Casanova."

Manny turns to me, not missing a step. "How do you put up with her, Skip?"

I bark.

"Not sure why you think I seduce women enough to compare me to Casanova, but then again, making assumptions seems to be your thing."

This is working out better than I thought. They are no longer even paying attention to the fact that we are all walking together. And they are releasing so many pheromones I can practically see their chemistry pinging and zinging on an attraction highway, even if they don't know about or won't admit said attraction.

From the way Tank is sniffing and glancing at the two of them as we walk, he smells them too. He may be dying, but he hasn't lost his keen sense of smell. *Catch the drift of what I'm up to, Tank?*

Lucy says, "We've been neighbors for four years. I see the women leaving your apartment in the morning. Puffy-eyed. Sad."

Manny did a *humph*.

"Nothing to say to that?" Lucy asks.

"Nothing that's any of your business."

"What happens if one of your beauties trips over a pot someday and breaks a nail?"

Lucy has said this before, but that was after John tripped over a pot going to the backyard. "I'm so sick of all his junk laying about," John had said. "What's it going to take for the property manager or the owner to do something about him?"

Lucy said, "Probably one of his models will trip over a pot and break a nail. Then all hell will break loose."

John snorted, "Sounds like a really bad movie."

"Fifty Shades of Hoarding," Lucy said, and John pulled her into a hug while they laughed together like naughty little kids.

I never got the joke, but no matter, Lucy doesn't finish it this time. Too bad. I'd like to see her and Manny hug and laugh.

Manny says, "I'll get rid of the pots once I find a good home for them."

"You do realize," Lucy says, "that's exactly what a—"

"—hoarder would say, I know. I'm really not a hoarder. I just don't want the pots to be separated. I'll tell you what, if you find a collective purpose for them, they're yours. But it can't be a thrift store or anything like that."

"Seriously? You don't like me, but you'd trust me with your precious pots?"

Manny says. "It's not as easy as you might think. I've tried to find the right place."

Lucy is quiet and lost in thought for a few minutes. Then she asks, "So where *are* we headed?"

"Donut shop."

Lucy grimaces. "I love donuts."

"Doesn't look like it."

She sweeps a hand over her outfit. "I didn't bring a wallet."

"My treat."

"I'll pay you back."

"If it's important to you."

"I don't need any favors right now."

He looks at me, the disobedient dog who made her go for a walk with him, and then her. His look says it all, but he speaks anyway, "We can agree to disagree."

"Okay, so I do need your help walking my dog this morning," she says, "or maybe he's walking me."

"Where does Skip usually walk you?"

"You're so funny. Baker Beach and Lands End during the week, and, before, the dog park on weekends."

"Should have known you're a dog-parker."

"What's that supposed to mean?" she asks.

Yeah, what's that supposed to mean?

"Bunch of couples and people looking for a club or relationship, bringing wine and cheese to turn exercising their dogs into a hipster event or a dating site."

If I could blush, or crawl into a doghouse somewhere, I would. Manny is right. John met Cecilia at a park, and it was just last night that I was thinking I'd use the dog park to find Lucy a new man. But that was before I realized Manny was my *numero uno* choice.

He nods toward Tank. "And Mastiffs don't get the warmest welcome there."

He's right. At the park, a few times, I've heard a horror story about two Mastiffs killing a woman in San Francisco and all she was doing was bringing home groceries. She didn't deserve that. Just tragic. But Tank doesn't deserve to be lumped together with those two devil dogs.

Lucy is nodding her head. "People are put off by Skip sometimes. The 'dog-parkers' used to be wary of him until they saw what a good boy he is." She wags a finger at me. "Not that he's been a good dog this morning. In any case, I don't want the other couples to ask me where John is or where he's been."

"You just gave me a good idea," my future alpha says.

"Really?" Lucy says, not really expecting a response.

"I'm surprised you're so chatty. You've said more words this morning than I've heard you use in years."

"Ha ha," he says, but he isn't really laughing.

"Okay. I give. What's the idea?" she asks.

"There should be an app for matchmaking at dog parks. You know, kind of like Tinder, where you can see where singles are, but it could tag singles in dog park locations. The whole #mustlovedogs thing. People could list what type of dog they have too. In fact, forget seeing the owner, someone could match up to a dog and see if they like their owner later."

Great minds think alike, Manny.

"There must be a better way to meet someone. Not that I'm looking. I never did the tech dating stuff." Lucy's nose, mouth, and eyes squeeze together with obvious distaste for all things dating.

That's okay, I want to tell her, we're *apping* Manny.

"My grandpa used to swear he could tell what kind of person someone was by knowing their favorite donut."

Lucy smiles. "With all due respect, sounds like your grandpa was missing a few donut holes."

"You'd be surprised how right he was. What's your favorite donut?"

She laughs. "Old-fashioned cake."

Manny rubs his chin. "Never kiss on the first date. You like it when a guy holds the door. Old-fashioned donuts are original and long-lasting. That makes you committed. Loyal. I'm guessing you don't like a lot of change. You're big on tradition. But you can go it alone sans glaze, or you can partner with glaze and be just as good."

Lucy nods. "I love traditions, and I'd rather be a partner. What's your favorite?"

He winks at her. "Bear Claw."

Lucy smiles. "Nice, Casanova."

"Strong. Protective. Loner. And like my grandpa said, I'm a healer."

"Mmm hmm," Lucy says. "The girls who leave your apartment don't look healed."

His jaw twitches. "Depends on how you look at it."

We're close to the donut shop, and Tank and I let our tongues hang out, unashamed of the drool running from our mouths. Donuts and love are in the air! Only thing that smells better than a donut is a bitch in heat. Bacon is a close second.

Manny jogs ahead and opens the shop door, bowing and swinging his arm to wave Lucy through. "My old-fashioned lady."

Nice touch, Manny.

Lucy laughs again. I've missed that sound. *Good job, Manster.*

As far as I'm concerned, this date is working out well even if Lucy and Manny don't know they're on a date. Manny says he likes this donut shop because the owner allows dogs and offers biscuits. *Works for me!*

"Good morning, Manny," the woman behind the counter says. "You brought a friend." She squeezes some tongs and sets a Bear Claw on a red plastic tray lined with wax paper.

"Tanya, this is Lucy. Lucy, Tanya."

"Welcome to my shop. What can I get you?"

"One old-fashioned with glaze, and one without please," Lucy says.

Manny leans to the side and whispers, "She orders with pride."

Tank and I follow Lucy and Manny to the table, eyeing

the handful of dog biscuits Tanya tossed on the side of the tray. We can't wait for our bounty.

Lucy takes a bite and closes her eyes as she chews. "Best donut I've ever had."

"Sit," Manny says to Tank and me, rewarding us with our treats.

"What would a maple donut mean?" Lucy asks between bites.

Manny eats his claw in three huge chunks and leans back in the chair, watching as Lucy savors hers.

"Maple? Balanced. Intuitive. Creative. Passionate. Sexual."

Lucy nods with each description, timed well with her chewing. "Sounds like my aunt, or at least what I know about her now. What about a jelly donut?"

"Not your average donut. Tricky. Won't give up a donut hole and wants to be whole, but can't be whole on its own, has to have jelly filling. But with the right jelly, good potential. I'm not a jelly donut fan. Too needy."

"Give me an example," Lucy says.

I'm listening carefully because I know why Lucy is asking: John loves jelly donuts. I remember how John would use his fingertip to scrape up any leftover drops of jelly when he ate a donut. If I had fingers, that's what I would have done too.

"Okay. Brad Pitt. I bet he likes jelly donuts. He left the Aniston chick to be with a Goodwill Ambassador for the United Nations. Before you know it, he's full of purpose and building homes for Hurricane Katrina victims."

Lucy bites her lower lip. I swear I'm going to freak out if she takes Manny's example to the next level. That John found a Goodwill Ambassador too.

"Why? Who's the jelly donut?"

"John."

Manny cringes. "Oh, sorry about that. Not trying to say John left you for Angelina Jolie."

Oh no. This isn't good.

"Wait, what?" Lucy looks devastated. "I hadn't even gone there!"

But now she is totally there, and being the smart lady she is, I know she is recalling her earlier hunch those first days when she'd texted John and asked if he'd cheated but he'd said no.

"Calm down, don't jump to conclusions. Stick to the facts," Manny says.

"Hard to stick to the facts when I'm hyperventilating."

"Get out of your head. Don't mess yourself up over hypotheticals. If you really aren't sure, ask him."

"I did. He said no." She releases a long breath.

"Good. That's all you need to know."

"But what if he's lying because he doesn't want to hurt me?" Lucy asks.

He shrugs. "You are hurt. Another woman or not."

"Yeah, but if there's another woman," Lucy pushes the tray away, "that's totally different. I can be angry. Pissed off. Not wait for him to come back. I can move forward and decide about our frigging honeymoon that I have to either cancel or go on alone."

I can't swallow my treat. John wanted to tell Lucy, but I barked him off, thinking it was selfish of him to fess up about Cecilia. To get her off his chest. But it was me. I was being the selfish one. If John had told her, she could move on easier. But . . . she'd want to move on without me too. Therein lies the dilemma.

Manny snorts and shakes his head. "You should be doing all that regardless. He left you. What does it matter why?"

Damn, the truth is ugly, but even if I didn't know about Cecilia, I'd agree with Manny. I don't think Lucy is going to take this well. She's too fragile, but instead she gets angry at Manny and whispers forcefully, I guess out of consideration for the baker, "You can be a real jerk."

"You know I like to make the ladies cry," Manny says.

And then to my shock, Lucy laughs.

He smiles and shoves his chair back. "I'd better get coffee and a maple bar for Eve."

"Manny," Lucy says, causing him to pause mid-rise, "what was your grandpa's favorite?"

He nods at Lucy's balled up napkin and stands. "Old-fashioned, glazed."

"And your grandma's?"

He grins. "Bear Claws."

28

LUCY

IF DOGS COULD TALK

WHILE MANNY GOT coffee and a maple bar for Aunt Eve, Lucy stared down at the donut shop floor. Did John need someone else to fill him up or make him whole? But if that were true, he wouldn't want to be alone. Had he lied when he said that was why he was leaving her? Or was the truth even worse: she wasn't enough jelly. Their relationship hadn't been enough. She didn't complete John. If her mom and Brené Brown could hear her thoughts now, they'd gag.

And then it hit her. Her stomach turned, and the glaze that had tasted so sweet only minutes before now felt like a pasty residue in her mouth. She was the one walking around like she'd lost her innards, her jelly. She was the one having an identity crisis. She was the one desperate to put her and John back together again.

Oh God! Was she the jelly donut posing as an old-fashioned, glazed?

Jelly or old-fashioned, how boring and uninteresting she felt. Did she rate low on the jelly scale? Was she Jennifer Aniston and now John had an Angelina Jolie? No matter;

both those relationships were over. And she liked both actresses.

She should get rid of her television and read more. She needed to get a life. She needed real people in her life. If she were to call any of her friends, they'd die of shock. They might not even return her calls. Pretty insulting, she thought, to start calling people now that she was single. Why hadn't she realized how much her life revolved around work, television, John, and Skip?

Manny walked toward her, cradling two coffees to go and a bag of maple donuts for her aunt.

"Ready?" He opened the door for her, and they walked out. Skip, for once, waited for her to exit. He even hesitated and waited behind Tank.

Phaius Tancarvilleae was moving slower and stiffer than he had on their way to the shop. She was surprised when Skip moved closer to Tank, as if offering his strength to lean on.

She figured she was seeing things, but Manny said, "Skip's a sweet dog. What is he?"

"A Wolador."

"Sounds like a *Harry Potter* name: 'Wolador.'" Manny's voice went deep and rumbled.

Clearly, Skip and Tank aren't the only ones being read to by Thomas. "Half Timber Wolf, half Labrador. He's illegal in some states."

She watched as Skip moved even closer to Tank, and Tank turned and licked him on his jaw.

"He's a monster all right." Manny sipped his coffee. "You might as well ask. I know you want to."

"I don't know what you mean," she said and looked away. But she did want to know if Tank was okay.

"Liar."

"I'm trying to change. Trying to start minding my own business."

"He's dying," Manny said.

She didn't want to say "I'm sorry" or offer any platitudes about Tank having a good life or suggest Manny could get a new puppy someday. That was kind of like people telling her she'd find another man. The idea of losing Skip was more than she could bear right now. Her life might be easier without a dog his size. She'd be able to save money if she could rent a studio, and she could do without the guilt she felt leaving him so much, but she'd be devastated to lose him.

What was wrong with her? This was about Manny and Tank. Why did she make everything about her? Had she always done this? Had she done this with John?

"How long?" she asked.

Manny shrugged his shoulders. "I guess it's up to me, which is messed up."

Lucy nodded. "You have to decide when to put him to sleep."

"I'm taking it one next right step at a time. I want him to let me know when he's ready, but that's selfish of me." He sliced his left hand in the air, careful not to spill any coffee, and then his right hand, which pulled on Tank's leash. "It's too much for me to jump from Point A: he's sick, so I'd better . . . Point B: put him down. My mind doesn't work that way."

"How does it work?" Lucy asked.

"Need a vision and a logical process," he said. "But there isn't one. You're a nurse. How do you do it? Deal with death?"

She didn't answer for a while. In many ways, she'd grown pragmatic about illness and death. Plus, working in Emergency, she never established a relationship with the patient. Death happened every day. She hadn't lost her first patient at Golden Years yet. What if Skip were dying? She wanted to grab Skip and squeeze him tight.

She tried to think through what her steps would be if Skip got sick and her nursing experience kicked in. "In trauma there's the physician's diagnosis, treatment options, quality versus quantity lifetime, treatment recommendation, and patient or family decision."

Manny didn't say anything.

"But dogs don't talk," she said. "And therein lies the rub. I don't know how I would handle it if Skip were sick. I'd have to do what you're doing. Take the next right step."

She thought about jelly donuts and John. What was her next right step in life? Maybe she could whittle each day down to the next right step.

"Manny, I think I like you. As a person, I mean."

"Don't sound so surprised," he said.

"It's been a while since I've made a friend outside of work. Don't know if I remember how to be one."

"Don't you think you're moving a little fast? Who says we're friends?"

She nodded toward Skip, who kept looking back at them, all the while propping up Tank. "Skip, obviously."

"Does his owner, agree?"

She pretended to mull it over. "I think she does."

29

SKIP

DUMB AS A DOG

WHAT DOES MANNY MEAN, it's up to him when Tank's time comes?

Humans. I swear, sometimes they can be so dumb. They think they can control everything. I look at Tank to see if he's paying attention to the silly conversation happening behind us.

Doesn't he know that Tank will know when and how to die? What's Manny going to do, command Tank to die like he would command him to sit?

Roll over and die, Tank. Good boy.

Yeah, I don't think so.

I'm not sick, but I've been sick, and dogs have a secret weapon. Unlike humans, we listen to our bodies. We know what we need to do when we aren't feeling well. It's in our DNA, our genes, passed down to us from our ancestors. We chew grass when our stomach aches and we need to vomit or when our digestive track is off. We know to eat our crap when we need Vitamin B (thank Dog I'm not Vitamin B deficient). And when our time comes to leave this world, we're going to know when that time is, and we'll decide if we want to do it alone or with our pack, our owners. Tank knows this as well as I do. All dogs do.

Snort. People. They don't get to say when a dog dies. And people have that saying, "Dumb as a dog."

Goofballs.

Manny and Lucy are chatting, so when we stop at the corner and wait for the light to change, I move closer to Tank and lick the side of his face. We make eye contact long enough for me to convey, *Tank, when your time comes, I promise to look out for Manny.*

Tank licks me back.

All for one and one for all.

30

LUCY

NEXT RIGHT STEP

AUNT EVE CAME into the hall and tightened her robe around her. "Ah, there you are." Her eyes lit up at the sight of coffee and the white paper bag with grease stains, "Please tell me that's a donut for me."

Her aunt seemed unfazed by the amount of wine they'd drunk the night before. Probably because she was so in love. The first blushes of love were a cure-all.

Lucy extended her hand, keeping it out of Skip's reach. His nose followed the bag. "Compliments of Manny."

"Manny?"

"Skip forced us on a walk today."

"If it includes a donut, I say *good dog*."

Skip barked and wagged his tail.

"Don't encourage him. He ignored all my commands and all but forced Manny on me."

"And was that such a bad thing?"

"Surprisingly, no," Lucy said, but she pointed at Skip. "That doesn't mean you weren't a bad bad bad dog. Don't let the treats and praise confuse you."

Skip jumped on her.

"Dammit. Down!" Lucy shook her head at Skip. Who was this kangaroo, and what had he done with her dog?

"How did Skip and Tank get along?"

"I could have sworn Skip was supporting Tank on the walk. Tank's sick."

Skip barked.

Her aunt frowned around a huge bite of the donut.

Skip licked up the flakes of maple that fell to the floor.

"Soooo, what did you talk about?" her aunt asked.

"He assessed my personality based on my favorite donut."

Aunt Eve's head bobbed. "I dig it. What's yours?"

Of course this was right up Aunt Eve's alley. Her aunt had always been into tarot cards, tealeaves, and horoscopes. That's where Lucy's daily astrology habit had begun, with her aunt.

Lucy wrinkled her nose and frowned. "You don't know my favorite donut? You took me out for donuts all the time." She had wanted her aunt to shout "Old-fashioned!" and save her the trouble of a donut identity crisis. One minute she was an old-fashioned, glazed or otherwise, and the next she wondered if she was the jelly donut, needing John to complete her.

Ugh. She was doing it again. Making everything about her. Being so self-centered was exhausting.

"Your mom's is a cinnamon twist. I'll have to ask George what his favorite is. So tell me, what did Manny say?"

"No huge surprises. Old-fashioned, glazed means I'm a traditionalist and don't like change. Basically, I'm totally boring." And wasn't that pretty much what John had implied about her Cherry Chip Cake? *Hmm.* What would Manny's grandpa say about cake choices?

"Come now. He didn't say that, or if he did there was more to it," her aunt said.

Great. Both Skip and Aunt Eve were on Team Manny now. Damn, there she went again with the Lucy Pity Party. She needed to grow up. Be different. Be thirty-something.

"Did you talk about John?" Aunt Eve asked.

"We talked about John liking jelly donuts." Lucy grabbed the mail off the counter. She normally looked at the mail daily, but this past week had been anything but normal. She walked to the couch and plopped onto it, mail resting in her lap. Her aunt followed her. Skip was hot on her aunt's crumb trail. Who knew he had such a sweet tooth? "Skip, I should have named you Hoover."

He stopped and stared at her. But not for long. Aunt Eve offered him a chunk of donut.

"Do you remember how Mom always said John was like Tarzan when I told her he had a long-distance girlfriend from high school when we met? He hadn't seen her in six months, and Mom said he couldn't let go of one vine until he found the next one."

Aunt Eve rolled her eyes. "Your mother."

"Was she right?" Lucy interrupted.

"Oh, honey."

"I got so mad at Mom when she said that. Like she was saying John only liked me because I was convenient. She never had anything positive to say about men during those years. I never wanted to ask her for advice or introduce her to anyone, so I just waited until college to date, when I had my own dorm room and space. Do you think John was ever happy with me? Or was she right? I was convenient."

"You were together for ten years. That's not about convenience."

Lucy thought back over the past few months and John's mood swings. She'd ignored his moods because she thought they were because *he* was adjusting to *change*. But what if there had been more to it? What if he'd found a new vine? New jelly?

"I remember when I met John. He was so handsome and funny, and he made me feel exceptional. We spent every minute together, liked all the same things, and he always praised my ability to plan for the future. He said until he met me, he only knew he wanted to go to law school but hadn't planned beyond that. We started making plans together. We started applying to nursing and law schools in the same cities. He supported all my decisions by following the plan. I thought we were meant to be. God, what if we are both jelly donuts?"

Aunt Eve sighed. "Couples are supposed to be supportive."

"But what if this is bigger? What if he met someone else? I asked him already, but why would he tell me? It's easier to break up with someone than to tell them you met someone else."

Her aunt shook her head. "John loved you. I don't see him cheating. Besides, where would he meet someone? Work? Where you know everyone? The dog park?" Aunt Eve laughed, making the idea sound ridiculous.

Skip whined and tried to climb up on Lucy's lap. "Skip, how many times do I have to tell you? You're not a lapdog. You're going to squash me."

"Would knowing he met someone make a difference?" Aunt Eve asked.

"If he cheated on me or left me for someone else, I'd feel like our relationship was a joke, and I wouldn't wait for him to come back."

"Then you should ask him again. You have to do what will help you move forward."

Lucy stopped sorting through the mail and paused with a flyer. Getting used to being alone would help her move forward. Planning to go on her non-honeymoon trip would help her move forward.

"Lately he's said that he hated that I wouldn't change, that I wouldn't detour from my list and plans, that I wouldn't try new things. But he also never suggested anything new. Except changing my birthday cake."

Aunt Eve leaned over her shoulder. "So what are you going to do about that?"

"I want to prove him wrong."

She wanted to take the next right step. She held up a flyer. "Get dressed. We're going to doga."

"Doga? Never heard of it." Aunt Eve clapped her hands like a little girl.

"It's something I've said I wanted to try but never have. I don't want to go to the dog park. I need exercise. I need friends. And because this flyer's right here, maybe it's a sign. I'm going to try something new."

31

SKIP

DOWNWARD-FACING DOG

I TROT AHEAD of Aunt and Lucy. Can humans walk any slower? I yank on my leash so hard I start coughing and huffing.

"Skip," Lucy warns.

I keep plowing forward, willingly strangling myself. I've never taken this route before. I'm like an artist with a blank canvas, and I can only hope my bladder has enough paint. I don't know where dog yoga will be, but I'm going to have loads of fun getting there.

In between leaving *Skip Was Here* on every hydrant, trash can, and light post we pass, I've been thinking more about humans and confessions. Lucy said she'd want to know if John cheated on her. That it would be easier to move on. And talking to Manny, Manny pointed out it shouldn't matter because Lucy was hurt either way.

But the thing is, if Lucy asks John again, I don't think she really wants the truth. I know, I know, it sounds like I'm trying to justify my betrayal and that her not knowing is self-serving because I don't want her to find out about

Cecilia because she might hate me, and when John pulls his head out of his butt she won't take him back, but I'm serious. Deep down, Lucy doesn't want to know John has cheated on her, she only really wants to know that he *hasn't*.

I have mixed emotions about going to doga. The last time I was introduced to a new group of dogs and their owners was with John, the day we met Cecilia and Bunny. *We all know how that worked out.* And since John left, Tank's the only other dog I've been around. I wonder how long I can be *dog in absentia* before no one in my hood will remember me, and I'll be the new dog on the block. Seven years of pecking order work down the drain. I'll have to start all over. *Ugh.*

I'm not worried about learning yoga. I'm a coordinated bloke. But I'm rusty on meeting a larger population of *nooches*; that's dog lingo for new pooches. I can't wait for the chance to be social again, but the first introduction to a group of dogs is critical. Any group of dogs is considered a pack, even if it's short-term and circumstantial, like this class. The manner of our meet-up will establish my place in the class-pack within minutes. Canine Credo dictates letting the weaker dogs come to me but being the first to greet the stronger ones. When uncertain if another dog is friendly, a dog will raise his hackles all along his spine. His whiskers will go back, flat against his face. His ears will move back too. His tail might even tuck. The stronger dog will make strong eye contact, whiskers forward and body tall. He'll lean on his front legs with his ears and tail high. The Pack Pecking Order Pyramid happens in rapid-fire succession. Weakest on the bottom and the Top Dog on, well, top.

Once we get that out of the way, though, I'm going to Namaste the heck out of doga. I bet there will be a dog there named Namaste. Just wait until everyone sees me. I'm going to be a natural, I think. Take Downward-Facing Dog for example. I've been starting my mornings and waking up from naps with that move since I was a puppy.

Legs out front, head down, butt up in the air. Stretch. Exhale.

My mom only had to show me how to do it once. Can't believe there's a class for it.

My bladder is about empty when we near the yoga center, and I know we're close because we start to see more and more people with dogs intersecting and turning in the same direction. My nose is bombarded with new-to-me-dog smells. I can't even imagine how I will relax with all this awesome stuff in the air.

There's a line outside the building, and a woman and a white Maltese with a bow on top of its head stand in front, greeting everyone. I'm too far away to tell if the Maltese is a she or a he, and there are too many dogs present to single the Maltese's scent out from this distance. As each person enters, their dog approaches the Maltese.

Ah-ha. Master Maltese.

In line, I follow protocol and exchange butt sniffs with the poodle in front of me and with the gray mutt behind me. Without words, we are saying, "It's nice to meet you." But something is different about the people. At the dog park, people are chatty, laughing loudly, often shouting at their pets, like they (the humans) need attention. I can't put my paw on it, but these people are so calm, and this makes their dogs calm.

Lucy and Aunt Eve follow my lead and shake hands with the woman standing in front of us. Lucy is fidgeting. I know because my leash is jerking against my neck. Forget doga, I'm going to need a chiropractor. She has got to be the only nervous person here. I want to tell her to chill out. I've got this. *Look around and pace yourself with everyone else's cool vibe. Like Aunt Eve's. They be chillin', and you should be too.*

The instructor turns to us, and her expression is open and welcome. I like her on the spot. But I look around, all cool-like and wait for the bow-headed Maltese to welcome me. It's a he. A *he* with a bow in his hair! He's not moving; he's just staring right at me.

I want to say he is challenging me by refusing to give up eye contact, but damn, like all the people, he's cool as a cucumber. I must be ten times his size, but his presence makes him seem twice my size. I don't know why, but I growl at his unwavering stare. This shocks me as much as it shocks Lucy. I came here to be friends with the leader, so what the heck am I doing? I'm off to a wrong start. I'm going to be known as Anti-Social Skip.

"Skip," Lucy says, turning to the instructor. "I'm sorry. He hasn't been around this many dogs for a while."

But the Maltese's little bow doesn't even jiggle. I can't shake him, and the kindness in his big dark eyes makes me feel ashamed. I lower my snout, lean forward, and wait for him to nudge my nose with his own. He turns his backside to me, and I return the favor. All is forgiven.

"We're all here in harmony," the Maltese's human says with an accent that sounds familiar. "I'm Natalie, your yogini."

She sounds a little like Marge, the travel agent who leaves Lucy messages, but not as scratchy. Natalie reaches out both hands to embrace Lucy's hand and then Aunt

Eve's. She nods down at the Maltese, "And this is Mantra, your dog's dogi."

Mantra? What the heck kind of name is that?

Mantra. Mantra.

Mmmaaannntttrrraaa.

Natalie holds out her hand for me to smell but doesn't lean over me. Dogs don't like to be leaned over by strangers. She smells like tree bark and grass after a warm summer rain.

"Say hello, Skip," Lucy says.

"Natalie," Aunt Eve says, "your accent . . . are you Australian?"

"I am."

Aunt Eve and Lucy look at each other and smile. Lucy says, "I'm supposed to be going to Australia."

Aunt Eve says to Lucy, "You said you were looking for a sign."

"Anything you need to know, I'm all yours." Natalie sweeps the doorway with a graceful arm. "Take some time to walk Skip around the room to meet the other dogs and then grab your mats and find an empty space. Try to find a spot near a larger dog since size makes a difference in the moves, and you can watch and learn from your neighbor."

Whoa, what? I can't start this visit with me going to all the other dogs! Doesn't this lady know it undermines my leadership of Lucy and makes me look subservient to the other dogs? They have to come to me first. That's how it works. I get it. Mantra is the head honcho, but this will put me on the bottom. They're going to eat me alive.

But when we enter the room, it's full of that same indescribable tranquil energy. There are more dogs than I can shake a tail at, and yet they aren't running around sniffing ass. The owners aren't loud and obnoxious. Nope. Instead, they're all lying on the mats with their owners, leashes dangling. Human hands-free. Gentle music is playing in the background, and there's a small fountain with running water.

Oh my.

All of a sudden, I know, I just know, that it doesn't matter if I'm on a leash, not on a leash, if I'm the first to approach another dog, or the last . . . everything I know about pack pecking orders is irrelevant here. From the easy breezy attitudes and body language of the dogs and owners, it's clear there are many packs here, but they are two-member packs. One owner and one dog. They move together as we walk toward them, and they greet us together, untroubled and relaxed. A woman with a Golden Retriever slides her mat over so we can be next to her. "I can help you with the positions," she offers.

I never knew a pack could work this way. When Aunt Eve goes home, I know Lucy and I can keep coming to doga and not feel alone as a party of two. In this place, it's okay if it's just Lucy and me.

A *dong* sounds from the front of the room. Natalie sweeps her arms wide as if she is going to hug the room and says, "Thank you, friends, for giving Lucy, Eve, and Skip a warm welcome. Shall we begin? Stand at the back of your mat and let your dog rest between your ankles or on the mat before you. Inhale. Exhale."

I glance at the Retriever next to me and decide to copy him. I sit in front of Lucy on the mat but turn to face her. I hold my head high. When my neighbor sighs, I sigh.

"We're here to find harmony with ourselves and our best friends. Let the chatter and energy of the outside world go.

You are here now. You are safe. Inhale love. Exhale your worries."

As I listen to Natalie and the soothing sound of breathing from humans and dogs, an aroma of peppermint toothpaste and dog biscuits fills the air. I am moved by the serenity that overcomes me. Oh, how I have missed feeling this unity. This understanding of being in the moment, feeling whole in my little pack.

"Now. Both of you face the front of the room. Stand behind your dog. We're going to go into Downward-Facing Dog."

Oh, I know those words. Without looking at my neighbor, I turn and stretch my front paws forward and lift my hips. I hear Aunt Eve and Lucy giggle behind me.

Our neighbor whispers, "Looks like he's a natural dogi."

Damn straight I am.

"Now," Natalie says as she bends over and places her fingers around Mantra's hips, "slide your hands under your companion's legs and pelvis, and lift the hips. Give them a wonderful stretch, lifting their feet off the floor into Downward-Facing Dog."

With my back toward them, I'm surprised when Lucy and Aunt each take one of my hips and lift me off the floor. Not only does it tickle, but I also only have my two front paws for balance. Oh, but then the best stretch I've ever felt extends from my groin to my chest. I groan and stretch my neck forward, causing more soft laughs from my ladies.

"Release their hips and now sweep your arms up, watch your fingertips, and reach for your sky."

I turn to watch Lucy. Her shoulders roll back, and her chin lifts as she raises her arms above. I am mesmerized, staring at her throat. I almost imagine a strong howl bursting from her lips.

"Reach toward your sky," Natalie says again.

Lucy wiggles her fingertips. She looks so tall. So grace-ful. Strength is in there somewhere; I can see that now. If only John could see her. He doesn't know what he's miss-ing. Or maybe he had an idea at one point because he was right: change suits her.

As we reach the end of the class, call me Jell-O Skip as Natalie asks us to lie down together. The smaller dogs crawl onto their owners' chests. I decide to lie between Aunt Eve and Lucy. *All for one and one for all*, Namaste style.

"Continue to breathe in tandem," Natalie says. "Close your eyes. Place one hand on your dog, and one hand on your stomach."

When both Lucy and Aunt Eve rest their palms on me, I feel full inside.

"Inhale to the base of your spine. Feel your stomach rise with air. Exhale. Make an affirmation today for you and your pet or human."

I like how Natalie treats us as equals.

"What are your intentions for your life together?"

I'm chillaxed, but Nat has my full attention. My ears perk.

"Envision your future. What do you see? What image of the two of you brings you joy? Embrace that image, and let's move into ten minutes of meditation."

Feeling Lucy's hand resting on me, I have a vision of us running in a grass field, laughing and smiling. We're playing chase. Once we are worn out, we lie down in the warm grass just like we are lying now, and Lucy stares into my eyes and smiles. We don't have to say a thing. We are sympatico. It's just the two of us. John isn't there. There is no fear or consequence for having betrayed Lucy. There is no betrayal. There's a new page. *All for one and one for all.*

I wake with a start. The class is still motionless. This class that we would never have tried with John. And it hits me, my secret will always be safe, and Lucy will always keep me if John never returns. I miss him. Lucy misses him. But look what we're doing. We're making new friends. We are finding ways to change and to be okay alone, if necessary. We don't need John. No, John could ruin all we are building. If John stays gone, our secret stays gone too. We will turn a new leaf. We *are* turning a new leaf.

Two *dongs* sound.

"Namaste, my friends."

Lucy opens her eyes and stares into mine. She smiles. We are in sync. Damn, I love her.

I will never let John come between us again.

32

SKIP

ASSUMPTIONS

On Sunday, before Aunt Eve leaves, we do a computer call with Grandma Sue, or as she likes me to think of her, Dogma Sue. We're going to break the news about the big breakup.

"She's just going to say something that makes me feel worse." Lucy chews on her nail. "Like 'I told you so.' And you know as soon as I do this, John's going to want to come back, and this will all have been for nothing, and then Mom will be all over me for taking him back."

"Give her a little more credit," Aunt Eve says. "She hates to see you hurt. You need her now. And she has more experience with men and breakups than either of us."

"Ack. Let's get this humiliation over with." Lucy turns the computer on. "I just hope she's in a good mood."

I wait beside Lucy, ready to lend what support I can.

Once we all say hello, Lucy gets to it. Well, Dogma gets to it. "Where's John?"

I lean into Lucy as she says, quite bravely in my opinion, "John has moved out. He wants time alone."

Dogma doesn't say anything at first. She glances at Aunt Eve. My head bounces from side to side as I try to watch them and read their body language. Eve's eyes are wide with warning.

Dogma takes a deep breath. "I'm so sorry, honey. Tell me about it."

So Lucy tells her about the Cherry Chip Cake and how John had been moody. I have a hard time looking at Dogma, or anyone for that matter. No eye contact from a shamed dog.

"I'm not doing well. I'm like a thirty-two-year-old going on sixteen."

I bark to vouch for her, and they all laugh. I'm pretty good at lightening the mood when necessary.

"Honey, everything happens for a reason. Who knows which this one is and how it will turn out in the long run?"

Lucy rests her chin in her hands and stares straight at the monitor. "Mom, what if I end up like you? Alone?"

Aunt Eve sits, calm as ever. Maybe, like me, she knows this conversation needs to happen.

And Dogma Sue says, "Then you're in for a good time."

Lucy's head tilts to the side, and she cries gentle tears. I wish I could get inside her head to learn what that sentence means to her. Her body relaxes like a deflated balloon, but at the same time, she seems more buoyant. I don't know how else to explain it. Maybe she's relieved her mom is happy despite Lucy's assumptions.

Aunt Eve puts her arm around Lucy's shoulder and hugs her. "Sue, we've had a lot of fun, haven't we?"

"We sure have. Now you're running off and getting hitched." These wonderful three ladies smile together. "I wish I could be there for a three-way hug."

I bark.

"Sorry. A four-way hug."

Before they ring off, Dogma Sue says, "Honey, I'm going to send you a book called *Love Is Toxic*."

"No, Mom. I don't have time to read anything right now."

"It's biology," her mom says. "You need to read it. It'll help."

After the call ends, Aunt Eve says, "I want to show you George's and my Facebook Page."

Lucy's eyes widen. "You're using Facebook?"

Aunt Eve giggles. "I'm hip."

"I'm impressed. I barely even use it. I haven't logged on for over a month."

"I guess that's why you've ignored my friend request. George posts fun pictures of us on our page. There are some from the reunion too."

"I'll log in to my account, then, so I can accept your friend request."

"Wait, sweetie." Aunt Eve puts her hand on top of Lucy's to stop her. "Does John have an account? You don't need to see anything about him you don't want to see."

Lucy hesitates. She blinks at Aunt Eve as if the thought had not occurred to her. Then she says, "No. He hates Facebook. He's sworn he'll never have social media accounts. Social media often comes up in court cases, so he avoids them like a legal plague. It's his firm's policy too."

I watch Lucy closely. She smiles and laughs at some of Aunt Eve's and George's pictures, but I can tell her mind is floating elsewhere. Maybe Aunt Eve's caution is catching up to her, or maybe it's temptation. Temptation to see just how much John has changed, and if he *is* on Facebook now.

Sunday night, before Aunt Eve leaves, she hands Lucy some money. "I want you to take this for a doga membership. It suits you. And treat Manny to a donut next Saturday for me."

33

SKIP

BRAINY BREAKUPS

EVERYTHING WENT AS WELL as the second week of a breakup could go. Thomas read to me. Some dark magic has petrified Hermione, Harry is speaking Parseltongue, and Ron has faced his fear of spiders. Lucy met me for lunch every day. Tank is still alive. We shared donuts this morning. That's two Saturday mornings in a row, so we're well on our way to a new pack tradition.

At the donut shop this morning, Manny asked, "Have you heard from Jelly Donut lately?"

Lucy said, "Stop calling him that." But then she answered around bites of her old-fashioned, glazed, "No. So far he isn't showing signs of missing my jelly."

Manny looked her over, though she didn't seem to notice as she licked her fingers clean (something I prefer she'd let me do, but Manny looked like he enjoyed watching her lick her fingers). He was giving her The Look. You know, *that* look. That I'd-like-to-lick-your-fingers look.

But alas, after a weeklong interlude with peace and

happiness, darkness has descended upon our apartment once again.

John has opened a Facebook account.

"Oh God! Why did I look?!" Lucy looks at me, both frustrated and crushed. She's being rhetorical, so I don't bother to respond with a whine or groan. Besides, I'm angst-ridden and speechless about the entire media-fest. I didn't have long to look at John's profile picture, but I had long enough to start obsessing about it too.

"I was just starting to feel better," Lucy says between cries. "The book from Mom warned me this could happen. I knew better!"

It's true. She does know better. This past week at bedtime, Lucy read *Love Is Toxic* aloud, knowing that I'm an avid reader myself. The theme is simple: *do not let your five senses be triggered by your ex.*

Makes sense really. Turns out that when you have a mate, any touch, sound, sight, smell, and taste responds to him and influences your body chemistry.

"This is why they call it the honeymoon period," Lucy explained as she turned the page. "When we first meet someone, our dopamine and scrotonin levels increase. It's the high of love. Love is a drug."

Over time, though, the brain chemistry regulates and finds a more reasonable and sustainable balance. The people, and the relationship, settle down. Not so many highs and lows anymore. Until there is a prolonged absence. Until there is a breakup. Then all hell breaks loose again.

With no sensory stimuli, the body chemistry gets whacked. Now the dopamine and serotonin levels crash to disastrous, tear-jerking levels. And only time, and zero stimulation of the five senses, will allow the body to rebalance. A new routine. New regulation.

"It's like withdrawals," Lucy said. "My brain chemistry is going through John withdrawals."

So it was obvious what we needed to do.

"As long as John wants to be alone, and as long as I want my sanity," Lucy said, "I can't hear, see, smell, touch, or taste him."

I sighed with relief. She'd never learn about Cecilia this way. I was grateful for brainy stuff.

Lucy patted my head and opened her calendar on her phone. "For every day we are John-free, we get a smiley face. We'll start counting tonight."

We racked up only six smiley faces pre–Facebook debacle. But it had been working.

No star for us tonight.

"God, I hate social media."

You and me both, sister.

"I can't handle this. Is he dating already?"

Close enough.

"Someone took that picture of him, and it wasn't me." She runs to the bathroom and vomits.

I wish we could go to an afternoon doga class. I want to remind her what Manny said last week, "Just stick to the facts. Don't get wrapped up in hypotheticals." Problem is, she's not wrong. Her instincts are right. I think I recognized Bunny on the sidewalk behind him in the photo, but it's hard to say without a scent stamp or a scratch-and-sniff feature. I think I recognize the alfresco cafe tables from Cecilia's bakery from that time John tricked me into going there.

It isn't all Lucy's fault she looked at Facebook tonight. It's Aunt Eve's.

Tonight, Aunt Eve called Lucy and told her wedding dresses were now posted on "Eve's Ladies In Waiting" Facebook page. And that's when it happened. Some elusive technological monster somehow discovered that John and Lucy know each other, and as I sat next to Lucy as she scrolled through Aunt Eve's dress photos, a red circle popped up with a white number.

Nothing good comes of red circles with white writing. STOP signs are red and white. But in all this techy crap, people think the red circle is a treat. People dismiss the obvious warning and twist it around in their crazy heads that it means, "Read me now." And so Lucy clicked on the circle of death. And John's face popped up on our screen. There he was in our John-free home, infiltrating our fragile hold on lightness.

Lucy is consumed by jealousy and rejection.

And I can't help but worry my betrayal is coming to a head. And all this because of Facebook. The danger was right there under our eyes. *Face*. It's all in the name. *Sight compromised.*

34

SKIP

GIRL ON A BEANBAG

IT'S PAST OUR BEDTIME, even for a Saturday, and Lucy has already taken me on three additional walks around our block.

"Exercise increases serotonin," she says each time we leave the building. Every now and then she says, "Stupid picture." Earlier, she shoved her phone in a drawer. "Must not call and ask who took it. Must not *hear* him."

Oh no, you mustn't. Be strong, lady. Fake it till you make it!

I'm proud of her for working on her serotonin levels. Her moods have been all over the place, like that stupid bouncing snowman-like toy she got me. It was an especially down moment when Lucy asked me, "Oh my God. What if I am becoming bipolar like my mom?"

Great. Self-diagnosing. She's turning into a hypochon-something.

"That was the last walk, I swear," she says to me as we enter the building and as if I've minded. "I'll take codeine so I can sleep, and then we'll wake up tomorrow, go to yoga, and start my John Detox all over again."

Now you're talking. We'll pick up where we fell off the John wagon.

Partway up the stairs, I can smell-tell someone is new to the premises. Someone who's wearing a hint of vanilla and smells of cigarettes and wine. But we're both shocked, Lucy more so than me, when we reach our floor to find a leggy blonde fast asleep on Thomas's beanbag, which has been relocated between our apartment and Manny's. It's as if the woman passed out halfway through her mission: *Must reach Manny*.

She's drunker than a skunk, though I must say winos smell better than skunks, so not sure who made up that incorrect metaphor. Or is it a simile or an analogy? I'm a dog. I can never keep them straight.

Drunk or skunked, I'm not sure how she managed all the stairs. Her slender ankles and shiny red high-heels extend far beyond the beanbag, preventing Lucy from marching past.

So Lucy snorts in disgust instead. "Yup. Seen this one around before." Lucy takes the woman's wrist gently between her thumb and forefinger, and turns to glare at Manny's door. "Her vitals are okay. As if climbing over his pots isn't enough, I have to climb over his women. Selfish men." Lucy raps on Manny's door.

Men. Plural. Methinks Lucy wants to take her frustration with John out on Manny. But I think that would be okay. Manny can handle it.

If Manny is inside, he isn't moving any faster than his beanbag woman. I hear a small movement, but it's quickly followed by Tank's sigh.

Lucy catches me licking the woman's exposed wrist.

I love vanilla.

"Some guard dogs you two make."

I know Lucy just wants our bed, but now she's staring at the girl with pity. Or a sense of responsibility. Maybe both. It's a hunch, but I think this is Lucy's work face.

"Skip, her pitiful-ness is so sad and in our faces."

Okay, so maybe it's not her work face. But I like how Lucy is talking to me like a partner.

"She came here on her own volition. She isn't any of our business."

Um, yeah, she is, Ms. Nurse. We can't leave her here.

"But I'm a nurse. I can't just leave her here."

Sweet. We're on the same page.

"And I don't want her to ruin Thomas's beanbag."

We're getting really good at this mind reading business 'cause I don't want to leave her to turn Thomas's beanbag into a barfbag either. Most dogs will eat their own vomit, and I've seen a few dogs enjoy someone else's, but I don't plan to eat hers, not even for Thomas.

Lucy covers her face with her hands. "I'm so tired, though. She's twice my height."

A bit of an exaggeration, but I get her point. She's too tall for Lucy to drag safely on her own. I could help by gently biting her arm and pulling, like the Newfoundland dogs do when they tow people and float ashore. Lucy showed me a video on the internet. It was amazing. I wonder if DOGTV has rescue shows? I will have to wait, watch, and see.

Yeah, yeah, yeah. If you're keeping score, I'm a convert. I frigging love DOGTV now, and I watch it when Thomas isn't reading to me.

"And she's deadweight right now." Lucy cries a fake sob and rubs her tired eyes. She kneels next to her. "Time to wake up."

But Sleeping Beauty doesn't move.

"Wakey wakey."

I do my part and lick her arm and face while Lucy squeezes her shoulder. After enough prodding and slobber, the girl's eyes open.

My big furry face makes her gasp, and Lucy says, "You're okay."

"Manny."

"He's not here," Lucy says and stands. "I'm calling you a cab."

The girl buries her face back into the bag. "No."

"You can't stay on this beanbag. It's Thomas's. But you probably don't care right now."

She scrunches up her face. "No, Manda's."

Lucy makes the same assumption I do: the chick's so drunk she's referring to herself in the third person.

"Listen up, Manda. This isn't Finders Keepers. It's Thomas's, and he works too hard for you to spoil it. So come on. Upsy-daisy, sweetie."

"Manda's."

Lucy rolls her eyes.

Even I'm getting tired.

"You know, you're not the only one. You might be better off without him."

I recall Manny saying the same to me about us and John.

"Need him," the girl says.

35

LUCY

GIRL WITH A HUMMINGBIRD TATTOO

AT LEAST I'VE never passed out outside John's new apartment; not that it was a fair comparison to the leggy blonde sprawled in the hall. Lucy had no clue where John lived. But if she did, she might have stormed over there to confront him in every single one of her weak moments, begging for a better explanation than "I want to be alone." Maybe she would have been like this poor woman, unable to ignore the temptation. Maybe she'd have curled up in a ball at his door. She really hoped not. She hoped she had more pride than that.

First thing Lucy was going to do once she dealt with Manny's girl was get on Facebook and block John so she wouldn't see anything about him. Stalking him on Facebook was no better than this desperate scenario unfolding at her feet.

Covergirl was like a Raggedy Ann doll, flopping in all directions when Lucy tried to move her.

"Help me help you. What if he comes home with

another woman? It'll be humiliating. You'll look like a stalker. Pull yourself together."

The woman's eyelids fluttered. "Gonna get sick."

Oh for the love of . . .

Lucy reached over and slid her arms around the train wreck and put her back into it. "Come with me. Let's get you into the bathroom. Don't you dare throw up on Thomas's bag."

"Amanda's."

"Enough already, Manda-Amanda."

By the time Lucy pulled the woman to her feet, her skirt was hiked up over her waist, her thong underwear on display for the world to see. Lucy felt like she'd just won California's Strong Woman competition. She wished she had opened her door first because it took a ton of coordination to do it with a ten-foot-tall Victoria's Secret model swaying in her arms, hitting her face with her perfect boobs. But they got to the bathroom. Just in time too.

Holding the mess's hair up while she vomited, Lucy admired the colorful tattoo of three hummingbirds and a flower on the back of her neck. Personally, she'd never wanted a tattoo, but it didn't mean she couldn't appreciate a beautiful piece when she saw one. Besides, it was better than looking at vomit.

Finished, the hummingbird wanted to flutter to the bathroom floor and sleep some more.

Lucy was tempted to leave her there and cover her with towels. Who hadn't thought about sleeping next to the toilet when they felt this bad? She'd probably throw up again.

"You can't sleep on the floor," the nurse in her said instead. Lucy wouldn't give up her bed for this woman, but she would make her comfortable on the couch. Who cared if her legs were too long? *Tall model problems.*

"Manny?" Hummingbird asked once settled on the couch. She looked up at Skip hovering over her. "Pretty puppy," she slurred.

"I left Manny a note," Lucy said. A bright-pink Post-it Note that said: *One of your éclairs is passed out on my couch.*

Lucy sat beside her unexpected guest and patted her flushed, yet still lovely, face with a damp washcloth. "Listen. You're young. You're beautiful. You shouldn't go after him like this. I get it. He's good looking and funny sometimes, but you need to move on. Treat yourself better."

Pot, please meet kettle. What would it take to start walking her own talk?

The girl's green eyes widened with brief clarity. "But he loved Mandy most." Tears slid from the girl's closed eyes. "Nightmares. Our fault Manda's gone."

Our. The swollen eyes and puffy faces in the mornings. Why nightmares? Who was Manda-Amanda?

There would be no more information from the blonde, who started snoring.

An hour later, Manny knocked on her door. He looked down at her, concerned. But not for her. "Where is she?"

"Comatose on the couch. She can stay, though." Lucy's attempt at humor was an utter fail. Manny's mind was obviously elsewhere.

"No, but thank you. She'll do better somewhere familiar."

He effortlessly scooped the woman into his arms and kissed her forehead. "It's me, Becca." He turned to Lucy.

"Thank you for taking care of her," he said, his face tired and seemingly older than Lucy had guessed him to be.

Lucy held her door open, and once he passed, she asked, "Manny, who was Manda or Amanda?"

"My little sister," he said.

36

LUCY
HEY, MATEY

A WEEK LATER, Lucy came home to another unpleasant to-do. This one was of her own making: a voice mail from her travel agent. She punched delete after she listened to Marge's message. Her travel agent was clearly nervous; it was the first time Marge hadn't faked an Australian accent.

"Lucy, honey, you haven't returned my calls. We're counting down to your honeymoon, and there are deadlines coming up for one of the most important trips of your life."

Like any grown woman licking her heartache and wounds, Lucy had avoided Marge and the decision that needed to be made.

After Manny left that night with the despondent girl, Lucy had surprised herself by crying for him. John was her greatest loss to date. She'd never had a sibling to love. Never one to lose, and she couldn't begin to imagine Manny's pain. Or the pain of the women he helped. Were his parents alive? Were they grieving the loss of a daughter? And now Tank was sick.

She hadn't seen Manny all week, not even for donuts

yesterday morning, and she suspected he was avoiding her. He was nursing wounds too.

Move forward or go under.

She dialed Marge's number before she could overthink it and before Marge left for the day. "Hi, Marge," Lucy said, "it's Lucy Bell."

"Lucy, honey. Thank goodness you've called." Her Aussie accent was back. "Let's talk honeymoon! I need to get yours and John's passport information and finalize your tour excursions."

It was now or never. "What if I need to cancel?"

Lucy was met with complete silence, an anomalous occurrence for chatty Marge. She could hear Marge's breathing, crackly from years of smoking, so she knew she was still there. Finally Marge answered minus the accent, "Cancel? Is everything okay?"

What was it about travel agents? That they so easily became a pseudo best friend and had the right to know what was going on in the innermost corners of your life? And you *wanted* to tell them everything?

"Right now, the wedding is off, but I'm not ready to say the honeymoon is off. I know that makes no sense. No wedding means there's no honeymoon. I just want to understand my options."

"Oh, sweetie," Marge said, "you're making more sense than you think. I've worn that hurt on my sleeve a few times. I've survived."

Lucy had to smile. Exactly what she needed to hear. "Thank you, Marge."

The sound of Marge's fingers punching away at her keyboard echoed in Lucy's ear. "Sweetie, you have a few options. You can cancel for a full refund. You can cancel the dumbass's portion and go on the trip yourself."

Lucy appreciated that Marge didn't say "alone." *Dumbass* worked too. Marge was on Team Lucy.

"You can also take his portion and upgrade to the premier package. You just need to decide by two weeks from Monday. You know what I hope you'll do?"

God, yes. Lucy was eager for someone to tell her what to do, for someone to make this choice for her, give her a survival guide. And maybe Marge was just the person to do it. Marge could care less about John. For all she knew, it was Lucy's choice to cancel the wedding. "I'd love to hear your opinion."

"Make this trip about you. Find a new reason to go. Grow and blossom in that Aussie sun. I've done this hike. It's amazing. You'll be totally safe with the tour group. No worries about being a woman on your own. With fifteen people going, you'll meet people from different countries. And, trust me when I say this, you'll be more social and willing to get to know them.

"Time and time again I see couples take these trips and then stay in their little bubble. Crikey, it defeats the entire point of exploring the world and gaining a new perspective."

Crikey was right. She needed a whole lot of new perspective.

"Thank you, Marge. I promise to call you on time with a decision."

Step one was to tell John. He'd paid for half of the trip (she would stop calling it a honeymoon from now on). Had he even thought about the events and dates that needed to be canceled? Did he even care? How selfish to leave her, the rejected one, to manage the details of their breakup. If John wasn't careful, maybe she wouldn't want *him* back when his short-term lease expired.

Her blood started to boil, and angry tears came to her eyes.

She dialed John's number before she could overthink it. She got his voice mail.

"John," she said, "sorry to bother you. Actually, no I'm not sorry to bother you." *Take that!* "We need to deal with the Australia trip." She mentally patted herself on the back for not saying honeymoon. "There are only two weeks left to make changes or cancel. What should I do with your portion of the trip? Please call me to discuss so I can update Marge." *So there!* Let him think she'd go no matter what.

She didn't have to wait long for an answer via text. Yep, he was avoiding talking to her.

John: *Are you still going?*

Of course, she typed but then second-guessed her faux confidence as soon as she hit send. What if he was missing her and now thought she didn't care if they reunited or not?

Oh, stop it! He let your last call go to voice mail, Lucy. Great, now she was talking to herself in the third person.

Three dots showed up on her phone; he was already responding. She waited and waited for his response to come through, but then the three dots disappeared.

Good. He could stew on it.

37

SKIP

REPURPOSED POTS

"Skip, want to take a walk *blah blah blah blah?*"

True story. Most of the time, once I hear the word "walk," that's all I hear. Anything that follows doesn't matter. John and Lucy used to employ subterfuge to hold off my enthusiasm for walks by spelling out *walk* until they were ready to leave: "You need to take you-know-who on a W-A-L-K." But with my high IQ, influenced by my Labrador genes, I caught on to their trickery pretty quickly. I'm not saying I can spell or read, but when you hear a series of letters often enough, the spelling of it just becomes another word: *double-u—a—ell—kay.*

Once we are on our way, Lucy tells me, "You get to meet Cranky Walter."

I'm looking forward to meeting Cranky Walter. I know little about him other than that Lucy works with him, and she's told me he tends to be grumpy. But I've been surprised enough by people of late, I decide I'll hold out judgment until I meet him myself.

It's a long walk in the sun, a perfect summer day, and

I'm happy as all get out when we approach a white fence that's connected to a large peach-colored single-level facility.

"This is where I work, Skip."

Cool.

We head to the back and pause by a metal gate, where Lucy enters a code. After a *click* and a *pop*, the gate swings open. Lucy peeks in before letting me inside. "Oh, good. You're already here," she says, but I can't see who she's talking to.

"I said I would be, didn't I?" a cranky voice responds.

That must be Walter.

Lucy looks down at me and rolls her eyes and mouths, "Good luck."

And then I enter a secret magical garden. The yard is four times the size of the one at our apartment building, and I'm gobsmacked by its beauty and splendor. It's lush and earthy with gravel trails throughout, and I want to roll around in the plants and fertilizer. How awesome one of our doga classes would be in this space.

Then I look up at a lanky man with a buzz cut. He looks like a shaved poodle. A disapproving shaved poodle.

Walter is hosing his flora and frowning at Lucy and me. His scowl reminds me of Manny's before Manny knew us, and before we understood Manny. We'd been wrong, so wrong, about Manny, all the way from the hoarding to the women in his life, so despite his glare, I continue to reserve judgment about "Cranky" Walter.

But he doesn't make it easy. He sets the hose down and points at me, "First things first. No pissing or shitting here. This is a garden, not some damn litter box."

Excuse me. I'm potty trained.

Lucy ignores him. I'm annoyed that she doesn't defend my honor. Maybe she's too distracted by the Garden of Eden.

"Walter," Lucy turns around, "this is unbelievable. It's like the *Secret Garden* by Frances Hodgson Burnett. I had no idea you have such a green thumb. I'm struggling to believe this has been back here the whole time. How have I missed it?"

Walter huffed. "Like most people here, you're running around like you're missing your marbles."

"If you mean I'm always busy, I agree. Is this all your work?" she asks.

I start to fall under Walter's green thumb spell. He makes me wish I had a thumb. Truth is *I* really don't even want to relieve myself in this haven. It's clear of all animal residue; no hint of cats, raccoons, or evil skunks. But there are birds. The birds love it here and are singing to prove it. He even has birdhouses set up for them. Okay, maybe he is a nice guy. Bird people are always sweet inside. Like Sleeping Beauty and Cinderella. He just needs to know I'm not a threat to his hard work and that I like plants and birds too.

"So what's this about?" he asks Lucy. "Why are you here on a Sunday?"

She gives him her sweetest, most hopeful smile. "I need your help. Have you met Martha Knight?"

"Yes." Walter picks up his hose again. He turns it on a gentle mist, my favorite kind of rain because the drops are like happy tears floating in the air, waiting for the perfect spot to land. I wish I could stand in his man-made rain and try to catch it on my tongue.

"And you know Enid," Lucy says.

He grunts. "Hates the food here."

"The one and only," Lucy says. "I have an idea. Actually, I *had* an idea." She looked around the garden again. "I was going to ask if there is a way to build a community garden for the residents. Martha Knight used to work in a garden at home, and she misses it. And we could have used the fresh veggies or herbs with the chef. But this is too magnificent to change."

"This is all my personal time and money," Walter says. "Never been a budget here for more than the typical landscaping, you know?"

"You're a garden whisperer," she says.

He has a crooked grin. I find his smile endearing.

"I got into it years ago. No one minded." He turns defensive. "You mind?"

Lucy is warming up to him. I can tell. Her shoulders have relaxed. The lines above her nose and between her eyes have softened.

I get it too. He's not Cranky Walter. He's Cautious Walter.

Her words come fast. "No way. You're a natural. Which was the very first plant?"

For some reason, he hesitates. He opens his mouth but doesn't say anything immediately. It's as if he isn't sure he wants to share.

Yup, cautious.

But then he points across the yard to a planter made out of pavers. "Fern over there. She's gone now, but many have grown from her since."

It's his tone that gives him away, the way he sounds

mentioning Fern being gone. Like Fern was a precious pet with a special place in his heart. Inside, Walter is a big fluffy marshmallow like me who just wants to belong. I fall in love with Cautious Walter then and there. These plants are his pack, and he will do anything for them. In return, they grow for him.

"Fern," Lucy repeats and stares at Walter as if she has never seen him before. "I'll come up with a different idea. I don't want to touch your work, but I'd love to add some benches so the residents might come out here and enjoy it. Would that be okay with you?"

But Walter looks like he is thinking. Maybe he's blushing, if a guy like him blushes. Yes, I think he *is* blushing. Even his big ears are turning red. He starts curling his fist, not in a scary-I-might-punch-you way, but in an I-can-make-it-work way. His arm tattoo of a woman with a buzzard sitting on her shoulder starts to wiggle. I'm not one for tattoos, and neither is Lucy, but this one is colored like a rainbow. I remember once John wanted to get a tattoo-like drawing for his leather briefcase, some legal symbol. As a surprise, Lucy started calling tattoo parlors to see if they might sketch the tattoo for her, but every time she said she didn't need an appointment to get it on her body, the tattooists declined. Finally she asked, "Why not? I'd still be paying for the art."

The tattoo artist said, "We never let our artwork leave the building."

"Wow," Lucy said. "What do you do with all the bodies?"

When Lucy told John the story, he laughed his ass off and said, "Telling me that story and about your effort is better than getting it. Thank you."

And that was that.

Lucy turns to leave when Walter asks, "You always give up so easy?" But he's not looking at us. He's looking at his plants, like he's piecing something together.

"Excuse me?" Her lips tighten, and she puts her hands on her hips, jerking the leash and my collar. "I'm not giving up. I don't want to mess with a good thing. I'm showing respect for your work."

"But I didn't say no. I kind of like the idea. Those people are cooped up too much. But I'll need somewhere to start the seedlings. I can't have the residents out here digging and watering every day. But if you want my help, I will help."

I'm concerned Lucy's smile might split her face in two. She's that radiant.

"That would be awesome."

"One condition," Walter says. "If I do this, I don't want the oldie-but-goodies coming out here and littering their bingo candy wrappers everywhere, stomping on my plants, or picking damn bouquets for each other. Look-don't-touch only. Got it?"

Lucy shakes her head. "But I want them to be involved. That's the point."

"I will move stuff around. I'll repurpose a few planters. I'll clear this spot by the door and put the new crates here. But that doesn't fix the seedling issue. Going to need a lot of pots and work space for the oldies."

Walter keeps talking, but Lucy and I look at each other, and I know that she's thinking what I'm thinking: *Manny's pots!*

"They could plant their seeds somewhere else if you can find a place inside. And when the new plants are ready, I'll move them out here." Cautious Walter blushes again. "And I can put a few benches over there," he says, pointing to the other side of the concrete patio, "so they can come out here and admire their handiwork."

Admire his handiwork too, I think.

"How many pots?" Lucy's eyes are sparkling and, no kidding, she is now jumping from foot to foot.

"You got to piss or something?" Walter asks.

"What? No! I'm excited! I know where we can get gorgeous pots. Free pots that need to be repurposed for good. What if we set up tables on the outskirts of the cafeteria, flush against the walls, near the bingo and craft tables? Those who want to participate can have a unique pot and care for their own seedlings. It will be easy to keep it swept up and cleaned, and when we're ready to move the seedlings out here, we can load them in that wagon over there."

Now Walter is nodding his head. His right cheek is twitching again. He *does* have a lopsided smile. "Damn, girl, that might work."

Lucy claps her hands. "Okay, I'm going to head out. We can pick up the pots this week. I'll talk to Dr. Ryan on Monday about the expenses."

"You move fast," Walter says. "What are we going to call this project of yours?"

"It's *our* project, Walter," Lucy says.

I think Walter might be about to cry because he swallows hard and blinks a lot, but he doesn't. He keeps his shit together.

I lick Lucy's hand, happy to see her turning Cautious Walter into our friend.

"Your garden adds so much life to this place. I'm sorry it's been ignored."

"Yeah," he says. "It just takes a little love and a memory about which plant needs what. Every plant has a purpose. Same as people do."

38

SKIP

THE DOCTOR IS IN

CANINE ANNOUNCEMENT! We're wrapping up four weeks without John, and I'm going to be a therapy dog! Not to be confused with a service dog. A therapy dog is a socialite, an excellent listener, comforter, and mind reader. Therapy dogs get to visit schools, hospitals, and nursing homes. *Bada bing*. Golden Years with Lucy! The screening process is less rigorous than it is to become a certified service dog. Okay, it's somewhat non-existent, but you still have to be recognized and accepted as a therapy dog; otherwise, the institutions will worry about liability. Lucy and I will train together.

"Busy is better right now," is what Lucy said when she first met the trainer and realized we'd have to do our training at night and on some weekends.

I agree. Busy *is* better.

I'm not worried about catching on because let's face it, I'm a natural. And Lucy is a nurse. What a team we'll make. Lucy already got me an engraved name tag that slaps against my rabies tag when I walk. *Jing a ling*. Just spells,

"Skip, Therapy Dog" right now. But I know it's only a matter of time until I'll be known as Dr. Skip. If I might write my own tagline, I'd add, "Bay Area's Best Cuddler."

Our long-term plan is for me to start working with Lucy at Golden Years in the fall. The timing works well for me. Now is not the time to be heading out for my new career during the day, because Thomas and I are committed to our book club for the summer.

In hindsight, one might wonder why it took us so long to consider my career. After all, working as a therapy dog is an obvious progression from my role with the neighborhood watch. And I've been raised by a caregiver. But I have to admit, the thought never occurred to me or Lucy when we were with John. If John were still with us, I wouldn't have "Donuts & Doga" every Saturday morning. That's what I've come to call our new tradition. And without doga, we would never have met the therapy dog trainer.

Funny, isn't it, how gifts can come out of such loss and tragedy?

Three things happened to point us in the right direction. Mrs. Brighton had mentioned how dogs can help with autism, like Thomas's and my book club. Then Lucy subscribes to Dr. Amanda Toler Woodward's newsletter. Dr. Woodward is Associate Professor of Social Work with Michigan State University, and she writes lots of cool stuff about elderly behavioral services. I'm not totally sure what that means, but Lucy says Dr. Woodward's insight is helping her improve life for her patients at Golden Years.

In a nutshell, Dr. W is smart and well respected in Lucy's field, *but if you ask me*, the doctor's true glory is that she has Loki in her pack: a Blue Heeler Australian Cattle Dog. And Loki is a therapy dog! Sometimes Dr. W shares pictures and stories about Loki in her newsletter. Lucy reads these bits out loud to me.

Loki cracks me up. She has lots of personality like me, and she is always up to something. At heart she's a cuddle-bug like me too, not what you might expect from a Blue Heeler. And she does yoga with Dr. Woodward. Again, just like Lucy and me!

Blue Heelers usually are bossy control freaks. I know because there are two at the dog park who try to herd me like I'm a stupid cow. They're named Fosters and Dundee. They piss me off sometimes, the way they forget we're supposed to be playing, but I also respect their commitment and their work ethic.

Only thing Loki and I don't have in common is I would *never* let two cats push me around or take my toys. 'Course, I've never had a cat before, only near dealings with Tom Cat, but someday I'll get my chance to show Tom who's the boss. Now this is important because, like me, an Australian Cattle Dog is not a breed typically thought of as a therapy dog. But they love people, they love their herd, and they love their pack. If there were a dating app for dogs, Loki and I would probably match up.

So Lucy was reading the latest newsletter, and she said, "If a Blue Heeler can be a therapy dog, maybe you can too, Skip."

That alone wasn't enough. I think Lucy was just making conversation with me, not really considering what it would take or what a perfect solution it would be for me to go to work with her sometimes. Her mind, as usual, was not in the Now as much as it was still on John and her new job.

But this morning at doga, I met a new yogi woman with a yellow Labrador who was wearing a red vest and other bling. Turns out he is a service dog, a different beast of dog therapy, but I was intrigued and wished I could read his fancy name tag. It was a large circle, the silver polished bright, and it had a cross on it. Lucy's hospital name tag had a cross on it.

Lucy joined us and started talking to the service dog's owner. Her name is Beth, and her dog's name is, wait for it, Doc. *Sigh*. Beth adopted him specifically to train as a service dog to work with people with PTSD. I'll have to learn what that means. Not sure if Beth's spelling out an important clue or if it's an actual word: *pee—tee—ess—dee*. You know, like *double-u—a—ell—kay*?

Doc won't be staying with Beth; that's another reason I don't ever want to be a service dog. Doc will be given away to someone with *pee—tee—ess—dee* when the time is right and he is called to duty. Not that I wouldn't be an excellent service member.

Anyhoo, once Beth explained the difference between the different care dogs, Lucy asked Beth if she'd be available to bring Doc to Golden Years to visit the patients, "for practice, if you want." At first I was peeved because what the heck am I? Minced dog food?

I barked to make my point. After our zen morning, my yogi-dogi peers all turned to stare at me, surprised by my outburst.

Lucy *shushed* me. I stopped at her command, not because she told me to, but to show Beth that I can follow instructions.

"I'm so sorry," Lucy said. "We've been through a lot of changes lately, and he's getting very bossy. I think he needs a dog trainer."

Then Beth said the wisest and best thing I've ever heard

a human say, "If a dog is acting more aggressive than usual, it's always something different the owner is doing."

Hear that, Lucy? You need the trainer. Not me.

They exchanged business cards and made arrangements for Doc's and Beth's first visit. And for Lucy's training.

39

SKIP

WALK IT OFF

I AM grateful my dog therapy training has begun because when Thomas goes back to school, I'm going to miss him. I'm not sure how much time we have left this summer, but we're reading the third book now, *Harry Potter and the Prisoner of Azkaban.*

Hagrid's pet Hippogriff (which is a bird horse), Buckbeak, has just attacked Draco Malfoy for being his usual punk-ass self during the Care of Magical Creatures class. Animals can always recognize a first-class jerk when they see one.

Without warning, Thomas stops reading.

Dawg, what's up? Don't leave me hanging. T-Dog never pauses when reading. No joke. Once he sits in his beanbag, he never stops reading until it's time to eat lunch or go home for the night.

He's quiet so long I'm about to quit him and go watch DOGTV, but then he says, "I will walk you."

Walk me? *Dude, I'd love that, but we have a door between us, so unless you have a magic wand from Ollivan-*

ders in Diagon Alley, I don't see it happening. He doesn't say anything more, and he resumes reading.

When lunchtime comes, Thomas doesn't run off like he normally would. Even though he knows Lucy is happy with his reading, he still has been taking off just before she gets home or when he hears the downstairs door open. But this time, he closes our book, stands in front of his beanbag, and faces Lucy when she reaches our landing.

"Thomas," Lucy asks, "is everything okay?"

I'm not sure how this is going to work out. Thomas still doesn't speak to Lucy, so he's unlikely to start now. But to my shock, he says, "I will walk Skip."

Just like that, in his monotone voice, a proclamation: *I will walk Skip.*

I'd give anything for hands to open the door so I can see Lucy's face. Superpower hearing is only good when people are making noise.

"Oh, wow," Lucy finally says. But she doesn't hesitate to add, "Let's talk to your mom tonight." She sounds skeptical, like she doesn't believe Thomas means it. But I know Thomas best, and he is incapable of saying anything less than what he means.

"I will walk Skip now." I hear Thomas shuffle to the side.

He's putting off his cheese sandwich for me? This is a really big day. Seriously. I don't know if Lucy realizes how magnanimous an offer this is coming from Thomas.

I hear the floor creaking as if Lucy is rocking from foot to foot. That's her undecided-let's-think-about-this move, probably because Lucy doesn't have Mrs. Brighton's approval.

"Okay. I will walk behind you and watch. And we will talk to your mom tonight."

When she unlocks the door and comes inside, Thomas waits in the doorway.

Lucy looks at me, smiles, and whispers, "He's talking to me."

I'm happy to see her rewarded for her efforts with Thomas even if it was really me that made it happen. I'm okay with her taking the credit. We all need treats and rewards sometimes.

I grab my leash, and we head toward the door. Thomas races ahead of us. I've never seen him run. He runs crooked. Like most things, he runs outside the line, or the box, *whatever*. I love this guy.

At the door, Lucy hands him the leash. "Always put a leash on when you walk him."

As if he will be contaminated if he touches the leash at the same time as Lucy, he lets it drop to the floor then picks it up. He clips it on, and we head out.

"We'll go around the block a few times," she says as much to herself as to Thomas and me.

I think it's a good choice. I'm sure I can get Thomas home, but I don't know if Thomas is good with directions. I don't usually like being limited to the block, but if Thomas is going to start walking me, bonus! Begging dogs can't be choosy.

The first time, about halfway around the block, we see three boys. They look Thomas's age. Fifteen years old or so. Thomas doesn't look up when they call, "Thomas!"

I'll tell you now. I don't like 'em. There's that movie about the little boy who sees dead people, well, I see and smell mean people. They smell like that gross propane gas hooked up to the outdoor grill. I knows what I knows, and I knows I don't like these guys.

Thomas starts humming to himself and walks faster.

I don't recognize the tune, but it sounds scary. *Duh, duh, duhhhhh.*

Lucy asks, "Are they your friends, Thomas?"

But Thomas has shut down, and I guess he's decided he's talked to Lucy enough for one day because he just keeps humming: *duh, duh, duhhhhh.*

When we make it around the first time, Lucy asks, "Ready for more, or are you done?"

He keeps walking. The boys aren't there the next two rounds. *Thank Dog.*

On the way up the stairs, Thomas goes to his apartment as if he is back to his routine.

Lucy looks hard at me. "Skip, I swear. If any of those boys are mean to Thomas, don't let them get away with it."

We'll be okay. We'll be safe together.

While Lucy and I eat lunch together, she talks non-stop about Thomas talking to her.

She is happy, so I am happy too.

That night when we talk to Mrs. Brighton, Thomas is in his room. I'm good at multitasking, so while I'm glued to Mrs. Brighton's reaction as she and Lucy sit on the couch, I can also hear Thomas practicing commands in his room: sit, heel, stay, speak, and two I haven't tried.

The first is "high-five." I've seen this on DOGTV. It's when the dog lifts its paw, higher than a shake. You know I won't shake, not even for Thomas. But I am amenable to doing the high-five. It's kind of cool and fits my personality. The other command is "sick."

Siiiiiiick. The middle is long, and the *ck* is hard. It's a strong, curt word. Aggressive. Not the same sick when my stomach is upset or when Lucy or John have had the flu. The way Thomas is saying it, it's an action word. I've never heard it on DOGTV. Never at the dog park. And not from Lucy or John. But it's a new word and a new day. I'm looking forward to learning something new, if Thomas can teach me. I'll do a lot for Bacon Bits. Lucy and T-Dog's mom don't seem to hear him; they are too wrapped up in their own moment.

Lucy is smiling but with her eyebrows raised and her nose wrinkled like she's not sure if Mrs. Brighton is happy, or if she's speechless because Lucy took her son on a walk without her permission.

Mrs. Brighton is shaking her head, jaw dropped. I can smell her lightness; it reminds me of a fresh ocean breeze.

"He went outside with you? Around this block?" Mrs. Brighton whirls her hand above her head. "Three times?"

"I know I shouldn't have without your permission, but I was so happy he wanted to, and I didn't want to scare him away by saying no. I told him we would talk to you tonight."

Mrs. Brighton grabs Lucy's fiddling hands. "I can't believe this. It's okay. I just, I just don't know . . ." Mrs. Brighton pauses, holding Lucy's hands, and turns to look at me with happy-tear eyes. "This is because of you, Skip. You're Thomas's therapy dog. His friend. Thank you."

It's my privilege. You're welcome.

And she looks back at Lucy, "And thank *you*, Lucy."

Lucy smiles and tilts her head to the side. "I've seen Thomas walking around the block before, though."

Lucy's right, he has walked around the block alone before. It used to be part of his afternoon routine, seven days a week. But if she'd ever done neighborhood watch with me, she'd know that Thomas stopped taking walks moons ago. Like a whole year ago!

"No, dear. He stopped. Out of the blue. No matter how much we worked with him, his teachers and I couldn't figure out what happened. And, sadly, as it can be with autism, some things just change for no reason. I was heart-sick when the walking fell out of his repertoire. It helps with thought process, memory, stress, and getting sunlight. Now he only spends time outdoors at his school playground or if I take him somewhere. But never here."

I think about the boys we saw and wonder if Lucy is thinking about them too. Will she say something to Mrs. Brighton?

"When we were walking," Lucy says, "three boys about Thomas's age called his name, but he ignored them." I know Lucy sensed the darkness about them, but she's being delicate. "Do you think something happened with them?"

Mrs. Brighton shakes her head vehemently. "Oh no, they are nice boys. They used to play with Thomas when they were smaller. I know their parents. They've always tried to include Thomas. But, eventually, they too fell out of his repertoire."

I think you might be wrong about this one, Mrs. B.

Mrs. Brighton stands and knocks on Thomas's door. He opens.

"Thomas, do you want to walk Skip when Lucy is at work?"

"Don't insult a Hippogriff."

Even Mrs. Brighton, who knows *Harry Potter* and is used to T-Dog using the books to communicate, pauses. "That's a yes, I think." Then she turns to explain to Lucy. "Hippogriffs are very loyal, and Thomas is saying Skip is loyal. I think."

Lucy says, "What's a Hippogriff?"

"Hagrid's pet," Thomas says.

Lucy smiles at Mrs. Brighton. I think she's keeping track of how many times Thomas speaks to her.

As Lucy and Mrs. Brighton talk about keys and rules, I respond to Thomas's "come." I join him in the room, where I do tricks for Bacon Bits. But he doesn't say the new word I heard earlier, so I guess I'll have to wait to find out what *siiiiiiick* means.

Afterward, Lucy and I head to my rescue dog Meetup group at Golden Gate Park, and by the time we get home, it's raining. I'm dreading watching more *Sex and the City*, but Lucy surprises me by turning on the first *Harry Potter* movie.

For the next few hours, I am glued to the TV and also watching Lucy's expressions. She finally sees the magic that Thomas has been sharing with me and how Thomas and *Harry Potter* make this world a better place.

Now, this is my idea of a perfect night with my lady.

40

SKIP

ABOUT DOGGONE TIME

THE "DAY YOU STOLE MY POTS" happens after Lucy knocks on Manny's door without getting an answer. "I still have no idea where and when he works," she says before asking Walter to help her carry them away.

If I could, I'd tell her that Manny rarely leaves his apartment. If he works, he works from home.

She speaks as she writes him a note: "I have found a new home for your pots. They are safe. Talk to you tonight."

That evening, as soon as Lucy comes home from work, Manny bounds over to our apartment. "You stole my pots!"

He's red in the face, a little sweaty. If you ask me, his sweat smells sharper than usual. Panic smells like the sharp cheddar Lucy melts in her quesadillas, and sometimes it oozes into the pan and burns.

Lucy lowers her voice. "Manny, I was going to talk to you tonight. You saw my note. They weren't stolen. They are in a good place."

"Where are they? I want them back."

"Manny," she uses his name intentionally, like she is trying to get him to focus on her (she's done this to me and John before when we weren't listening), "you said I should take the pots if they were all kept together for a really good purpose. You'll be so pleased."

He shakes his head vigorously. "I should never have said that."

"They are all together, right this very second, at Golden Years. I will take you to see them after I walk Skip." Now Lucy's voice is less stern and more like the voice she used once when we saw a little girl drop her ice cream cone on the sidewalk. I'm not going to lie. I would have eaten it if Lucy had let me.

Manny runs his hands through his hair. "They're all together?"

I want to remind him to breathe and that he needs oxygen to live.

"Yes. And not going anywhere. They will be well appreciated. More appreciated than sitting here, unused. They can grow things now."

"Okay." He nods and takes a deep breath (*Whew!*), like one of those inflating hot air balloons that Lucy and John once went for a ride on in the wine valley. I wasn't there, but I pieced their story together. They have a picture on the bed stand of them standing in front of the basket. Well, they *had* the picture. I saw John slide it into his suitcase when he left us. Manny's shoulders drop, and his arms hang like noodles at his sides. "I won't see them. Have to let her, I mean them, go."

"If you ever want to talk about Amanda, I'm ready when you are. That's what friends are for."

"I don't need you to rescue me." He turns to leave.

It's the same thing Lucy said to him when he fixed our toilet. And just like when Lucy pushed him away, Manny isn't really talking about the pots; he's talking about something bigger. And he's wrong. He does need Lucy's help. Just like we need his. Just like I need Thomas's, and just like Thomas needs me to protect him from the neighborhood thugs.

We be a pack, dude. And what do pack members do? We step in and fill a need. *All for one and one for all.*

My sweet Lucy handles Manny well by responding, "Good. Because I'm not rescuing you. I rescued your pots."

Manny pauses and turns back to us. "So now you're stealing my pots and my lines." Even though no one can see it, both humans and dogs hear the smile in his voice. Pots crisis averted. Still, Manny doesn't go to Golden Years with Lucy. He isn't ready to see Amanda's pots in their new home.

You know that human saying, "Time heals all wounds"? I don't know if I believe that. But I will concede our attention to our time without John is adjusting. When John first left, we hurt every second of the day. Each minute was a mission of survival. Then we graduated to taking it day by day. And except for the hiccups, such as our setback after John's mug popped up on Facebook, we're getting by week by week now. I wonder when we will move on to month by month? Maybe we'll never stop grieving. Maybe we'll just get used to our new life or a new normal. Maybe time doesn't heal all wounds; it just forces us to move forward. "Time waits for no one." Now that's a saying I agree with. Time waits for no one.

"There are five stages to grief," Lucy has read to me: denial, anger, bargaining, depression, and acceptance. But as it is with humans and afflictions, each person can present in different orders and take different amounts of time to move on to a new level. Kind of like the video games John used to play. Some peeps are better at figuring out those games and moving through the levels more quickly. John was faster than Lucy and me.

Man, life would be easier as a video game. Maybe that's why John played the video games so much toward the end. Maybe he was looking for easy push buttons to move on to the next level. He always used to chant, "Almost there. Almost there." Just before he'd howl a war cry when he succeeded.

This breakup business is no joke. I think I'm in the acceptance stage about John, but sometimes I'll go down a few rabbit holes of depression. But I know all the facts. And I worry if he came back at this point, Lucy would uncover our betrayal. There's always a trail back to betrayal. Just like Big's wife finding out about Carrie, or with Ross and Rachel in *Friends*.

Yeah, Lucy's been watching reruns of *Friends*, but it beats *Sex and the City* any day. Ross and Rachel are on a "break," and bozo grass-is-greener-and-different Ross sleeps with that other cute woman. Just like there was a trail from Ross's betrayal to Rachel (that rascal, Gunther!), there's a trail from my betrayal to Lucy. And that trail can only be broken with John staying gone. John is my Gunther.

I still love the heck out of the guy, though. I'll always love him. But I want him to be happy in his new pack even if being jealous of Bunny makes me feel like I have tapeworms again. There comes a point, though, when you just gotta accept that if you love someone enough, you'll care more about them being happier without you than just kinda happy with you.

I think Lucy is in a hybrid stage of denial and bargaining but also has sinkholes of depression, denying that John could be happier without her and bargaining that if she lets him be free, he'll come back. *That's just stupid. Makes no sense. Let someone go and they'll come back? Um, I don't think so.*

But Lucy and I have been John-free for almost five weeks now. Lucy says, "We deserve a reward, like the chips that people get in Alcoholics Anonymous." So I get a Dentabone, and Lucy eats a whole bag of Twizzlers.

I know, it seems backward: why graduate from hourly to weekly to monthly if we can get a treat every hour instead of once a month? The more treats the better in my book, but Lucy says, "Someday the reward will be John is back, or we'll be happy without rewards. We'll just be happy."

It's the first time I've heard Lucy even mention John not being in our life and a potential for "happy" in the same sentence. She's making progress toward *acceptance*.

Right now, though, we still need the treats for motivation and a sense of accomplishment.

Manny realized his pots were gone in a matter of hours after Walter came and helped Lucy load them up. And everyone is still avoiding the topic of his sister, even over donuts. At one point, would Manny have noticed the *second* the pots were gone? The *minute* they were gone? If Lucy had waited or taken one pot at a time, would Manny have needed a week or more to notice?

Is Manny still grieving for his little sister, and what

stage is he in? And how will he handle Tank's departure to the Rainbow Bridge? What happens when new grief stacks upon old grief?

41

LUCY
FORWARDING ADDRESS

LUCY HOPED absence was making John's heart grow fonder. Otherwise, what good were these age-old clichés? They were supposed to be tried and true by generations of people. They just needed to be true for her too.

Though she did have that moment walking back from therapy dog training the other night. A slight, gentle moment where a happy inner voice chimed in and said, "In some ways you're happier."

She'd lost weight. Was getting more exercise. Loved her job. Was sleeping more regular hours. Was eating healthier (mostly because the only lunch she could tolerate at Golden Years was the salad, but she was working on a new local menu with the chef, and the garden was underway).

Part of her had wanted to wrap her arms around the gentle hope that she could be happy again, hold it dear, and encourage it to grow, just like the seedlings her residents nurtured. Another part of her wanted to bury the feeling and make sure the initial thought never saw the light of day. She hadn't had the guts to dissect why she wanted to shun hope at the time. What was a good metaphor for finding hope in something but also being terrified to face what she'd be disavowing? If she could be happier without John, was there such a thing as true love?

He was her true love, dammit!

Then two things happened. First, when she and Skip got home from his training, she'd been in a "rearrange the furniture" kind of mood. As she moved furniture piece by piece, she swept and mopped. She'd started in the living room and made her way to the front door. The hallway was her last area to clean. When she'd shoved the chest in the foyer aside, she found a piece of mail that had slid under the chest some time ago, judging by the dust bunnies and fur it had collected. It read: IMPORTANT NOTICE in red caps, and it was from the United States Postal Service: *Forwarding Address Confirmed for John Dryden.*

It was postmarked the first week she and Skip had been alone.

So John had permanently forwarded his mail to his short-term lease address. Not so temporary, was it? Okay. He had to get his mail even though most bills were now digital, etcetera. But this was the federal government officially mocking her: *John has left you.*

John had foreseen that she would contact him with anything important in the mail. But he wanted to be alone, so he didn't want her to contact him. He'd crossed the T's and dotted the frigging I's. *Damn.*

She was being stupid. *It's just mail.* She started to tear it in half but paused. The envelope all but winked at her, beckoned her with a finger, and said, "Come on, take a look inside. You have a right to know where he lives now."

She could open it and find out where he lived. No, she'd

end up becoming a stalker, wearing dark clothes at night and spying on what "being alone" meant.

Skip came up beside her, probably picking up on her pathetic-ness. "You're right," she said aloud and tore the notice in tiny pieces. "His address and mail are none of my business."

She'd just finished when her phone rang. *Oh no.* John's mom. Was she calling about the wedding or the annihilation of her world? Had John broken his promise and told his mom without warning her?

Just get it over with. She'll just keep calling. She could let it go to voice mail, but then she'd have to work up the guts to call Marianne back. She wasn't about to ignore this woman she considered a second mom.

"Hello?" Lucy answered. Her teeth started chattering like she was standing in Iceland in that scary series *Fortitude*, not her warm apartment in sunny California.

"Lucy, I'm so sorry," her maybe-not-ever-mother-in-law said.

Lucy's surge of anger surprised her. She could take John's choice out on Marianne and sarcastically ask, "What for? The breakup? For a son who's making choices rooted in his parents' relationship years later?" But John was a grown man. It would be ridiculous to take his choices out on Marianne. And Lucy didn't really even feel like doing it. She loved Marianne.

"Hi, Marianne. I'm sorry too. I'm sorry I haven't called. John and I were waiting, I had hoped . . ."

"I know, Lucy. Believe me, I know."

Lucy and Marianne had never talked about her failed marriage, even John had never discussed it with his parents, so why would Lucy? And yet, here they were, separated by phone waves, evolving from future in-laws to two women who'd been thrust into heartache by men. Both rejected. One, so a man could be alone. The other, so a man could be with another woman.

"I'd like to see you," Marianne said. "I've already told my foolish son that he wasn't ending my relationship with you."

Lucy didn't make any commitments, she said it was hard to talk about, and she asked if she could take some time. Marianne understood, but she said, "Lucy, don't wait for him, dear. He's having a premature midlife crisis. And the outcome is hard to predict." Then she hung up.

And there it was, a decree even more official than the one she'd received from the federal government: *Mom said so.*

John had ended their relationship.

Not temporarily. Not for a short-term lease. Not for a trial period. Ended. Marianne hadn't said, "If you love him set him free, he'll come back because it's meant to be." Nope. She'd said, "Don't wait."

Lucy texted John without thinking, her thumbs moving fast and furious. *You could have warned me you were telling your mom!* Her dopamine spiked. Her pain was starting over again, but she was finally pissed! What an asshole!

Skip nudged her. "Not now, Skip!"

Screw a response from him! She texted him again. *I've canceled your portion of the trip.* She wouldn't give him the honor of typing "honeymoon." *And I'm taking your deposit to cover your half of the lease.*

He finally responded, *Okay . . . Does this mean you're still going?*

Hadn't she already told him she was, even if she'd been

bluffing before? He hadn't believed her. She bet he didn't think her jelly was adventurous enough. She'd fix that. *You bet I am*, she replied. She turned off her phone as soon as she hit send.

Move forward or go the hell under.

42

SKIP

EMOTIONAL DECISIONS

MY LEASH IS LOOPED over a parking meter on busy Geary Boulevard. I ignore the cars flying by. I am captivated, watching Lucy through the large storefront window.

An illusive force has possessed my Lucy. She's running around the store like a squirrel on a mission to collect every nut in a forest, like she's the master nut collector. Or the nut. I'm not sure. A store clerk follows her, catching the items she tosses to him seconds after he points to them on display.

I've missed something. Some epoch-making button-pushing right under my nose while we were back at our apartment, just returned from my latest session of dog therapy training. I'm rocking training, by the way. The trainer loves me. She keeps saying, "You're going to heal many hearts, Skip." *Damn straight I will.*

Anyway, one minute Lucy was cleaning and staring at some mail she'd found under the hallway chest, and the next, John's mom was calling. Okay, I get how Marianne's call could push a button. But we knew John was bound to tell his mom. Just a few days ago, Lucy even said to me, "I wonder when he'll tell his parents."

After the call, Lucy had texted someone, her jaw mulish and lips pursed. I suspected it was John, but I was positive she'd tell me if she were breaking our sobriety. Her shoulders had rolled forward and up toward her ears as she thumbed out her techno message quicker than I've ever seen her text. *Clickety clickety clickety.* The noise always puts me on edge, but it was worse this time. I sensed a digital storm brewing.

She wouldn't look me in the eye, so I nudged her hands, fumbled her texting.

"Not now, Skip!" she shouted.

And then it happened. Whatever happened. The phone dinged with a response, and like a spastic Jack Russell Terrier puppy, she grabbed my leash, yanked on her tennis shoes, and dragged me out of the apartment. We walked at a fast clip for several blocks. I didn't even try to stop her with a piss or sniff. No way. I was not going under the firing squad. She tied me up outside a store. I think John and Lucy have walked me here once before, but we only window shopped.

So now I'm waiting outside the store for Lucy. The store clerk looks happy, but Lucy resembles an angry lunatic, her arms grabbing and waving about. Must have been John she texted. Is it safe to say that Lucy has entered the anger stage of grief?

Here's what I know about stores: they take money for things. Money Lucy doesn't have. Money for things as small as a battery to things as big as a backpack. And Lucy has a lot of things piling up in the man's arms. At the counter, she starts shoving her purchases in the backpack as the man hands them to her. I lose track of her at this point because the sun is setting and shining on the window. The glare makes it hard for me to track her.

When she comes out, the gigantic full backpack is slung over her shoulders with a belt fastened around her waist. She leans over to untether my leash and almost tips head over feet.

Our walk home is silent except for Lucy's labored breathing. I take the lead. *Where's a pop-up doga group when you need one?* Lucy needs to zen the heck out.

When we get home, she dumps the backpack's contents onto the living room floor. She goes to the entertainment center, where the wedding invitations and honeymoon file have been hiding, and takes a list out. She is checking off items when someone pounds on our door.

Lucy opens the door, and Manny marches inside, talking a mile a minute. Very un-Manny-ish.

Oh jeez. Pots. He wants to talk about the pots again. I wish I could tell him this is not a good time. *Look around you, buddy. DEFCON 5, dude!*

He almost trips over Lucy's sporting goods store explosion. He looks at me.

I beg him with my eyes: *Tread carefully.*

I think he gets it because his energy chills out a bit.

"Everything okay here?" he asks.

Lucy says, "You're not the only one dealing with life, you know?"

I hope Manny doesn't say something foolish, like, "Obviously." He doesn't. *Whew.*

"Yeah, sorry. I'm worried about my pots." His hand shakes as he scratches his head. "I found a few more. So they aren't all together like they have to be."

His tone or words break through some of Lucy's tunnel vision. Her eyes stop darting between the mess on the floor and her list. "More? Where?"

I know what she's thinking: *Impossible*. She and Walter carted away every pot from every corner, step, nook, and cranny. It took two trips!

Manny looks away. "I may have a room of Amanda's stuff in my apartment, and I might have found more in there."

"A room?" This pulls Lucy out of her myopic state.

We've never been inside Manny's apartment. John and Lucy always suspected he hoarded more inside (case in point, the beanbag). But an entire room for Amanda?

Lucy sets her list aside and faces Manny. "I promise I will take the pots to the other pots. Can I see this room?"

Yeah, can I see it too?

Manny's upper lip starts to sweat, and his eyes dart over her mess. "Um, doesn't look much worse than this thing you've got going on here on your floor, which is what, by the way?"

Lucy says, "Show me the room. Tell me about Amanda if you're ready. Then I'll tell you what's happening."

Hallelujah! Take the offer, Manny. Help this dog out. I need to know what the F is happening. And I want to see your apartment and hear about Amanda too.

"This isn't a game. Tit for tat."

"Of course it isn't. But aren't you sick of being such a mystery to me?"

"No, not really."

"Aren't you sick of me asking questions?"

"Definitely."

"Then answer them, and I'll stop."

"That makes no sense. Codependent really."

"Question for question. Come on. Show me the room."

"And you'll tell me about all this?" Manny points at the floor and her paraphernalia.

"I will. And if it makes you feel better, I really don't want to."

"That does help. Let's get this over with."

43

SKIP

MANNY'S WORLD

WHEN MANNY PUSHES open his door, Tank is waiting in the hallway.

"Show them the way, Tank."

Can turtles lead? 'Cause that's the rate Tank walks us down the hallway. I nudge him from behind. *How you doing? I'm worried about you.*

He turns his head and sighs.

Once we're all standing before a closed bedroom door, Tank crawls into his fur-covered bed, which is spread out beneath a large window and next to a wide neat desk with a large computer and a laptop. Jealousy doesn't quite touch how I'm feeling. Even though I have my Thomas, I picture Tank and Manny working side by side all day, and my heart aches briefly for my John, or Bunny's John now. But at least soon I'll be working with Lucy at Golden Years.

And Tank's bed is Facebook post–worthy. Lucy should share the hell out of this thing. Not only is his bed large enough to hold a grizzly bear, but it is so furry and lush that once Tank is settled, the bed hugs him like a larger-than-life teddy bear. His bed is one dog-loving hug. Even his toys are being embraced. Can anything take the place of curling up with Lucy in bed? I think Tank's bed might. I think he's already asleep, like in two seconds! His chill-lax-tude is a sure sign that his bed is a drug, or our pack and pecking order is established. I'm no threat to him, even with him being sick. He doesn't even stir when I start sniffing out the rest of his joint or the door to "the room" as Lucy ends up calling it.

"Manny," Lucy says, "it's very neat and techy in your apartment. Not what I expected."

Nope. We thought he was an apartment-wide hoarder.

Manny ignores her and takes his time deciding if he's going to carry through with his agreement and open the bedroom door. He has time because, like me, Lucy is trying to take in the living room and craft a story about Manny. I imagine the list of questions adding up in her head are similar to mine.

Does he work here?

What does he do?

Why does he need so much equipment?

His TV is bigger than our apartment. No, not really, but might as well be. And so few cords! We have so many computer and television cords, it's a hazard to go anywhere near the walls.

There's that saying: *You are what you eat.* I've always hated that. I'm not dog food. Maybe it should be *You are how you live.* Manny's apartment makes one thing clear: Manny is a neat freak. A lovable neat freak who likes to be with his dog all day. What does our apartment say about Lucy and me? Does it reflect who we are as a family? Maybe it once did when John and my ottoman were still there. Like our heads, I guess our apartment is having an identity crisis. It will evolve as we do.

Eventually Lucy focuses on Manny. "Don't overthink this. Just open the door. You'll feel better."

"Says the queen of overthinking."

Lucy smiles. "See? I know what I'm talking about then, right? Open it up."

Manny's hand shakes as he turns the knob and lets the door swing open. It doesn't swing all the way but stops at a 90-degree angle and rests against something.

That's because the room is piled high with boxes and things. John used to watch that show *American Pickers*. Frankie and Mikey would be in picker's heaven right now.

I recognize a smell, though. I call it the Haight Street smell. Whenever John, Lucy, and I used to take Aunt Eve to Haight to stock up on tarot cards and vinyl records, I'd smell like the incense store we visited for two days after.

Anyway, the room is packed but orderly. Frankie and Mikey would sort through this stuff in a jiffy. Each box is labeled, and items are hanging from the walls like a fancy secondhand boutique. And there, right up front, are three stray pots.

"Manny?" Lucy's eyes are wide. "What is all this?"

"This," Manny says, sparing a bittersweet glance at Tank, "is what's left of Amanda."

Manny's hanging hand is salty where I lick it. Yeah, he's been grieving too. He has a room to prove it.

"Can we go in?" Lucy asks.

We. I like how Lucy is including me. I'm dying to get my nose and paws in there.

He crosses his arms as if hugging himself. "Just don't touch anything."

Nothing about not smelling it. *Whoop!*

There's not enough room for all three of us, so Manny pulls up a chair outside the door like a security guard at the drugstore and watches us closely.

Lucy reads one box. "Amanda's journals."

"They're her botany journals. Not diaries."

"And this one?" She points. "Amanda's notebooks."

"Notes for the post-doctoral thesis she was writing." He's sweating now. "I need a beer. Want one?"

He doesn't wait for a response. He jumps up, strides off, and is back in a flash with two beers. He sets them down and pulls up a chair for Lucy.

She sits next to him while I lie down close to Tank, a corner of his bed underneath me. *Scooch over, Tank. Let's have a huggable moment.*

"What happened?" Lucy asks, taking the beer he offers.

Manny shakes his head. "A stupid risk. And she was so damn smart." He takes a drink. Lucy too. "She was a botanist. Studying at USF. Four years ago, she and her friends went out. She had never been a partier, never even smoked a joint."

His tone makes it clear this was unheard of, but I'm not sure what a joint is or if Lucy and John have ever had one. I wish I could talk and ask questions.

"But these were her friends from high school. They lived in the city, and they'd get together every now and then to catch up. They'd all been different but had always stuck together. But this night, they wanted to go clubbing. The fools bought some Spice or K2 off some guy."

I have no idea what Manny's talking about. Spice is for cooking, I think. And the last time I heard *kay-too* I think it had something to do with a ski trip we took in Tahoe with John.

"One girl's boyfriend found them the next day in agony when he was bringing them Gatorade after his girlfriend called for help. They had blood running from their noses, vicious cramps. They were so out of it, they thought they had bad hangovers. But Amanda must have gotten the worst of the four synthetic joints because she was already dead. They thought she was just passed out. Sick like them. But she'd been dead for hours."

With her years of nursing, Lucy obviously understands. I'm still in the dark, but I understand loss and pain. Grief.

Lucy reaches over and takes Manny's hand.

"The boyfriend called 9-1-1. Thank God." He swallowed hard. "Synthetic had rat poison in it. They all could have died."

Lucy dashes away her tears. "And sometimes they wish they had."

I think of the drunk willowy blonde and how she had said Manny loved Amanda the most. She'd mentioned nightmares. Now I get it. This is why the girls always come to Manny. He doesn't blame them. He cares for them.

Lucy wipes her eyes on her sleeve and sniffles. "The tattoo with the three hummingbirds and the flower? They're the hummingbirds and your sister is the flower."

Manny clears his throat a few times, but never speaks.

"I'm sorry I thought you were a player," Lucy says.

Manny gives a sad laugh. "I preferred you thinking that. Much better than the truth that my sister's friends blame themselves and are slowly killing themselves over it. She wouldn't have wanted this. She loved them."

Lucy nods. "How long are you going to hang on to her stuff?"

"I'm losing a little everyday." Manny looks at Tank. "You'll add these pots to the rest?"

"Yes."

They sip their beers. For a long time, no one says a word.

"Your turn," Manny finally says. "What's with the extreme world tour explosion in your place?"

"I'm going to go on my honeymoon alone."

"What sparked this?" he asks.

"The United States Postal Service and my previous future mother-in-law."

Manny nods, but that's it. Guess he doesn't feel the need to know more, but Lucy volunteers.

"I kept thinking John would change his mind, so I never canceled the honeymoon. And I was angry he hadn't warned me about telling his mom. We had an agreement. So I bluffed and texted him that I was keeping his portion of the honeymoon deposit and still taking the trip. I thought he'd argue with me."

"And?"

"He didn't."

Manny bobs his head, staring forward at Amanda's room. I wonder if Lucy will tell him about the garden at Golden Years now.

But she is still on John. "I hate that he assumes I can't, or won't, do this trip alone. I don't know. I just went crazy and bought all my supplies. I can't even afford them."

"Go, Lucy. And keep his portion. He didn't argue. Done. Go."

"I don't know," she says. "There's Skip to consider.

Who will take care of him? Maybe my Aunt Eve or Mom? I guess I could ask John if I have to. Skip loves him, but he's been through so much change. It's not fair to him."

They sit in silence, blind to the freak-out session imploding my soul. I am stupid sometimes. Why didn't it occur to me that I, of course, won't be going on the trip with Lucy? How long will Lucy leave me? Do I want to stay with Aunt Eve? What if I love living with John and his new pack? What if Lucy asks John and he says no? He could choose Bunny and Cecilia over me too. Complete and utter rejection.

"I will keep his portion. Maybe I should just keep working and save the money to help with rent," Lucy says, but she sounds uncertain. Uncertainty smells like that scent between savory and sweet. Which one should a person choose, knowing they will probably wish they'd chosen the opposite?

"You won't regret going," Manny says, "but you'll regret not going."

Lucy looks around the room. "When's the last time you went somewhere?"

He doesn't say, but Lucy and I both guess the obvious: before Amanda's death. Before he had Tank to raise.

Lucy satisfies our curiosity. "So, Mystery Manny. What do you do anyway? You work from home."

"You're looking at it," he points to his big computer that can also be a standing desk. It looks out over the backyard. "I'm a software engineer."

"What do you create?"

"I used to own a company that developed drone software and that was bought out. Now I develop apps."

Ah-ha. The dog park dating app!

"Seriously?" Lucy asks.

"Seriously. Listen, I think you should go on your trip. It's what, two weeks? I can watch Skip for you. Don't call John."

Oh my Dog. I like this idea. This is brilliant. I can stay with Manny while Lucy is gone. She'll have to come back to our apartment, and I'll be here! And if Tank's time comes, I'll be here for Manny.

"I don't need you to rescue me," Lucy says.

"I'm not rescuing you. I'm rescuing Skip," he says, and they both smile.

"I'll think about it. I think there's a one-pet maximum."

"It's temporary. No one will care."

"How long have you lived here?" Lucy asks. "You were here when we moved in."

"Eleven years."

"Longer than the Brightons even," Lucy says. "Explains the owner's partisan tenant loyalty to you." She rocks to the side and nudges his shoulder with hers.

"Some of it. I own the building."

Lucy shouts and punches him in the arm. "You what?"

"Ow." Manny rubs his shoulder. "What's the big deal?"

"What's the . . ." Lucy looks wild as she stands up and grabs the last pots. "You've been lying to us!" She marches toward the door, arms full. "Open the door. Skip, come now!"

Manny follows us. Even Tank is curious enough to wake up. "Maybe you should wait and take the pots when you're not so—"

"Pissed?" Lucy turns on him.

My opinion? She isn't pissed. She's humiliated for all the times she and John have complained to the property manager and the owner . . . Manny, as it turns out. Humans hate looking like fools. If she were really as angry at him, she wouldn't care enough to take the last three Amanda pots and keep her promise to Manny to house them all together.

It's moments like these that I'm glad humans don't always understand their own actions in the heat of the Now, because they aren't always what they seem. Manny might believe that Lucy is thoroughly annoyed, but my Lucy is compassionate. The truth is, her faux anger is the kindest way she can take a few more pieces of his sister away.

44

SKIP

TOM CAT

It is pitch black when the bone-chilling caterwauling rips us from our sound slumber. I'm not sure who jumped more, Lucy or me.

"What in the hell was that?" Lucy covers her chest as if to hold her heart in place.

When the unearthly cries rise again, we scramble out of bed. I want to scream at Lucy, "Get our brightest flashlight! Grab some earmuffs and soil! We need soil!" Because there is only one beast I can imagine would make such a noise, and that would be a Mandrake from *The Chamber of Secrets*.

I thought I'd have nightmares after Thomas's reading from the second *Harry Potter* book. An unearthed Mandrake's cry can be deadly. A mature Mandrake's screams will kill any living creature. Even a young Mandrake seedling's banshee shrills can knock a dog or human out for hours. And Oh My Dog! The only way to stop one from screeching is to put it in a pot and cover it with soil. We are out of pots and soil! The irony! *I need a wand! I need a Hermione! We need supplies!*

A low moan haunts us now. In fact, now it sounds like Moaning Myrtle might be out there. I'd pick Myrtle over a Mandrake any day. Myrtle's a big crybaby, but she isn't lethal.

It's on the back stairs, like the skunk that one day. This is proof that nothing good comes of dark, narrow stairways. I pray the Mandrakes haven't gotten to my Thomas's ears.

I crouch and slink toward the back door with Lucy behind me wielding a frying pan from the stove. It isn't a wand, but it will have to do. Maybe it's the pan-wand, not the wand, that chooses the wizard.

Lucy flattens the side of her face against the door. The monster is scratching around out there, probably with long black fingernails like I always imagine Dementors have. But then I recognize the smell.

Tom Cat?

What in the hell is he doing here? The pots are gone. The bags of soil too. No excuse for his sneaky urine attacks. He grows more vocal like he knows he has an audience now, and he's angry that his litter playground has been dismantled and decimated.

The nerve. The nerve of the mangy cat to voice his displeasure. As if he is entitled to Amanda's pots or to our stairway. If Lucy opens the door, I'm going for him. I'm going to scare the cat shit out of him so he never comes back here again. For Dog's sake, I thought he was a Mandrake. He's gone too far this time.

I hear more movement, and Manny's back door opens. I can tell he flips on the porch light because a glow seeps through the bottom of our door. If I didn't know the light was Manny's, I'd be convinced we were victims of a feline alien invasion.

Lucy hears him, of course, and is ready to leave Manny to deal with the intrusion. She whispers to me, "He owns the building. He can deal with it." Yeah, so I guess Lucy is a little miffed after all.

Then Manny says, "Whoa. What in the hell happened to you?"

We are both too nosy and curious to go back to bed now.

Lucy pushes me away from the door and cracks it just enough to look out. "What's going on?"

"Something got to him. He's bleeding."

"Why did he come here?" Lucy asks.

I wish I could see Tom, but I can smell it now. His blood. His fear. He mewls again, and though I didn't previously speak Feline, I am a fast learner. I appreciate now that his cries are cries of pain.

His pain brought him here. Animals know who the good humans are. Animals instinctively know where to hide when they are in danger, harmed, ill, or even dying. But when they are ready to throw in the towel and lick their wounds, they don't cry out. They don't draw attention to themselves. No, Tom's not giving up yet. He wants help. And if you ask me, he came to the right two people. I still don't like him, though.

"It's okay," Lucy coos in that soft voice that usually calms me, steps out onto the porch without me, and closes the door. "It's okay."

"You're a nurse. Do something."

"I don't know anything about cats!"

"Shhh, keep your voice down. You'll scare him."

"He's not going anywhere. He's too hurt."

"I'll get something to put him in," Manny says, "and call the vet's emergency line. Get dressed."

Of course Manny has the ER number. Tank is getting sicker. He's hanging on to Tank for dear life these days. But Tank and I know, Tank is just waiting to choose his time.

"I can't take him to a vet," Lucy says. "I can barely afford Skip."

Ruh-roh. I hate any topic about not being able to take care of me, aka keep me. Tom's already digging up a touchy subject. *Drats, cat!*

"We'll both go, and I'll pay, but you have to take care of him."

"What? Why me? It's your fault Tom started coming around here to begin with. This is *your* building."

I sense a subtle shift through the door, and Manny says, "Right. The pots. What if he came here to find comfort in the pots? Now they are gone. I should never have gotten rid of them. It's my fault he's hurt."

Lucy sounds exasperated. "No, you did the right thing about the pots, I promise. You'll see someday. Right now we need to focus."

"I'm allergic."

"Take a Benadryl. Skip hates Tom."

Lucy's right, I have hated him, even as recently as one minute ago. But, hey, I'm training to be a therapy dog, after all. My mind-set is shifting from second to second. I find myself intrigued by Tom's perseverance, his nerve, his cheek. His cat's meow.

I also like this partnership between Lucy, Manny, and me. We'd all be involved on Project Tom Cat. Besides, and maybe most importantly, Manny is going to need our help going to the ER once Tank chooses to leave this world. This is good practice. Kind of like what the dog parkers talk about when a woman is pregnant. They always say they are doing practice runs to the hospital for her delivery.

I bark from behind the door. A light bark. A bark that says, "I think we should help Tom." I don't know how else to let Lucy know I'm okay, but Manny understands and says, "See? Skip's happy to help."

The back door downstairs opens, and Thomas whispers, "Too loud. Too loud. Too loud."

Mrs. Brighton sticks her head out. "Is everything okay?"

Manny gives Mrs. Brighton the rundown. "Lucy and I will take care of it."

"I can't believe I'm going to do this," Lucy says just before she slides back into our apartment. I wait and listen to Manny coaxing Tom into a box.

From our front window, I watch Manny, Lucy, and Tom leave the building. It's the first time I've been left alone in my apartment at night, but I don't howl. I know Thomas is downstairs if I need him, so I crawl up on the couch and wait for the trio to return.

All for one and one for all.

45

SKIP

I'M A CAT DOG

IF ANYONE HAD ASKED me a few months ago what my life would look like today, I would never have said, "Well, John will be gone. We'll eat donuts with Manny and Tank most Saturday mornings. I'll be in a *Harry Potter* book club with Thomas. I'll be hooked on DOGTV, and I'm training as a therapy dog. And, oh yeah, Tom Cat will become my cat."

And if someone had tried to tell me that I'd really like my new life, I would have thought they'd swallowed one too many hairballs and cut off the oxygen to their brain.

But they would have been right. I *am* starting to dig my new life.

Sure, I still have meltdowns when I worry about Lucy and what could happen if she finds out about me and Cecilia, but the longer we go without John and the more our pack grows, the more my fears fade. And so does the loss of John. My heart is healing. Acceptance and a new routine will do that to a dog.

Manny and Lucy are splitting Tom Cat's care. Manny via his wallet. Lucy is putting the roof over Tom's head, or the bed over his head. He's been under our bed for three days and only comes out when necessary.

At first, Manny and Lucy came home from the vet ER empty-handed, and I assumed Tom Cat didn't make it. I didn't have time to think about how that made me feel because Lucy quickly updated me that he had needed stitches and "to get fixed," so the vet was keeping him for forty-eight hours.

When Lucy picked him up three days ago and introduced him to our apartment, he was in a cat kennel. I thought it looked more like a tiny prison or a toolbox with holes and a gate. "To keep him from hurting himself," she said when Manny set the whole kit and caboodle on our floor. She wagged her finger at me. "Remember, you're a therapy dog now, Skip. He needs your help."

Intending to formally introduce myself, I looked through the prison door, but Tom hissed at me. Not only was he in a claustrophobic box, he was shaved, bandaged, and wearing the dreaded cone of shame.

I was awestruck by how he had such fight in him even with that confidence-sucking funnel around his neck.

I've worn one before, when my balls were snipped off as part of my initiation to join the *John & Lucy* pack. I promised myself I'd never wear one again. Now and then I see dogs at the dog park wearing them. Sometimes for an injury, sometimes as the rite of passage into their new families, but the reason doesn't matter. The cone changes a dog, consumes him. Even if you are the toppest-toppity-top dog at the park, you are relegated to the bottom of the pack. All the other dogs will ignore or bully you. The cone is a signal, "You are a weak link." And forget trying to drink or eat.

Itch in your groin? Forget it. You're not getting to it. It sucks.

And there is nothing, absolutely nothing you can change to rid yourself of that plastic halo of shame. Even if you figure out how to wiggle your way out of it, your human will just put it on tighter. They don't care that it's an identity shredder or that it'll render you incapable of making eye contact with anyone.

Until, one day on a whim, your human will decide you're ready and remove it. Your old self will be back quicker than you can wag your tail.

But Tom? There's no shame in that cone-headed cat. Nope. In fact, the first night when Lucy opened the kennel to feed him, she didn't think he'd try to escape, but any creature in that crate contraption would. He darted under our bed. And, so far, he hasn't fully come out except to nibble at some food or use his litter box. Maybe he's embarrassed about being shaved bald on part of his head, his shoulders, one hind leg, and his underbelly. Lucy told me that his stitches were catgut sutures but not made of cat. I'm still confused about that.

At first I wondered how Lucy would manage walking us both, but get this: cats get to piss and poo *in the house* and *in a box*. Who decided that a cat should have a box and a dog should have the great outdoors to do his business? Even though it means Tom Cat doesn't have to hold it in while Lucy is away, I don't think I'd like having a box. It's demeaning. Okay, sure, a cat might argue that it's more humiliating to have a human following me around with a recycled grocery bag while I defecate, but hey, look at the facts. First, a human is cleaning up my excrement; I'm not cleaning up theirs. So if anyone should be embarrassed, it's the humans. Secondly, at least I don't have to *live* with my crap until someone comes along with a little plastic shovel and cleans out a litter box.

The only reasons I can come up with for the discriminatory poo process is that A) a dog would need a huge litter box, and apartments in San Francisco can be small, and B) humans don't want to walk cats. I mean, think about it. Have you ever seen a cat park? Me neither.

So Tom and I have been roomies for three days now. We're still pussyfooting around each other, and feeling each other out. But if I'm honest, I kind of like having him around. Sometimes when Thomas is reading from his bean-bag, which he pulls a little further inside the apartment every morning now that he has a key to walk me, Tom Cat will move to the floor under the foot of the bed. I think he likes Mrs. Norris, the cat who belongs to Hogwarts' caretaker, Argus Filch, and Crookshanks, Hermione's cat. He purrs when their names come up.

Thomas likes Tom, especially his name, but he plays his cards much cooler and ignores Tom for the most part. Not like Lucy and me. No, we are waiting for him to like us back.

Lucy has said to me a few times, "He's still in pain. We have to let him come to us." But I've also heard her mumble in the middle of the night when Tom Cat mewls beneath our heads, "Damn Manny. How'd I let him talk us into this?"

But in the mornings when Lucy sets Tom's canned food near the bed and takes a few steps away, she always smiles when he comes out to eat, and her fingers wiggle like she's itching to pet him and give him some comfort.

You'd think I'd be jealous, but I'm not. If I had fingers, I'd pet him too. What will it take for Tom Cat to come to me when I don't have food or treats to offer him, only comfort and protection? When he trusts me, I might even lick him and help him tidy up his remaining fur.

And Lucy has shown me some pictures on Facebook of cats and dogs who cuddle together. Last night, she found a picture of a cat and dog taking care of baby geese. Can you imagine? Apparently there are packs of dogs, prides of cats, and flocks of birds.

I guess we all just want to belong to something bigger.

I have so many responsibilities right now, even with my neighborhood watch sabbatical. I'm feeling more and more complete, like I belong. I miss John, but I love all these silly gooses in my flock-pack. Funny how love makes room for more love, isn't it?

46

SKIP

WHO LET THE DOGS OUT?

THOMAS SETS the book down and says, "Time for a walk."

He's a superb dog walker and cat sitter. He always puts me on the leash before he opens the door, and he always closes the bedroom door first so Tom Cat can't get out and hurt himself worse.

What a gorgeous summer day. *Doo-do-doo.* Even my tail has a few extra wags in it. There's nothing wrong with my world in moments like these, these in-the-Now-right-now times.

We're halfway through our walk-around-the-block-walk when Thomas's fist tightens on my leash. He puts his head down and starts walking faster.

I think he's seen something. My hearing superpowers are called for. Footsteps are gaining on us. I can't turn to look, thanks to the chokehold Thomas has on my leash, but a gust of wind carries all the information I need.

Not-Thomas's friends are coming at us from behind. They stink of bicycle metal, sweat, and teenage boy testosterone. Ask any mother out there and she'll tell you that boys going through puberty can stink, like that Chinese Shar-pei at the park. Those puberty-teeter-tottering-shits' hormones are all over the place, and all I can say is Axe's men's body sprays have done mothers, teachers, and teenage girls a public service. Hell, I'm grateful that Thomas is wearing syrup from his pancakes most of the time.

Male hormonal haywire equals male haywire aggression. And those Testosteronosaurus Rexes don't waste any time proving me right.

"Thomas! Thomas! Thomas!" First one calls out then the other two. Their repetitive shouts layer each other like the damn annoying seagulls down at Baker Beach. They somehow know Thomas's secret three-times code, but they are abusing it and using it against him. Thomas rushes on, and I want to growl and shout, "Shut up! Leave him alone!"

But, alas, they catch up to us and surround us. Thomas stares down at the ground as if he's trying to count every speck of dirt on the sidewalk. His hand spasms on my leash. Claustrophobic doesn't even begin to explain how I feel.

Dogs don't like to be surrounded by people we don't know, and we definitely don't like people leaning over us. It's the first mistake people make about dogs, even when they are just trying to be friendly. Strangers should never hover or lean over a dog they don't know, not even to pet them. It's threatening. Stranger Danger. How would a person like it if a stranger twice, maybe three times, their height came at them from above to touch or hug them without permission? Huh?

And that's what these little a-holes start to do as they lean toward Thomas, shouting in threes. Worse, they're hovering over me to get in Thomas's face.

I barely hear Thomas say, "Speak. Speak. Speak."

So I bark and pull a bit on my leash to move backward and away from the mean shadow they're casting, and I show my teeth.

"Speak, speak, speak," the *Harry Potter* Draco-like little prick says. "Even the dog speaks, Freak."

My Thomas is not a freak!

And then Thomas whispers, "Sick. Sick. Sick."

I still don't know what that command means, but it doesn't matter because the fur rises on my neck, and I instinctually lean forward, curl my lips, and growl. When I look up at the three dicks looming over me, I recognize the testosterone-charged jerks for who they really are: Draco Malfoy, Crabbe, and Goyle.

Damn Slytherins. Why do they insist on being such assholes?

And Thomas is Harry, and I'm Buckbeak, and even with me knowing about Buckbeak's almost-execution for attacking Draco, I know what I have to do. I need to teach Draco a lesson.

Because here's the thing about Draco: he has the potential to become a nice guy, he just isn't one today. And he needs to learn that he can't treat us this way. No one treats my Thomas like this.

And so I let all three of those stinky Slytherins have it. I lunge for Draco and snap my teeth together. I bite air, just as I intended. I have no intention of harming any of them, only scaring the Slytherin shit out of them so they'll never do this again. I growl, bark, gnash my teeth, and pull at my leash. I'm a mad dog. Thomas has the good sense to release his tight hold on my leash and gives me another four feet of attack radius. I don't have time to look, but I sense T-Dog has his head up now and is standing taller. He takes a step forward, as do I, and the boys jump away.

"Let's get out of here!" Crabbe screams, and the three boys start running.

It's not enough for me. I'll never know if Thomas lets my leash go intentionally or if he is in shock watching his tormentors flee, but I become the hunter and chase them.

"Help! Help!" crybaby Draco bawls.

A good stretch, and I'll have Draco's shirt in my teeth.

I'm wild. I'm my mom. I'm my ancestors. My prey stumbles, tripping over his own fear after looking over his shoulder at my demonic display, and then he falls to the ground. Crabbe and Goyle don't hesitate to leave their buddy in the dust. They escape to the other side of the street.

I lean over Draco like he leaned over me not more than a minute ago. I bully him like he bullied Thomas. My breath is hot, and it blows all over his face, my slobber too. My snout wrinkles, my bicuspids sharp and snapping as I lean as close to his face as I dare. His tears start to fall.

I don't succumb to his tears. No, I wait for Thomas so we can finish this together. Thomas catches up and grabs my leash. "Down, Skip," he says.

And with one last meaningful glare at Draco, I move away and heel next to Thomas.

Draco is leaning back on his elbows, staring up at Thomas like we are both mad. "Your dog is crazy!"

Thomas says, "Sick. Sick. Sick."

I still don't know what that means, but Draco must because he squawks and puts one arm out. "No! Stop! I'm sorry!"

Our work here is done.

Thomas and I leave Draco behind and continue on our merry way. We walk three more times around the block. The Slytherins don't come near us again, and once we get home, Thomas gives me extra Bacon Bits.

"He what?" Lucy shouts at Mrs. Brighton and the cop standing in our living room.

Thomas immediately starts shouting from his room downstairs, his voice carrying through the floor and walls, "Too loud! Too loud! Too loud!"

Mrs. Brighton has her palms open at her sides. "One of the parents called."

I smell another dog on the cop, who is standing beside her. Oh, what I would do to take a good whiff, but Lucy won't let me past her. She's using one of the new hand signals we've learned in training to wait behind her. More importantly, she's standing between me and the cop like a protective mother moose. Even I'm scared for the copper.

Lucy looks at me, horrified. "But Skip has never attacked a person in his life!"

Exactly, so there must be a good reason for it. *Tell the cop about my neighborhood watch role.* I'm part of his Team Blue. *All for one and one for all, sir.*

The cop pats the air as if to stamp out her protective-ness. "No one is in trouble. It's a warning."

Mrs. Brighton says, "A neighbor saw it happen and said it was the boys' faults. They were egging Thomas on."

"It's not okay, Mrs. Brighton. Skip could have hurt someone."

But I wouldn't have. She should know me better than that.

"But he didn't," Mrs. Brighton says. "He protected Thomas. I found out those boys aren't his friends at all. They've been teasing him for a year now. And I finally got Thomas to admit it's why he stopped taking walks." Mrs. Brighton blinks away tears. "How had I missed that?"

"But he told Skip to 'sick'?" Lucy asks. "That's what the boys said? I didn't even know Skip knew that word."

I don't.

Lucy marches into the living room and grabs the purple monkey that I haven't touched since she gave it to me and drops it on the floor. She points aggressively at it and commands, "Sick!"

I have no idea what she wants me to do, so I smell the monkey and then lick it. *Dang it!* I forgot about that stupid faux fur. I start to gag on my faux hairball.

"See?" Lucy says. "He doesn't even know what it means!"

Again from Thomas: "Too loud! Too loud! Too loud!"

"Mrs. Brighton is correct," the officer says. "The boys were taunting her son. I have a German Shepherd in my patrol car right now. I know how dogs think. My guess is Skip, here, was being protective but was also scared. They probably backed him into a corner so to speak."

Holy moly! There's an honest to Dog cop dog outside? I run to the front window and look out. I can only see the cop car. I can't smell or see the law-enforcing dog. *My hero!* What I would do to meet and sniff him. If he is real. But why would a policeman lie? It must be illegal for policemen to lie. And as Dumbledore would say, just because you can't see something, it doesn't mean you shouldn't believe in it. Or something like that.

Lucy exhales. "So this is a warning? I promise you,

Officer, I will make sure Skip will be trained to never attack again."

Mrs. Brighton is nodding. "I've explained it to Thomas too. He thought the command meant protect, not attack."

I'm relieved that there is no talk of Thomas not walking me again.

"Yes, this is a warning. But do have your dog trained."

"And the other parents?" Mrs. Brighton asks. "Are they being warned to teach their boys better manners? To not pick on my son?"

The cop says, "At first warning, they said, 'Boys will be boys.'"

"What?" Lucy and Mrs. Brighton shout in unison.

Thomas joins the choir from below. "Too loud! Too loud! Too loud!"

Mrs. Brighton puts her hands on her hips and faces down the cop. "And how did you respond to that?"

The cop winks at me. Me! As he turns to the door, he says, "I told them that, in that case, they'd better understand that dogs will be dogs."

Touché, Officer, touché.

47

LUCY

GOT TO SEE IT TO BELIEVE IT

PAINT GUN WARS would have been less destructive to the Golden Years craft area than Enid Gray in charge of scrapbooking. Unused magazine clippings littered the floor like New Year's Eve confetti. All those little bits would be impossible to clean up, and they'd be finding scraps here and there for weeks to come.

Walter shook his head at the dozen scrappers but pointed directly at Enid and June's magazine cuttings, pet rocks, and painted shells. "Ladies, if I knew you'd make such a mess, I never would have brought those rocks and shells in for you."

Enid only laughed and kept painting. June smiled.

Walter turned to Lucy before he started sweeping up the glitter and paper. "And this is exactly the kind of thing I'm talking about when I said no bingo candy wrappers allowed in my garden. Litterbugs. All of them."

Lucy recognized the real Walter now: all bark, no bite. Yes, June, Enid, Martha, and the others were making a fine mess, but they were having a blast making it. Thank goodness Lucy had the common sense to give them craft aprons; without them, the residents' clothes would have been annihilated. They looked like a painting crew on a break, but with paper trimmings, glue, and glitter in their hair.

Watching June and Enid broke Lucy's heart. The two friends did everything together, but they wouldn't for much longer.

They'd found out last week that June had late-stage pancreatic cancer. June had simply nodded when they told her and had reached over to squeeze Lucy's and Dr. Ryan's hands to reassure them. She'd only said, "I have people to meet," and had looked up toward the heavens.

Enid was in denial except to insist she and June finish their vision board for Camino de Santiago and their pilgrimage through the French Pyrenees and Spain. "No time to waste."

Enid was talking non-stop to June as Lucy leaned over them. "Mind if I take a look?" As if Enid would ever turn down being in the spotlight.

Enid added a final touch of a sunflower on a rock; it wasn't half bad. Then she added it to the pile before sliding their joint collage spread toward Lucy.

Images of people hiking, fields of flowers, ocean views, campfires, almond cakes, and croissants were carefully arranged across the posterboards. Across the top, cut out letters spelled *Camino de Santiago*, and across the bottom in larger letters, it read: *Let Go*.

Maybe Lucy should start collaging. Serenity settled over her as she looked at the spread. Was she feeling a sense of adventure? John had always said she wasn't an adventurous person. That wasn't entirely true. He'd said she wasn't spontaneous. She had to wonder if he didn't have a point.

Her honeymoon in Australia was something she'd planned since childhood. Maybe her hike wasn't so adventurous or spontaneous.

When she finally looked up, June was watching her with kindness and generosity.

Lucy held her welcoming and comforting stare.

Enid was being Enid and chatting away, seemingly unaware of June and Lucy's silent connection. Enid always chatted more when she was scared, and Lucy knew Enid had a right to be terrified about losing June.

Already, June had lost twenty pounds she couldn't afford to lose and was confined to a wheelchair. She said, "I'm ready to let go."

"Save it for the trip, June," Enid said, refusing to meet her friend's eyes. Enid soldiered about, egging June out of bed each morning, chauffeuring her around Golden Years.

"Don't you quit on me," she'd say as she combed June's hair. And June, Lucy suspected, wouldn't have it any other way: Enid at her side, bullying her, "Buck up, soldier."

In that moment, Lucy knew. Finishing the collage was June's gift to Enid. Her way of helping Enid to start letting go.

June tipped her head toward Lucy's iPad. Lucy smiled and hit her music app and turned up the volume to Backstreet Boys' "I Want It That Way."

Enid groaned. "For the love of God, June. I swear, the only thing good about you dying soon is I won't ever have to listen to that song again."

Lucy winked at June. Little did Enid know that June had solicited Lucy's help to plan something special for Enid once June transitioned to hospice care, and June's favorite song was part of it.

June tapped the collage and then the skin above her heart.

"Have you walked the Camino de Santiago, June?" Lucy could picture a young June making the pilgrimage that thousands of people hiked each year to Santiago de Compostela, Spain.

June gave a thumbs-up just as Enid said, "She sure has. Back in 1972 with her sisters April and May."

Of course June's sisters were named April and May.

Enid was a walking encyclopedia about June. Enid probably knew more about June than Enid knew about herself.

"Not me, though. So that's why we're going. Right, June?"

Two thumbs-up now.

Lucy played along. "Are you religious, Enid?"

Enid cringed as if she'd eaten a slug. "Hell, no. June isn't either. Okay, okay," Enid amended as June tapped the table, "June is *spiritual*. Says she has people and pets to meet in the universe above."

June was thoughtful as she painted a shell white and then added whiskers.

I think those are whiskers. Lucy took a closer look.

Enid rattled on. "You don't have to be religious to do the pilgrimage. Yeah, some people want to go see the bones of Saint James the Apostle. But did you know you can hike to the coast instead and figuratively or literally throw something into the ocean to let it go? That's what these shells and rocks are for. We're not going all the way to the coast, because the best almond cakes are in Santiago de Compostela, so we're ending the trip on a high note. We'll leave the rocks throughout the trail as words of encouragement for others." Enid held up a rock that said *Keep calm and hike on*. "At the end of the journey, we will toss our shells, which symbolize the baggage we need to let go onto the trail, and be free from whatever it is that's weighing us down."

Each word scratched an itch that Lucy didn't know she had. Something was growing inside her, and it felt like hope. Who'da thunk she needed a sense of letting go when all this time, she'd been holding on?

Enid said. "You can go with us, Lucy, if you want. What will you let go?"

Oh God. Where to start? "How do you decide?" she asked instead.

"What's a burden to you?" Enid showed her shell of a broken heart.

Lucy would never have guessed she and Enid might have anything in common. Did it matter the source of love or heartache? Or only that it had been love and was hard to lose? The loss of John's two hundred–pound body was what weighed her down. The fear of being alone the rest of her life froze her in her tracks.

She surprised herself by admitting, "My fiancé, John, left me. I'm afraid I wasn't enough, that he didn't really love me, and that I will never love someone like this again."

The Backstreet Boys had good timing, singing: *Ain't nothing but a heartache. Tell me why.*

June reached for Lucy's hand while Enid said, "Good riddance. What a dumbass."

Dumbass again. That's what Marge had called John too. Her travel agent and Enid would make good friends. Laughter rumbled from Lucy's solar plexus. "You don't even know him."

"Thank God," Enid said, "I'm too old to spend time with a fool. You can let go of that relationship on our sojourn. And there will be men waiting for your love. Or a companion." Enid winked at June. She passed Lucy a shell. "Start painting."

Lucy liked how she'd become a member of this make-believe future trip. Or, wait, could it be something real? *Could she?* Marge had said to forget her honeymoon and make it a trip for her: one where she could blossom.

Lucy stroked the blank shell before her and then looked at Enid and June's pile. "But how do I let go of a relation-ship I want more than anything? Letting go of someone you love isn't nearly as easy as taking a long walk and throwing some things into the sea or onto a trail."

And then soft-spoken June spoke. "You're letting go of the old relationship, making room for something new. Even when he comes back," Lucy liked how she said *when* not *if*, "it will be a new relationship with a new John. You'll both have changed. You'll have to meet each other and start again."

Enid slapped the table. "Too true. June, when you do speak up, you always say the right thing, Cookie."

Light was churning in Lucy. A new idea. A new spark. Letting go of the past. Making room for the future. *Move forward or go under.* She needed to talk to Marge.

"I love you, Enid," June said.

Enid's eyes filled with tears. "See? She really always says the right thing."

Lucy watched the dynamic duo. Her heart ached for what lay ahead. How could they be there for Enid when June's time came?

June blew softly on her finished shell.

"What's that you've painted?" Lucy asked. "A dog?"

Inevitably, Enid spoke for her. "That's Lady."

June's sigh was pretty mournful. "Letting go."

"She's always felt guilty for giving up her dog and her pups after her husband died, but she just couldn't handle them. Lady was part Timber Wolf and very headstrong. If I were a dog, I bet I'd be a Timber Wolf."

Goose bumps raced up Lucy's neck, arms, and legs. *What?!* How many Timber Wolf mix dogs could be in the area? "When?" Lucy asked. "When did you lose Lady?" The world could be small, but this small? *No way.*

"Seven years ago," June whispered. "Tragic mistake."

Enid protectively took the shell from June and put it aside to dry. "And it's time for you to let go of your guilt and of Lady." She turned to Lucy. "June has always worried about what happened to Lady and the pups. I keep telling her they all will have found good homes. Even better homes, but she won't listen. She wants to see it to believe it."

Oh my God. Me too.

"Where did you live at the time?" Lucy asked, trying to calm her own hopes and keep her breathing even. If she could give this to June, oh what a gift.

"Outside of Half Moon Bay," the encyclopedia chimed in.

"Do you by chance have any pictures of Lady?"

"Oh, crap." Enid rolled her eyes. "Just great. Another dog person. I'm a cat person myself. She has a picture on her bedside table."

Lucy's phone buzzed. It was her mom. Mom would have to wait. Lucy stood, anxious to rush to June's room, but Enid called after her.

When the old woman caught up, she took Lucy's hand. Her eyes pleaded as she spoke through building tears. "Lucy, when my bestie's time comes, can you be with me?"

Willing back her own tears, Lucy hugged her. "There's no other place or person I'd rather be with."

"Good." Enid fanned her face and, after regaining her composure, shuffled back to the collage table and June.

Lucy jogged to June's room. There on the bed stand was a picture of a dog who could easily be Skip. How had Lucy missed this picture before? She reached for it and sat on the side of June's bed. The large white dog, Lady, was surrounded by several black puppies and one lone white one. Skip. Brushing her thumb over the little body, her tears welled. It had to be Skip. She needed to find out for sure before she told June, before she brought Skip in.

Never had she wanted to call John so badly. She thought about the day they found Skip, the three of them in love at first sight. They'd promised Skip a family. Never had she wondered about what or who Skip had already lost.

She was staring down at the framed photo when Sheila came huffing and puffing around the corner. "Your mom just called the front desk. She's been trying to reach you. There's been an accident. It's your aunt."

48

SKIP

THOMAS and I are watching DOGTV when there is a tap at the door. I assume it's Mrs. Brighton checking on us. No one rang the building buzzer. I don't even bother to smell-tell or follow Thomas to the door. I'm obsessing about Aunt Eve. And Tank. The whole afternoon has been one attack of bad news after another.

Thomas squawks in surprise, and there's a crash as if someone has been pushed out of the way. I run to see what's what. I hear Thomas's bumbling run echoing from the stairs then the slam of his front door.

And there, standing in my doorway, is John. *My John.*

"Lucy?" he calls out.

Of course, she can't respond because she isn't here. She's at the emergency room with Aunt Eve.

"What in the hell is going on?" he asks me. He hesitates a second before stepping over the threshold. Setting an envelope on the side table, he squats down, arms wide.

I run to his open arms. I need a hug and some reassurance. I've lost all control of my tail, whines, and tears. My feelings for him are such a complicated package. I know John feels the same because he wipes his face in my fur.

"God, I've missed you, buddy." He kisses me.

Me too, man. Me too.

He stands up, shuts the door, and asks me again, "What in the hell is going on?"

I try to tell him how Manny told me that Aunt Eve was in an accident and Lucy asked Manny to check on me, but then something horrible has changed with Tank, so Manny rushed him to the animal hospital, and I used to think that humans had no say when a dog would go to the Rainbow Bridge, but Manny said, "This is goodbye, Skip." I try to tell John how Thomas is keeping me company so I won't fall apart, but as you know, I can't speak human, so it all comes out in a series of cries, groans, and angst.

"It's okay, buddy," John says and sits on the living room floor with me so I can lie across his lap and calm down. As he pets my back with strong reassuring strokes, he notices DOGTV and chuckles. "You watching dog soap operas now, Skip?" Then he just shakes his head. "Where's your mom? She isn't returning my texts."

After a good scratch behind my ears, he says, "Let's go talk to Mrs. Brighton. I'm afraid I scared Thomas."

Okay, this is good. We are already putting things back in order. Let's go fix Thomas. But as we pass the bedroom door, I see Tom Cat poking his head out to check on me. We've become really good at picking up on each other's mood. He's only worried about me, but you know, John doesn't know about Tom's new status.

"How did he get in here? Get out of here!" John shouts.

Before I can even try to protect Tom, John chases him out the back door, clapping his hands to scare him far away.

Noooooooooooooo! Tom Cat! Come back.

I stare at John with disbelief. Can't he see that Tom Cat is rehabilitating? Is John blind? *Hello, shaved fur and stitches!* I try to follow Tom outside, to catch and reassure him, but John just doesn't get it. He grabs my collar and says like he always said before when we were a pack, "Don't hurt him, Skip. It's Hoarding Manny's fault the dirty cat comes around. Have no idea how he got in the apartment, though." John looks out the back stairway. "Well, well. Manny finally cleaned up his act, huh? At least all of those trashy pots are finally gone." He slams the door shut.

Me? Hurt Tom? John, you have no idea what you're talking about. Manny isn't a hoarder. The pots weren't trash. And Tom Cat is my *cat!*

And with my rose-colored glasses and rose-tinted nostrils off, it hits me: John doesn't know us anymore. For us to truly understand each other, we'd have to start all over. I don't even know what he's doing here or if he plans to stay. And I don't even know that I want him to stay. What about Manny, Thomas, and Tom Cat? How will we be there for Manny now that Tank is leaving? What about Lucy and Cecilia?

I can't take this. John is ruining everything. He should have just stayed with Cecilia and Bunny. As we walk downstairs, I sniff his pants. I don't smell Cecilia or Bunny, but I was rolling all over him just a little bit ago, so I can only smell my anxiety.

Mrs. Brighton opens the door on the first knock as if she has been waiting for us. Her hands on her hips are a bad sign.

"I'm sorry I scared Thomas, Mrs. Brighton. We

surprised each other. I was expecting Lucy to answer the door."

"I bet you were," she says, sounding like Lucy's lioness. "Thomas sits with Skip when Lucy is away, and Manny had to rush off."

This is the coldest I've ever seen Mrs. Brighton.

I wonder how John will react to Lucy and Manny's names being used in the same sentence. I don't have to wait long.

His eyebrows crash above the bridge of his nose. "What's Manny got to do with this?"

Mrs. Brighton just shakes her head like John is a big nincompoop. "A lot has changed since you left."

Exactly!

John lifts his cell phone helplessly between them as if to show Mrs. Brighton something. "I can't get ahold of Lucy. She's not responding, which isn't like her. Is that where she is? With Manny?"

Mrs. Brighton rolls her eyes. "Manny had to take Tank to the vet. The poor, poor man. And I'm sorry because this might upset you . . ."

"Lucy went with him," John assumes.

Mrs. Brighton and I both look at him like he's an idiot. I wish I could raise one eyebrow like she is doing right now. It's very effective body language if you ask me.

"There was an accident with Lucy's aunt. She's at San Francisco General."

John pales. To know Aunt Eve is to love Aunt Eve. He is as blank as the Lucy-text-free phone in his hand. Anyone in their right mind can read his face: he wasn't Lucy's go-to guy or person. Manny was. Thomas and Mrs. Brighton were.

"Thank you, Mrs. Brighton." He turns.

"John," Mrs. Brighton says, "don't hurt her."

John frowns and tilts his head like I do whenever I see something for the first time. Maybe he doesn't know what to do with Mrs. B's warning. A relationship with Mrs. Brighton never existed in the *John, Lucy, Skip* pack. He doesn't know where he fits in our world anymore. I want to tell him that he doesn't.

To prove it, he rushes back upstairs without caring or asking if Thomas will return to me. But it doesn't matter. Thomas might never want to return; John's appearance is too great a disruption to our fledgling pack.

Mrs. Brighton pats my head. "All will be okay, Skip."

That's what *she* thinks. She doesn't know we lost Tom Cat. She doesn't know about Cecilia. Or Bunny.

When I reach my apartment, John is leaving Lucy a voice mail. "I just heard about Aunt Eve. I'm on my way." Then he hangs up and dials someone new and asks about Aunt Eve's status. He drops his head and rubs his temples with his free hand. "If you see Lucy, tell her I'm on my way."

Oh Dog. Is Aunt Eve dead?

"Skip," he kneels before me and holds my face in his hands. "Aunt Eve is going to be okay. Everything's going to be okay."

Oh, thank goodness! Aunt Eve is still with us. And that's the second time within minutes that someone has tried to tell me everything is going to be okay.

If I could talk, I'd tell John as he prepares to leave me alone that nothing is going to be okay. And it's his fault. Again.

49

LUCY

PLUS ONE

A MIDDLE-AGED BALDING man with a round midsection charged toward Lucy as she blocked Aunt Eve's hospital room. "That nut almost killed my wife! She's going to pay!"

Lucy braced herself in the doorway. She gripped the doorjambs on either side. He wasn't getting past her. It was one thing to be working and responding to trauma, it was another to be at the hospital on personal reasons with her defenses down after nearly losing Aunt Eve. She sensed George, Aunt Eve's fiancé, come up behind her but urged him to stay back. "I can handle this."

The man thought she was a nurse attending to Aunt Eve, not the injured woman's niece. Her Golden Years scrubs were one-tenth of the confusion. The other nine-tenths was due to his grief. During her career, she'd seen it a thousand times. His pain was talking, and he thought he was addressing a minion, not a real person.

His eyes were dilated, and he had a bruise and cut on his forehead. Had he been checked out yet? Had he put his wife first and ignored or declined medical attention for himself?

Nurse Lucy kicked in. "Sir, let's have someone look at your head wound."

"It's her fault! I don't care about my head. I want my wife out of pain!"

Fear was ugly. Fear and pain filled every space, nook, and cranny in the room and every cell in this man's body. Out of the corner of her eye and down the long hall, she could see the nurses scrambling to get security's attention. She wasn't worried about her safety. She was worried about this man and Aunt Eve and all they had to recover from, physically and mentally. There had been a head-on collision, and it remained unclear who was at fault.

The man clenched his jaw. "Where's *her* family? They here? I'll break *their* ribs and legs. Then we'll be even. Oh God, my son and daughter. How will I tell my family?"

"Sir, we need to get your head checked. You must put your health first right now. This is the best way to help your wife."

"*My* head?! You think there's something wrong with me? It's that crazy bitch who needs her head checked." He jabbed the air above Lucy, reaching into the room where her aunt rested. He wanted at Aunt Eve.

Security wasn't here yet.

"Sir, you have a wound—"

One minute the distraught man was reaching for her shoulders to shove her aside, and the next John slid in front of her like a solid wall of protection.

Where did he come from?

"Mr. Jordan," John said, "step back."

What was John doing here? How did John know the man's name? How did he find them just in time?

"I'm Eve Bell's lawyer. I can assure you we will be in

touch, but right now, you need to have your head wound checked as the nurse," he pointed at Lucy behind him, "advised. Your family and your lawyer, when you get one, would want you to do the same."

Based on his posturing, Lucy was worried the man was inconsolable and that even John couldn't stop him or avert his wrath, but John seemed to get through to the man. Maybe it was his steady and authoritative voice or his legal title.

"Mr. Jordan, this is not the way to handle this. It will only make everything worse. I know that doesn't seem possible right now, but I've seen it happen time and time again."

Security was three yards away now, but John put his hand up when one of the guards pulled out cuffs. "That won't be necessary. Can we get Mr. Jordan some medical attention instead?"

Mr. Jordan looked past John to Lucy. He looked confused and shook his head. "I'm sorry. My wife . . ."

John helped him take a seat in the wheelchair, and he squeezed the man's shoulder.

His kindness brought tears of relief to Lucy's eyes.

John handed Mr. Jordan one of his business cards. "This is my contact information. In the meantime, whom can we call for you? Do you have family we can bring to the hospital?"

Lucy watched, stunned as the now-exhausted and numb man started to cry. "My sister. Can someone call her?"

John looked over his shoulder at Lucy. He mouthed: *I'll be right back.*

She covered her cheeks with her cold palms as John walked beside the man and the nurse, wheeling him toward an examination room. John kept his large reassuring hand on the man's back. He'd taken out his phone and was now speaking to someone on Mr. Jordan's behalf.

Returning from the restroom, Lucy's mom rushed toward her and almost stumbled when she saw John. "I thought you said you didn't call him."

"I didn't," Lucy brought her up to speed, as much as she could.

"Then what is he doing here?"

"I have no idea," Lucy said, swallowing tears, "but I've never been more happy to see him."

When they walked back into Aunt Eve's room, George was cradling her aunt's hand in his. "I'm right here by your side, where I will always be."

Lucy's tears trickled out, but when her mom started crying, Lucy let the floodgates open. She'd been so scared that they'd lost Aunt Eve. The taxi ride from Golden Years (thank goodness Sheila had insisted she take a cab) had been the longest drive to the hospital Lucy had ever made in all her years working there.

She'd wasted no time calling her friends in trauma to find out what she could, to be prepared before she arrived so she could be strong for her mom and George, a man she'd never met. When her former coworker told her Aunt Eve had been in a head-on accident and had a minor stroke, Lucy had been struck by what loss could truly mean. Loss wasn't letting John go to sort things out even if it meant he wasn't in her life. Loss was losing an incredible woman who'd changed her life and her mom's life. And George's life too. He was still staring adoringly at her aunt.

John reappeared then. Her mom squeezed John's wrist

and wiped her tears with her free hand. "I don't know what you're doing here, but I'm glad you came."

Lucy and John stepped outside the room to be alone.

He took Lucy's face in his hands and looked down at her. "Are you okay? He didn't hurt you?"

She shook her head, and he pulled her close.

His embrace felt sooooo good, so John. His smell and chest against her face was home as she remembered it.

But she was confused. She pulled back enough to ask, "How did you know?"

"I stopped by the apartment to see you."

He'd stopped by her apartment? "Why?"

"I wanted to see you. Talk to you. I tried to call first, but you didn't answer."

No, she wouldn't have. Her phone hadn't left her purse since she'd called Manny to keep an eye on Skip. She wondered how that confrontation went, but just as she was going to ask about Manny and how Skip was, Aunt Eve called weakly from her bed.

"Lucy. John, is that you?"

John turned Lucy in his arms and anchored his hand on her hip, keeping his arm around her as they approached Aunt Eve's bed.

Her sad eyes peeked through the bruises and her swollen left cheek, but she tried to smile. "Thank you." She lifted her hand, and John took it.

"Aunt Eve, you scared me," he said.

Aunt Eve started crying. "That man, is he right? Did I hurt his wife?"

And wonderful John said, "It was an accident, sweets."

"But my fault," she said.

"No, it doesn't sound that way. I've already talked to my

contacts. Mr. Jordan and his wife were driving the wrong way. But I don't want you to worry about any of this, Eve. That's my job now. My firm is going to represent you, no matter what."

No matter what. No matter if Aunt Eve was in the right or wrong? No matter if she and John were together or apart? There had been brief moments over the past week when Lucy had a sense that maybe John wouldn't be back, and she didn't want to regret the time they'd had together. She hadn't wanted it to be for nothing. And now, with him promising to be there for Aunt Eve, she was grateful for his support, "no matter" the peripheral hurt, strings, and unknowns.

"That poor man," Aunt Eve said.

"You just get some rest for now. I understand you have a wedding to recover for." He pulled out an invitation from his pocket.

What was he doing with that?

Perplexed, Lucy asked George and Aunt Eve, "You sent John an invitation?" She hadn't even received one. Even Aunt Eve, the hopeless romantic she was, wouldn't dream of trying to play reunion matchmaker at her wedding.

"No," John said and handed Lucy the envelope. "The post office accidentally forwarded it to me. But," he looked at Aunt Eve before he turned to face Lucy, "I hope to be the plus one."

Plus one? Lucy would have to be a moron to miss his meaning. She hoped she was wrong, but she thought she might be blushing and smiling like a clown. But why now? So much had changed in her life. What had changed in his?

Aunt Eve smiled at John. "I want you to meet George. You could learn a thing or two from him."

This had been a horrible way to finally meet her aunt's fiancé. Aunt Eve and George had just returned from moving his things from Reno to Oakland and were on their way to pick up Lucy's mom to drive into San Francisco and show George the city when the accident happened. Lucy had intended to meet them for dinner later that night after Skip's training session.

Post introductions, Lucy led John outside the room. "You don't have to stay."

"I want to, if you'll let me."

She'd waited so long for this moment, but not *this* moment. Not like this.

"I can't believe you're here." And would he stay, or was this just a one-time thing?

"I am. And I meant what I said. I'll represent Aunt Eve. We'll all straighten this out together."

Together.

Lucy started to shake her head, and John cupped her cheeks again.

"Don't say no. Not yet. Not until we talk. That's why I went to the apartment tonight. The invitation was just an excuse. I miss us."

No one was more surprised than Lucy to hear June's advice echoing in her mind: *You'll both have changed. You'll have to meet each other and start again.*

She put her hands around his wrists, and he pulled her forward to kiss her forehead. His warm lips against her skin were nirvana.

"Aunt Eve can't afford you," she said, skirting the other issue.

"It's pro bono." John attempted a smile. "What is family for?"

Lucy looked into his eyes for a long time. *But we haven't been a family for weeks now, have we?*

In all the ways she had imagined John coming back to her, she would never have imagined this awful situation. It was rather reminiscent of one of Aunt Eve's romance novels, and it lacked as much clarity and confidence too. There'd been a time she wanted her life to play out like a romance novel, but now she wasn't so sure.

"Now," he said, sliding his hands from her cheeks to her shoulders, "when's the last time you, your mom, and George ate? Let me get you some food. Then let's get you some sleep." He dipped his head and gave her a lingering kiss.

She'd ask him later how he knew how to find her, but for now, she would focus on her family and how to best support her mom, aunt, and George. While John got them some food, she went to check with her friends and staff to see if there was anything she could do for Mr. Jordan and his wife. She also texted Manny that Aunt Eve was okay, but he didn't respond. She knew Skip and Tom Cat were safe with Manny. Manny had indeed rescued her tonight when she'd learned Aunt Eve was in the hospital. One call, and Manny had said, "I've got this. Take care of you and Eve."

She was just reading her horoscope when John returned with food for each of them.

Taurus: Some things happen to help us become our better selves and, therefore, better with others.

50

SKIP

COMPROMISED

SPOILER ALERT: Lucy and John mounted each other after slipping into the house, locking lips, and running their hands everywhere until most of their clothes were gone. Neither one of them acknowledged me.

Earth to John and Lucy. Is Aunt Eve alive?!

I'm guessing Aunt Eve is fine, or they wouldn't be so, I don't know, making up instead of breaking up?

I can't tell you how they even made it to the bedroom. John was all over Lucy like she was new grass, sniffing and marking her everywhere with his saliva.

All five of her senses have been compromised. Lucy's lost her mind and memory for all we've been through. I think of *Sex and the City* and all she should have learned but didn't. At one point, Lucy even makes a comment like, "You're kissing different." If John hears her, he ignores her, and since she lets it go or loses the thought as they conquer one another's bodies, it's a moot point.

I can't bear to keep watching, so I move to the living

room and watch DOGTV, where I am positive I won't see any humans humping.

Lucy hasn't even noticed that Tom Cat isn't making noise under the bed because he's gone. And she hasn't asked about Thomas, but she didn't know Thomas was here because she doesn't know that Manny had to take Tank to the Rainbow Bridge. She's lost touch with everything but John's tongue and skin. I want to believe if she knew, she wouldn't be humping away in there. No, she'd be with Manny. Supporting him. I hope I'm right about this anyway.

She deserves to know. She'd want to know. I decide to go back to the room and try to tell her.

They are still going at it. The perverts don't even notice me walk up to her side of the bed and stare. It's like I'm wearing Harry's cloak of invisibility.

When they're done, gasping for air and playing dead, John reaches between them and pulls away but then shatters the postcoital mood, saying, "Shit. The condom broke."

What's your point? I want to ask John. *I'm surprised the bed didn't break.*

Now there's a flurry of activity. They jump out of bed and run to the bathroom, where they inspect something slimy in John's hand. This has never been part of their bed routine in the past. When they return to bed and curl up in the middle of it like they used to, they leave no room for me. I've been evicted, and I can't even take my doggy bed on the floor because I forfeited it to Tom Cat a few days ago. Even with him gone, I don't want to take my old bed back. I want him to feel missed and irreplaceable when he returns. *If* he returns. If I ran away and came home, I'd want to know someone missed me.

With John here, will Tom Cat even want to be here?

Will Thomas return? How will Manny fit in? And, worst of all, what if we lose Tom, Thomas, and Manny only for Lucy to discover Cecilia (and Bunny!) and then I will truly have lost everyone I love?

I get up and find John's shirt in the hall and push it around with my nose. I don't smell Cecilia. His pants are on the bedroom floor where they fell with a clank when his belt buckle hit the wood floor. I bet it startled Thomas. I sure hope Mrs. Brighton doesn't know what was happening up here. Not like it hasn't in the past, but still. I wonder if they feel as betrayed as I do.

With John back and walking me at lunch, who will Thomas read to? Who will protect Thomas from the Slytherins on his walks? Or worse, will he stop walking again? What about Manny? What about doga? I'm having a hard time picturing John at doga; he's never been very flexible. Athletic, yes. Limber, no. I'm a therapy dog now. What happens with my training? I just got my official tags in the mail, for crying out loud!

And this is when my life crumbles before my eyes, ears, and nose. I want John gone. I prefer our new life and routine. Our new life is bigger. Fuller.

John is snoring on the other side of Lucy. Of course he is, he's probably the happiest man in the world right now, getting Lucy back. He's Big. He isn't the one risking anything. Plus, he got laid.

I can't sleep. And I know Lucy can't either. I don't have to stand up to see her open eyes. I can feel she's awake, that slight energy in an otherwise still home. She isn't moving. She either can't still her thoughts like me (whatever hers may be), or she doesn't want to burst her little two-member-club-no-dogs-allowed bubble with John by moving. I don't know which I feel stronger: bitterness that they've excluded me or obsession with all I stand to lose. When Lucy peeks over the mattress at me, I shuffle around on the floor until she can stare at my back.

I sigh, worried about my pack, confused by my wishy-washiness.

"Skip. Come up here," Lucy whispers.

I'm fragile enough that I need a good cuddle more than I need to make a point, so I stand up, and she moves to the middle of the bed, pushing John to the other side. I wish she'd push him off the bed.

He turns to spoon her as I take my rightful place in the bed.

Lucy and I keep each other company as we lie awake the rest of the night. The three of us are together again.

Hmph. All for one and one for all. Only I don't feel all that complete.

51

LUCY

THE MORNING AFTER

LUCY HEARD John's cell phone vibrating from the other room; it was his third call in the last few hours. She wondered who would be calling him so early. A woman?

Oh God, what have I done?

As morning light arrived through the rain dotting the windows, Lucy wasn't sure if she was relieved or resentful. She took a deep breath, inhaling John's cologne. The smell and warmth of him in her arms, in her bed, and in her apartment were welcome but disorienting after having him gone for so long. Two months!

She wanted to close her eyes and pretend he never left in the first place, that he'd never left *her*, never rejected her. But she couldn't. Her backside was warm, cuddled up against him, and his arm cradled her waist. Skip's breathing rumbled through her chest where he slept against her. She didn't move for fear of bursting their bubble and facing reality. But she'd have to eventually.

The condom. *Ugh.* But not yet.

Less than eight hours ago she had been on the verge of

losing Aunt Eve, grateful for John's unexpected arrival and care of her and her mother during those dreaded hours. It would be difficult enough to relax or sleep, when she wanted to spend every waking moment with Aunt Eve knowing they'd come so close to losing her, but add to it that less than six hours ago a possible baby wasn't on her mind . . . sleep was impossible.

How could life change so much in the past six hours, eight hours, twenty-four hours, or two months? How much more would it change in the next six hours, eight hours, twenty-four hours, or two months? *Nine months?*

Countless times, she'd imagined John coming back to her, telling her how much he missed her, how much he loved her, and how he wanted to spend the rest of his life with her. But she'd started to accept the importance of timing. She wanted to get back together at the right time, and she'd thought she would leap at the chance whenever that was. Now she knew she had her limits. Could she trust a new beginning of a relationship that came out of Aunt Eve's life-and-death experience, or because of a possible child?

She could be pregnant right now, or within the next three days. It all depended on if and when she was ovulating. And right now, for the life of her, she couldn't know because she'd gone off the pill six weeks ago, and she hadn't had a normal period yet. Add stress, and her system was haywire.

She could be pregnant with their child. They'd be back together because it's what he said he wanted, and what she thought she'd always wanted with him.

In all her dreams about them getting back together, it was never because she was pregnant. Heck, for all her dreams about having a family, it was never because of an accident, a birth control malfunction in a glorious moment of emotional rawness and vulnerability brought on by the reminder that their time on earth together was priceless.

Near-death could do that. Seeing her aunt and her fiancé, George, had been so bittersweet and evocative. Love like that. Almost lost. Hearing George say, "To love is to live, and to live is to love," just before she left the hospital.

Aunt Eve had taught her about true love. George had proved it existed. Did she and John have what they had? June's Backstreet Boys' "I Want It That Way" echoed through her skull. Did they have true love if they needed a car crash and an accidental pregnancy to bring them together?

Oh, but it would be so easy. So easy to use a pregnancy to pull her life with John back together. So easy to go from being afraid of being alone to growing her family from the inside out. Cocooning their child from the inside, and loving John from the outside. Yes, it would be so easy to be pregnant and to let doing the "right thing" make a mockery of the past two months. It would be so easy to say, "It was meant to be." And yet, this timing, this way, had never been her snapshot of what becoming a mother would look and feel like.

Is this what love looks like?

Or did love look like George sitting by Auntie's bedside and stroking her right hand, reassuring her that he was with her and still thought her the most beautiful woman in the world despite the slightly paralyzed left side of her face?

Her mom had gotten pregnant with Lucy by accident. Look how that had impacted her mom's life, and even Lucy's life until her mom received therapy. She could get back with John, be pregnant, have a baby, and there was no guarantee they'd work out. She could end up a single mom just like her mom, trying to pass Cherry Chip Cakes on to her child.

The mattress shifted, and Skip's nails clattered against the wood floor as he left her side. He looked under the bed and sighed for the millionth time.

What would he say if he could talk? She and Skip had worked so hard to move forward. What was best for him? What was best for her? What would happen to Manny, Thomas, and Tom Cat? Would she and John go back to the way they were before, content with just each other? Could they have a better relationship now? She couldn't see Manny and John becoming friends, even for her sake. What would happen to the Amanda's Garden that she, Martha, and Walter were working on for Manny? And would Thomas still read to and walk Skip? Would she make time for her new friends and projects if she were pregnant and rebuilding a life with John? Or would she slide back into being old Lucy? They could carry on, like nothing had happened.

But something had happened. June had said, no matter if he came back, they'd have to begin anew because Lucy was new.

She had changed. She knew this now. She felt more confident about her new life, more curious about who she wanted to become as Just Lucy. She hadn't crumbled when John left. She wasn't alone; if anything, she had more people in her life now than she'd ever had. And John must have been changing too. Didn't they need time to get to know each other again? To rediscover each other?

She was just discovering herself. Would she continue to

do that with John in her life? She'd made him her every-thing, and she might be too fragile to resist doing that again. She was afraid to give up today.

Wow. Did I just think "give up"?

And John? Did he truly know if he was done being alone? Shoot. Had he even been alone? They'd had no time to talk while tearing off each other's clothes. Was he ready to give up his new life? Just like that? Could he so easily "give up" on her and now on being alone? Where was his conviction? His commitment?

John's arm tightened around her waist, and he kissed the back of her neck. As his hand slid suggestively down her arm to her waist and then her hip, she stiffened. They didn't need to double down on an accidental pregnancy.

John said, "You're worrying. I can tell. It's going to be okay. If you're pregnant, we have each other. I promised you I'd be here for you, and I am."

She turned on her side to face him. "How? How will you be here? Would you want to get married? Go back to the way our relationship was?"

"Of course," he said and tried to pull her close. "It's why I came back last night. I wanted to ask you to take me back. I've missed you. Us."

"But what about being alone? It was important enough to you to leave us, to risk *us*." She moved back so she could see John's face. "John, I just . . . this isn't the way we should get back together, you know? A baby? We'd be giving a baby a job, a responsibility to make us work. This just isn't the way I imagined our life would be."

John smiled at her and cupped her cheek in his hand. "Honey, sometimes life happens. There isn't a list. We have to take risks. Sometimes they are blessings in disguise. Who cares if it isn't how you imagined it. What if it just is? What does it matter so long as we're both happy? Together. So I thought I wanted to be alone. Maybe I don't anymore."

"Maybe? See, that's just it. You don't know. It matters to me that it would take a baby to change your mind."

They were both quiet for a few minutes. Then Lucy said, "The past two months have been hard, John. I have wanted you to come back so badly, but I can't pretend that you didn't leave us with little to no explanation, and if we hadn't almost lost Aunt Eve—"

"Don't," he begged. "We can't do *if*. This *is*."

She sighed and frowned. "This matters to me. If we hadn't almost lost Aunt Eve, and if the condom hadn't broken, would we be talking about getting back together?"

John rolled onto his back and rubbed his face with his hands.

"Yes. And I am here now."

"You weren't here before."

"I was here for ten years!"

"And you left."

"But I'm here now," he said again.

Skip was now pacing along the bedside.

John reached up and brushed her hair. "So it's not ideal, but it's real. Eve, a baby . . . they are both good reasons in my eyes."

Lucy started to cry. "I don't want to always wonder if we're only together because I got pregnant."

"Lucy—"

She got out of bed and yanked on her clothes and shoes to walk Skip. "Really, where would you be right now if Auntie hadn't gotten hurt?" Lucy crossed her arms and waited.

"I'd be at my apartment. Maybe. Because I came here last night to talk to you."

"And if I'm not pregnant? Then what?"

John groaned and got out of bed to dress. "You surprise me. A family is what you've always wanted. I'm sorry I left to be alone. But I did. And now, yes, we could be pregnant. Why do we have to dissect this?"

"Because this is my life we are messing with like some whim!" Lucy yelled in the early morning hours, which caused Skip to start barking. She was waking up the entire building.

John stared at her from across the bed. The moment was all too reminiscent of her Cherry Chip Cake.

"John," she started, not sure she was ready for the answer, "have you been dating?"

He sighed and rubbed his face. He nodded. "I was seeing someone." He put his hands up in surrender. "But it's over. I ended it. No one compares to you."

"You wanted to be alone!" Lucy shouted. "You never said, 'I want to date.'"

"Keep it down. Do you want our neighbors to know our business?"

She glared at him. "*My* neighbors are my friends, and they know more than you think. How could you? Is that who has been calling your phone all night?"

John patted his pockets and looked around for the phone.

Guilty.

"It's in the living room. It's been vibrating all night. Tell me."

"No," John said, "I have not been seeing anyone. Bad choice of words. I've dated, yes. I need coffee."

"I want you to leave," Lucy said. "I need to think about all of this, and I need to get to the hospital to check on Mom and Aunt Eve."

"Okay, okay. This is too much for you, too soon. I get it. I left, and now you don't trust my intentions. That's fine. I deserve that. But think about what I'm saying. We can talk about dating, or whatever time you need, but no matter what, you have to tell me if you're pregnant, and we'll take this one step at a time."

"I don't have to tell you anything," she said and sank to the floor next to Skip to look under the bed and check on Tom Cat. They'd probably scared the catnip out of him. *Oh no, where is he?* She scrambled to her feet to walk around the apartment, John and Skip on her heels. "Skip, where's Tom?"

"Who's Tom?" John asked. "Are you telling me that cat was supposed to be in here?"

Her heart froze. "What did you do to Tom Cat?"

Skip looked at her like she should have asked that a long time ago.

"I'm sorry. I thought he snuck in here. I can't believe you invited that dirty cat in here."

"He's not a dirty cat!" What would happen to Tom back on the street? Would he come back?

"Tell me exactly what happened when you came here last night, John."

"Thomas freaked out when he saw me and ran down-stairs. But don't worry. I already spoke to Mrs. Brighton. She told me about Aunt Eve. And I didn't know about the cat. How could I?"

Yes, how could John have known? He'd left them. He wasn't a part of their lives anymore. *But wait, what was*

Thomas doing here instead of Manny? She'd check on Manny and Thomas as soon as she could get John out the door. Then she'd go find Tom Cat. Skip would help.

Just then her phone rang. She'd left it on all night in case the hospital called and Aunt Eve's condition changed, but it was Golden Years. It must be important since it was a Saturday and her day off.

"Hello?"

"Lucy, Dr. Ryan. Enid is asking for you. It's time."

Oh God. June. "I'm on my way! You have to go, John. I have to go. I have to get to Golden Years for a patient."

"But it's your day off now, right? You get weekends? I thought we'd go get breakfast."

Truth was, even if she didn't want and need to be with Enid, she'd rather find Tom Cat, smooth things over with Thomas, and have donuts with Manny, Skip, and Tank. Now there was a choice she never thought she'd make! She left the back door open for Tom Cat just in case he was hiding in the stairwell. Skip was going with her to see June. His therapy collar suited him when she clipped on the red tag. She could swear he nodded at her as if recognizing he was about to go to work.

"Skip's a therapy dog now?" John asked, incredulous.

She paused, looking into Skip's eyes. John didn't know them anymore.

As she all but pushed John out of the building before her and they stepped outside, Manny returned. His eyes widened when he saw John. Lucy blushed as Manny took in John's bed head and rumpled clothes. Lord only knew what she looked like. She couldn't meet his eyes when she said, "Good morning, Manny."

Manny shook his head as he went into the building and closed the door with a thud.

John turned to her. "Some things never change."

Anger and resentment burned hot as she snapped, "That's where you're wrong. Wait here, John. Skip, stay."

She went back into the building. "Manny."

He paused, "How's Eve?"

"She's going to be okay."

"I'm glad." He started to climb the stairs.

John poked his head back through the door. "Lucy."

"Just wait a minute!" She lost her cool. "Manny, please wait."

He stopped and turned, his face hard.

What was he so mad about? It was none of his business that John was there. Why was he overreacting? *Wait a minute.* Lucy looked around for Manny's sidekick.

"Where is Tank?" she asked, dread pooling in her stomach.

He looked past her shoulder and said, "He's gone."

She knew he didn't mean John. Manny had lost Tank and another part of Amanda.

"Oh, Manny," her eyes filled with tears, and she reached out to touch his arm.

But he nodded toward the front door. "Jelly Donut's waiting." He turned and walked away.

52

SKIP

SOFT VOICE

Lucy parks at Golden Years. I'm suited up with my therapy tag and red vest. I am a pro, so I push the John fiasco aside. I push my pain for Manny and Tank aside. I have a job to do. Someone needs my care.

While I have visited Walter's garden, this is my first time stepping paw inside Lucy's work. We are greeted by a large woman. I like her at first sight. Her aura is like a bouncing ball of sunshine. Like me, she has her game face on. Her name is Sheila.

Something serious is happening. I can smell scrambled eggs cooking somewhere, but the place is silent. The silence turns to energy. People are waiting, but what for?

The place has so many smells that the dog in me wants to dissect each one. I recognize some of the cleaning stuff Lucy uses at home such as our laundry detergent and toilet bowl cleaner. I already know about the scrambled eggs. There's a mustiness that I recognize as age despite perfumes and soaps trying to cover it up. The oldest dogs at the park can't disguise the smell of age even when they roll repeatedly in the grass and weeds.

As Lucy, Sheila, and I start walking, I get a whiff of something familiar, only I can't recognize it. I tremble. All of a sudden, I am overcome with fear and loss, like something really really really bad is about to happen. Something irrevocable. I start to breathe quickly, but this makes it worse because the trace of whatever it is I'm picking up on only infuses my senses more. I am pulled to the familiar smell, and at the same time, I am terrified of it.

Lucy looks closely at me. "Skip, are you okay? There is someone special for you to see."

Someone special. A million images and smells flash before me. Mama, my siblings, the caretaker at the pound who told me I'd need someone special and then . . . And then I recognize the smell, and I take off, dragging Lucy with me as I follow the scent.

Soft Voice! My Soft Voice is here. She has come back for me!

53

LUCY

GROWING OLD TOGETHER

IN ALL HER years in the hospital environment, Lucy had never cried so much.

Skip had gone crazy. She'd actually feared he wasn't ready to be a therapy dog despite all his training and trainer-approved temperament. A compulsory wild behavior had overtaken him, and instead of her leading him to June, he'd led her to the very room where June lay dying. Enid sat at her side.

He was so focused that she was afraid to let his leash go, but once they reached the room, he paused and walked cautiously to the bedside. As he sniffed June's hand and started to whine, Enid gasped in awe.

Lucy knew then she could drop his leash. As he trained to do, Skip gingerly climbed up beside June and stared her in the face. His was a cry Lucy had never heard.

He was larger than June as he spread out beside her. And then June opened her eyes.

She asked, "Lady?"

Skip mewled and tucked his nose into her neck just like a puppy with his mama.

The two cried together, and Enid dabbed at the tears running down June's weathered face.

"Lucy, however did you find her?" Enid asked.

Lucy wiped her own tears. "Lady was his mama. John and I rescued Skip from the pound outside of Half Moon Bay several years ago."

June was too weak to lift her hand, but her finger pointed through Skip's fur at Lucy.

Lucy covered June's hand on top of Skip's quivering body. She leaned over to kiss June's face and then Skip. "He's the best thing that has ever happened to me. Thank you for making the sacrifice."

June's face crumpled, and she cried. She whispered, "Happy tears."

Enid lay down on the other side of June, resting her cheek on June's shoulder and her hand on Skip. "You can let go now, honey," Enid said. "You can let go. See you in Santiago."

54

LUCY

PLAN B

Lucy sat on the floor next to the couch with Skip's head resting on her thighs. "You are amazing, Skip. The best therapy dog ever."

He sighed.

She sighed back and stared down at the morning after pill in her hand.

"This is for the best. I'm not selfish enough to have a baby just to hold on to a dream."

He said nothing. His eyes did not judge her. No, they only shone with love.

"I love him, but I don't want my old life back this way." She shook her head. "I can't believe I am saying that, much less really believe it. But something's happening, isn't it? You and I? We are building a new life together, and I just don't know how John fits into it anymore. It all feels too fragile to push it. I don't like a lot of change, but I've been changing. I have."

Skip barked, stood up, and wagged his tail.

"See? Even you see that I'm changing."

Skip barked again.

"It's strange to miss my old routines and life as much as I fear having them back. And at the same time, I'm scared. What if this is my only chance to get John back?"

She texted her mother that she needed to walk Skip and then would head to the hospital to check on her, Aunt Eve, and George. Tomorrow morning, she would return to check on Enid and fulfill the promise she and Sheila had made to June about Enid's first morning alone.

Tom Cat wasn't home yet, and she needed to look for him too. She prayed he'd return to them. Mrs. Brighton had assured her Thomas was okay and ready to read to Skip; apparently they were on a very good part of *Harry Potter*. Manny? She only hoped she could find a way to support Manny and that he'd still let her be his friend. She'd knocked on his door, but he hadn't answered. He was grieving, and as his friend, she'd give him the time and space he needed. Grief was like DNA, unique for each person.

Lucy swallowed the pill and the hypothetical pregnancy. She let it all sink in. What was, what could have been, what should be. She had worked too hard and come too far on her own to let heartache and a broken condom dictate her future.

She was on the cusp of something. She wasn't sure what it was, but she felt both afraid and excited to find out.

Now she and Skip needed to take a walk and try to find Tom Cat before she headed to the hospital for the afternoon.

55

SKIP

THE CAT IS OUT OF THE BAG

WE HAVEN'T FOUND Tom Cat on our walk yet. We never knew where he hung out before he joined our pack, so we don't know where to look. I can't even catch a whiff of him.

"Maybe we should put some old pots and dirt on the stairs and lure him back to us."

Good one, Lucy.

"I do hope he comes back to us, Skip."

Me too, boss. Me too.

"Let's walk to the dog park. We'll ask people if they've seen Tom anywhere. Then I need to check on Aunt Eve."

Whoa. We haven't been to the dog park since John left us, but it's time. It's not the new dog park, mind you; it's *our* dog park. We need to reclaim it. We can arrive as Skip and Lucy and announce to the world that we are no longer Skip, Lucy, and John.

So much has happened. We are letting go. I found Soft Voice. Soft Voice found me.

I felt her love when I lay in bed with her. I found so much healing in that moment as we cuddled. She still smelled like Mama did, or maybe Mama always smelled like Soft Voice. Her friend Enid told me, "She always regretted losing you."

It's amazing how much those words healed me, and how much lying with Soft Voice until she left me again set me free. Lucy told her that I am the best thing that has ever happened to her. And in those moments of saying goodbye to Soft Voice, I knew Lucy and I would be together forever.

John is gone. Lucy's already taking steps to put our life back together, and she even said, "But what happens happens. We move forward. We don't go under."

Fine by me. All of this means Lucy and I are a true team. She'll never know of Cecilia because John is gone. The past is behind us. We've been repacked. *All for one and one for all.*

Oh, how life can change from one hour to the next. Lucy and I are having a rousing game of fetch to burn off our energy when my life falls apart. That damn ball. I should have known it would lead to my final ruination!

I've just caught my latest ball when someone calls, "Skip!"

That voice. That biscuity scent. I freeze and the ball falls from my mouth. How did I not realize she was here? Bunny too? What is she doing here at our old park? I panic. Is John with Cecilia? It will be too much for Lucy to see them together regardless of her epiphany. I don't bother to look for them. I have to get Lucy out of here. Fast! But I hesitate too long. Lucy and She Who Must Not Be Named have caught up to me on either side. I am trapped.

Lucy asks, "How do you know my dog's name?"

Cecilia pauses and says, "I know John."

"How?" Lucy asks defensively.

I cower and look everywhere but at Lucy or Cecilia. I even ignore Bunny's behind when she offers it to me.

"How well or how long?" Cecilia asks.

"Both."

I run before Lucy can do the human math. Before she can add up how Cecilia knows my name and how I know Cecilia. I run before she can look at me with shock, hurt, and hatred. I run before she can reject me. I ignore her demands to return, which don't last, and I run far and long. Far enough to find myself in a strange neighborhood where no one recognizes me, no one knows my gentle side, and they can only see the wildness of the genes and appearance passed on by my mother. But truth be told, I am wild with fear. It doesn't take long for Animal Control to sniff me out and haul me off to the place I'm destined to die.

It's better this way. It's better that I return myself to the pound so Lucy doesn't have to. She's been through enough.

56

LUCY

THE LONG RUN

WHEN SKIP IGNORED HER CALLS, Lucy had to make a choice. Find out more from this woman or find Skip.

But Lucy already knew. She knew deep in her heart what this woman meant. John had never left her to be alone. And she'd have to deal with this and her feelings, but only after she saved her dog. Her precious dog that somehow knew this other woman. She had a million questions for the woman, but she had a million reasons to put Skip first.

"He wants to get back together with you. He left me, you know?" the woman said as Lucy turned to leave.

Lucy paused and turned back. Skip's deserted leash hung lifeless in her hand, his absence heavier than any void John could have left. "I'm sorry," Lucy said genuinely. "I know how that feels."

57

SKIP

IMPOUNDED

WHEN JOHN and Lucy rescued me from the pound seven years ago, I bow-vowed I would never do anything to lose them, and yet here I am, being guided by a leash pole and muzzle into the animal shelter. If I wasn't so depressed, I might be impressed by how much warmer and friendlier the place is compared to the cold place I was dropped when I was a puppy with my mom and sibs. I might even summon the energy to hope that I might get adopted again. But I've become a realist in the past few months.

The odds of me being adopted a second time are like one to fifteen million. Besides, just because I don't want to die here doesn't mean I don't deserve to be here.

What good is a disloyal dog to someone as sweet as Lucy? I'm a disgrace to the Canine Credo: *Be Man's Best Friend.* I can argue that I was John's best friend even if being one started me down the path that has landed me in the pound again. But Lucy? No, I had a big paw in John's betrayal and her heartbreak. Some best friend I was, right?

It's hard for me to believe that three months ago I was

tied up outside a store as Lucy held wedding dresses up to the window to get my opinion. I barked at the ones I liked. Okay, I barked at all of them because she was so excited to be marrying John. If I could turn back time, I wouldn't beg John to take me to the new dog park a second time. But I did. There's no turning back.

My captor doesn't take me straight to a pen like they did when I was a pup. He clips my leash to a metal table and says, "Let's see what we can find out about you and if you've had your shots."

Of course I've had my shots. What kind of owner do you think Lucy is? Can't you tell from looking at me how loved I've been?

He waves a box above me, and when it starts ringing at the back of my neck, he says, "Excellent." He leaves me to make a phone call. When he comes back, he says, "Let's get you settled."

Settled. Right. Settled only to be taken away from life. No more dog days of summer for me. It occurs to me that I've been wrong about more things than Lucy's ability to lead. Like how I've bragged about how dogs choose when and how they will die. Because look at Tank; humans *do* decide when dogs will go to the Rainbow Bridge. I mean, look at me. I've lost all control of my life, even how long I'll get to live. I could cry.

We walk down the concrete aisle, and I look from side to side at each dog and each pen. They look as anxious as I feel. I know I should assert some authority and toughness, but I ain't got it in me. I'm tired of being tough. Hasn't gotten me anywhere I want to be. I'm shocked when my captor stops at a kennel with a puppy yipping and staring happily at me. His feet are too large for his tiny body, causing him to trip over himself and tumble onto his back. I can't believe it when the guy opens the gate. He's putting me in with this little puppy? After watching us for a few minutes, he removes the muzzle and leash. "Looks like you'll be gentle with him. They said not to put you alone."

Who said not to put me alone? I lick his hand with gratitude and enthusiasm. The man trusts me. He senses my sweetie-pie side. He knows I'm a good dog at heart. Maybe my last days won't be as depressing and lonely as I thought.

"Warm up this little one, Big Guy. He's the last of his litter."

Ugh. I was the last of my litter in this hellhole too. Boy, do I remember that horrible feeling. I lie down next to my eager roomie, and it's all the invitation the squirt needs.

As I let the little whippersnapper climb all over me, the man pats my head and says, "Good boy. With any luck, we'll find a home for this little guy before your owner comes to get you. But it won't be today. It's closing time."

It's another one of the few times in my life I'm glad I can't speak the human language because I don't have the heart to tell him, or even hear myself say this out loud: *Lucy won't be coming for me. She's not even going to look for me. She knows the truth about me and John by now.*

Squirt (yeah, I have to call him something) is sitting on my head, biting my ears, and begging me to wrestle with him. His tiny bark that says, "I'm so happy you're here," is a salve to my soul. I've failed Lucy, but if I can care for this little guy until he has a new home, at least I can be proud of that.

58

LUCY

A DOSE OF THEIR OWN MEDICINE

HOW MANY TIMES had John texted her in the past twelve hours? At least a dozen times before she stopped counting. She knew she had to face her feelings and misbeliefs about John and how he had cheated on her, lied to her. She would when she was ready, but right now she had more important things to address. She hit ignore on John's call once again.

Sure enough, Enid was curled up in bed just as June had anticipated. And per June's dying wishes, Enid was about to get a dose of her own medicine. "Project Buck Up, Soldier," June had called it.

Sheila and Martha waited just outside the door and out of Enid's line of sight. She was grieving, and if it had been anyone else who needed the time alone, such as Martha, Lucy would have respected the isolation, but June had known Enid better than anyone, even Enid herself. So Lucy followed the plan and script she and June had decided upon.

"Enid," Lucy said with a tough tone she wasn't entirely used to using. "Time to get up, soldier."

"No. Can't you see I'm in mourning?" Enid mumbled and stared at the wall.

"The entire world can see you're mourning. As you should be, but 'either get busy living or get busy dying,'" Lucy read from her mental lines, regardless how much she just wanted to coddle the barking Enid. June had been so quiet and gentle, yet she had known how to write one heck of an Enid script.

"No," Enid said.

"Well," Lucy said dramatically and waved Sheila and Martha into the room, "then you leave us no choice."

They had Enid's attention now.

"What's gotten into you?" Enid glowered at them. "Leave me the hell alone."

Lucy set up her iPad as Sheila and Martha got in line at the foot of the bed with Lucy. They handed Lucy a hairbrush. Now all three women held brushes like microphones.

"Don't say you weren't warned," Lucy said as she turned the volume full up and hit play.

Familiar music filled the room as they began to lip-synch to the Backstreet Boys' "I Want It That Way."

You are my fire.

My one desire.

Believe, when I say,

I want it that way.

Enid sat up in bed, stunned tears running down her face as the trio and their brushes started to dance in a circle at the foot of her bed,

Tell me why

Ain't nothing but a heartache

Tell me why

Ain't nothing but a mistake

Tell me why
I never want to hear you say,
I want it that way

Shaking her head and trying to pretend she was annoyed and angry (though the tears and twinkle in her eye ruined it), Enid swung her legs over the side of her bed and slid her feet into her slippers. She yanked on the sash of her robe, grabbed her walker, and walked by the singing and dancing trio. As she passed Lucy, she said, "I always knew June had it in her. Time for some eggs."

After high-fiving Sheila and Martha on the successful execution of Project Buck Up, Soldier, Lucy raced to her car. She had just enough time to reach the pound when the doors opened. Time for Project Jailbreak.

59

SKIP

CHIPPED AND SQUIRTED

THE BELLS JINGLE on the kennel hall door, letting us all know that the day crew is returning. Last night it wasn't pitch black the way I remember the pound being when I was a puppy. Instead, lights were strung up by the ceiling, spreading a little cheer.

I survived my first night in the pound, thanks to Squirt. Every time I had a nightmare about losing Lucy, I'd wake up to find his roly-poly body warm as a toaster oven against my belly. Even now, he is curled up under my front leg. I've heard people talk about a good night's sleep, saying, "I slept like a baby." I think true sleep would be to "sleep like a puppy." Even in this cage, Squirt was a ball of energy last night until he finally wore himself out. When the crew left and turned out the lights, he fell fast asleep and didn't move all night.

His rapid heart rate and puppy breaths flutter against my chest and leg, giving me purpose. I can't help but think of my long-lost mother and how calm, assertive, and loving she was or how it must have felt to have all eight of our hearts thriving against her. Or how devastated she must have felt as, one by one, we were taken from her, or how she must have felt when she was pulled from me, forced to leave me. If not for Squirt, I think my heart would have broken overnight.

More than once during the night as I stared down at Squirt, I was moved to tears. I think I'd make a good father. Teaching, leading, and caring for him feels more natural and less scary than any of the days I tried to lead Lucy. I'm going to do everything I can to help him get adopted. I am going to miss him when he's gone, at least for the days I have left in this life.

Squirt turns to my minuscule male teat and tries to suckle. He did this a few times during the night. At first, I tried to teach him that it was fruitless by pushing him away with my snout and licking his back to comfort him. But now I just let him. He's soothing himself, and I'm okay with that. He's using me like one of those chew toys I've seen babies sucking on in their strollers when their parents are walking them.

Looking down at Squirt's brown and black stripes, I'm reminded of Tank. I wonder how poor Manny is doing. I hope he will understand why Lucy has to give me up, despite his own loss and powerlessness to bring Tank back.

I can smell coffee in the air, and not long after, I hear the staff getting into work mode, getting ready to take care of us dogs. I can hear the slap of the hose against the concrete. I remember how it felt when I was a puppy and how the floor was hosed down with cold water under my feet, and I'm not looking forward to the disruption, or seeing how it will upset Squirt, but I'll do my best to be a good example. I'll teach him it's better to have a clean cage than not. What family is going to adopt him if our crap's all over the place?

The other dogs are starting to wake up and yawn and stretch like Lucy and I learned in yoga. *Oh how I miss doga.* There's anticipation and dog breath in the air. Morning feeding will do that to any animal. No matter what the day ahead looks like, it always starts with breakfast.

But this morning, I lie still, content to let Squirt stay warm beside me for as long as possible. After all, I've got nowhere to be. What's the rush?

The high-energy mutts walk outside; yes, it's true, each kennel has a plastic door, and we can go outside if we want. It's at the backside of the kennel, and I suspect I can go there and stay dry with Squirt while they clean our cages. The flap also lets in fresh air and outdoor noises, such as cars and people in the parking lot. I can hear people arriving. I can make out their chatter as they walk to the building. People coming to work. People volunteering. Owners looking for their babies.

The hum of human voices almost lulls me back to sleep, but a sound startles me awake. I hear something. Someone. A something-someone that I've been drawn to most of my life. And I'm afraid to believe it. Am I dreaming? I hold still, all of my instincts on high alert, my ears straight up in the air, desperate to hear the sound again.

Silence. Silence. And then, "Excuse me. Are you open yet? I'm here for my dog."

Wait, what? She can't love me enough to keep me after all of this, can she?

A man's voice says, "Wolf mix?"

And the doggess's voice says, "That's my Skip."

And I know. Yes she does. She does want me after all

this. I start to whimper uncontrollably. I can't stop. Can't even.

That's my Skip repeats in my head. I stay next to Squirt. I close my eyes. Lucy loves me. She really does.

The door at the end of the walk opens, and there she is. Her lavender with a hint of Cherry Chip Cake (someone's been baking) washes over me. I almost pass out. She is so beautiful. More beautiful than the first time I ever saw her. I am frozen in place. Squirt sleeps so innocently next to me, completely clueless to the torment and elation I'm experiencing.

Lucy spots me down the way and moves slowly toward me.

She has no leash with her. She isn't smiling, but she lets out a long breath, and as her shoulders drop, all of her stress leaves her body. These are good signs, and yet, I can't move. I just stare at her with my wide eyes, my jaw almost touching the floor as I pant. I think I'm hyperventilating. I can smell my own desperation, and it reeks like vomit. TMI, I know. All the other dogs smell my weakness too. If I were in a pen right now, they'd all win dominance over me. Every dog wants to get a piece of me, and all the while Squirt keeps sleeping, clueless. This little guy needs to be a bit more alert in this dog-eat-dog world. But he rests easy under my care.

Lucy stops in front of my cage and stares down at me. She sees Squirt curled up under my leg. A small smile touches her face, and she covers it with her fist like she's trying to hide it from me or to hold it back.

She meets my eyes, and then I hear her lovely voice. She's determined but calm, and she points a finger at me.

"You will never run away from me again. You will love,

honor, and obey me. I am top dog. I am your alpha. If you can't handle that, speak now."

I've done some stupid things in my life, but I'm not a complete idiot; I remain silent.

"I had no idea John put you, or us, in this position. Now, that's the last we will speak of it. Let's go home."

Home. A smile bursts from my being in such force I can barely catch my breath. My tail thumps against the concrete so hard, I bet somewhere a seismologist thinks the Bay Area is having an earthquake. I'm being given another chance, and I'm never going to mess this up again. I'm going to be the best dog to Lucy. I'll do whatever she tells me, and I am never going to question her love again. I have no idea what has happened since I ran away from her yesterday, and I'm going to follow her lead.

Squirt whimpers, yawns, and opens his eyes.

Oh no. What about Squirt?

As puppies can do, he goes from sleeping like the dead to a manic mutt in half a breath, and when he sees Lucy looming over us, he goes bananas.

Bittersweet. That's how this moment feels. To feel put back together again by Lucy but torn about leaving Squirt alone to face this world, not knowing if and when he will get his special person.

Nothing is going to stop me from leaving here with Lucy, but it doesn't mean I'm not devastated about being Squirtless. This must have been how my mama felt.

I lick his head and belly and climb to my feet. Squirt runs against the gate to greet Lucy. She sticks fingers from each hand through the fence; one for me to lick and one for Squirt to chew on.

"You've been taking care of this cutie pie. He looks like Tank."

A staff member stops next to Lucy. "I wish everyone chipped their dogs," he said, "and brought us cupcakes." He licked his fingers.

I have no idea what he means by "chipped," but Lucy can chip me anytime if it keeps me in her life.

Lucy stands and smiles. "I actually got Skip from this exact shelter over seven years ago, and the attendant recommended I chip him so I could always find him."

So I could always find him?

For the first time in my life, I lose all my senses. I can't smell, see, or hear. I can only feel inside. Lucy found me because she decided the day she adopted me that she would always find me.

"Thank you for putting him with the puppy. What's his or her story?"

"Him. Mastiff Pitbull Terrier mix." He points around the pound. "You'll see we have mostly Pits here. Vastly misunderstood dogs."

"Skip too, at times."

"I believe it," he says.

By now, Squirt's jumping up at me, trying to get me to lie down so he can play Canine of the Mountain. Normally I would indulge him because I instinctually know it helps puppies learn about being dominant, but I have a harder lesson to teach him: I can't stay.

I need to create distance, but the little muttchkin just crawls under me and lays down on his belly and starts waving his little feet right between my front paws. I can't help but sigh and smile as tears fill my eyes.

He does look like Tank. Manny could use another Tank.

I get dog–goose bumps when Lucy peers back into the pen and asks, "Skip, are you thinking what I'm thinking?"

I'm good at deciphering body language. I read smells like nobody's business. I can hear through walls, I swear it. But I need them all to guess a person's thoughts. I can pick up on energy, but I can't read minds, not like Lucy and John used to be able to do with each other. But as Lucy and I look at each other, I know exactly what she will say next, and she knows I'm on board.

She turns to the staff member and says, "I'll take them both."

I howl until the entire place joins me in joyful song.

SKIP

RESCUING MANNY

BY THE TIME we get back to the apartment, I am emotionally exhausted. And Tom Cat is waiting for us. *Thank Dog.* Lucy left the door open, and he came back to us by choice. Right then and there, we fall asleep in bed together. I don't even have time to notice what he and Squirt think of each other. The last thing I remember is Tom purring against my belly.

Now Lucy is petting me awake. I can tell by the toys thrown around the room that Lucy dog-sat Squirt for me while I napped. She clearly wore him out because he's sound asleep in a cardboard box. Tom Cat has taken his place beneath the bed again. Baby steps.

Standing with the box, she says to me, "Let's go. Now or never, right?"

Oooh. It's time to give Squirt to Manny! *Right. Let's do this!*

"If Manny won't take him, we'll keep him, but if he does, everyone will be happy."

Seriously. I'm not worried. Who can resist Squirt? I

hope Squirt stays asleep or he will ruin the surprise. I'm just so proud and happy that I get to see Manny's face when he first sees him. He's irresistible, this little guy, and now we can be neighbors.

Lucy opens the door. Sticking to my new commitment to be the best dog ever, I wait until she tells me I can follow her. I'm silent as a mouse as we walk across the landing to Manny's door.

Lucy looks at me and giggles, both nervous and excited. I'd giggle too if it were biologically possible.

It's early, but we both know Manny is up. As she knocks on his door, I jump in the air. I can't contain myself. I can hear him walking through his apartment, and I think Lucy can too, but I hear better than she does. He's being purposely quiet. He's taking cautious steps, not like he's just being slow or in a normal flow. My guess is he knows it's Lucy. Maybe he's avoiding us. But, boy, is he in for a surprise because it's not just Lucy and me.

He's at the door now. I can smell him and hear his hesitance. He's probably staring through the peephole, and I know I'm right because Lucy leans toward the eyehole.

"Open up, Manny. I know you're in there."

I hear him groan. He opens the door.

"Do we have to do this now?"

"I want to introduce you to someone."

Manny frowns, looks past her at me, her seemingly sole companion, and then he looks warily at her beaming face and the closed box in her arms. "Lucy, what have you done? You promised not to."

"I promised I wouldn't find a replacement for Tank, I know, but believe me when I say this is all Skip's doing."

That's right, Manny. And I'm proud of it!

Lucy adds, "Sometimes things happen for a reason, and you have to take a chance."

I wonder if she realizes how many times John has said this very thing to her, and how many times it annoyed her. But just as John was sometimes right, Lucy is now.

She pushes the box toward Manny.

"Lucy," he says, physically recoiling, preparing to close the door. "No."

"Skip," she says.

I jump around her to sit in Manny's doorway.

Manny glares at us both. "Great. Weeks ago, you had no control over walking Skip, and now he is reading your mind."

That's right, I am. It's a new day, Manny.

Lucy bends over to set the box on the floor. We hear a decisive yip. A startled Squirt makes his presence known.

When she first opens the box, I wonder what Squirt is thinking as Manny stares down at him.

"He's yours," Lucy says.

Manny reaches in and pets Squirt.

She rushes on. "He's not a replacement. He's fate. Skip ran away—"

His head jerks up. "What?!"

"Skip ran away, and when I found him at the pound, he had this little guy cuddling with him."

"I don't believe in fate."

"Well, it doesn't matter because Skip and I do. This guy was there, and he had your name written all over him. Skip agrees."

I bark to prove it.

Squirt starts to chew on Manny's fingers hanging over

the box. I lick Manny's fingers to show Squirt that biting and chewing is for bad puppies.

Lucy bends over and scoops Squirt up and cuddles him to her chest before handing him to Manny. "He has puppy breath," she says.

Manny takes Squirt in his large hands. At first, he holds him at arm's length. "What's his name?"

"You tell us."

"I didn't say I'm taking him."

"Oh, but you are."

Manny settles the squirming Squirt against his shoulder and moves his chin away so the puppy can't lick it. Manny's expression is sad, but his eyes sparkle. His shoulders relax.

"I don't need you to rescue me," he says to her.

"I'm not rescuing you." She reaches over and scratches Squirt's back. "I'm rescuing him."

"Come, Skip." She picks up the empty box and heads back to our apartment. Just before she shuts the door, she says to Manny, "Let us know his name once you decide. And," she hesitates but then says, "when you're ready, I have something to show you."

Manny looks at us over the puppy's head. I know she's talking about the Amanda Garden, and even though he doesn't know about it, Manny understands too. He swallows and nods.

I'd do anything to spend the rest of the day watching Manny and Squirt together. I can't wait to learn his name. But Lucy's so smart. She knows this is bonding time for them. Even so, we both slide down to the floor at our door to eavesdrop, and we smile together when we hear Manny chuckle and say, "Now, now. That's enough, little guy."

61

LUCY
BIG REVEALS

LUCY WAS nervous as Manny followed her to the cafeteria at Golden Years. What if he didn't like how they'd commemorated his sister and Tank? On the other hand, how could he not? Martha and Walter had spearheaded the project, and the results wowed even Enid, who was now nurturing her own seedlings and taking some of the credit for the project.

She wished Skip could be here for the reveal, but when she'd gone home for lunch to check on him and had heard Thomas reading to him once again, she hadn't wanted to disturb the much-longed-for *Harry Potter* reunion.

So far Tom Cat and Thomas had forgiven her for the John-relapse. Manny had said, "Being at my side when Tank passed wasn't your responsibility, but as a friend, I wish you could have been."

She did too.

Lucy was still in the process of forgiving John. This morning she finally called him and told him that he needed to give her space so she could mourn the end of their relationship. And though he'd said he'd left Cecilia, that he'd made the worst mistake by leaving Lucy, she'd held firm: *Don't call me. I will call you.* And then she'd thrown her wedding invitations into the recycling bin outside and called Marge to say, "I'm ready to change my trip."

"I should warn you," Manny said, "I left Bear with Thomas, Tom, and Skip."

"Then they're all happy," Lucy said. Sometimes Bear even slept over. Tom Cat would sleep in the entire dog bed, and Skip seemed content just to have a paw on the bed. He was happiest with Tom Cat happy. And little Bear just loved to be with his "big brother" Skip.

"Sometimes I get the impression that Skip doesn't like Bear's name," Manny said. "You notice how he sighs when I say Bear? But he does look like a cub."

Martha and Enid were waiting for them as they stepped up to the arranged pots. After introductions were made, Martha said, "We start the seedlings here within a controlled environment then we move them."

Lucy looked at Manny out of the corner of her eye. He was shyly wiping his eyes.

"Her pots, all lined up and being used," he turned to Lucy. "God, I can't tell you what a relief this is. I was just holding on to them, wasting them."

"Well, kiddo," Enid said, "if you like Phase One, you'd better hold on to your belt buckle for Phase Two. Ready, Martha?"

"There's a phase 2?" Manny asked. "I don't know if I can take it."

Lucy hung back and let Martha and Enid run the show. They'd put their hearts into the project. She followed Manny, knowing Walter was ready at the end of the hall to open the door to the newly renovated garden. The big reveal was finally happening.

Lucy's earlier doubts faded, and she thought, *Manny, your flipping mind is about to be blown.*

She wished she could race ahead just to see his face when he saw the new garden. But she didn't need to. One step through the door, after he digested the colorful flowers and garden beds blooming and growing in the large boxes decorated with the words *Grow and Glow*, Manny leaned his head back to take a deep breath, only to gasp or choke on a sob. Hanging in an arch above the blossoming boxes was a beautifully crafted wood sign: *Amanda's Garden.* The sign was compliments of Walter.

Enid high-fived Walter and Martha. "I knew it! I knew we could make a grown man cry."

Success, Enid. Success.

62

SKIP

HOT DOG

I MISSED Manny's reaction to his little sister's garden, but I don't mind. Tom Cat is upstairs in our bed, and Squirt (I can't bear to call him Bear just because he looks like one), Manny, Lucy, and I are sitting in our backyard.

Manny still can't get over Amanda's Garden.

Lucy says, "That's what friends are for."

Okay, I know it's too soon and that Lucy is still grieving John, but if you ask me, Lucy and Manny might think they are just friends, but I smell the blooming pheromones.

Hot Dog! These two are going somewhere someday.

"I changed my trip. I'm going alone, and I'm hiking the Camino de Santiago. Have I gone crazy?" she is asking herself more than Manny. I think he knows this, but he answers anyway.

"You'd be crazy not to go."

Lucy nods her head. "That leaves Skip and Tom Cat."

The most important part, if you ask me, but I'm no longer afraid that Lucy won't come back for me. We will be together until death do us part.

No, I don't want to go to a dog sitter for a whole month. I can handle living with Aunt Eve while she recovers, that would be okay, but I'll miss Tom, Thomas, Mrs. Brighton, Manny, and Squirt-Bear. But I also want Lucy to go. When she told me about her trip the other day, she said, "I'm ready to let go." I knew she didn't mean let go of me.

"I'll take care of him while you're gone. Tom too."

Lucy and I both look at him with shock. I start wagging my tail and jumping around.

"What?" Lucy asks. "I thought you were allergic to cats?"

"I can take Benadryl, and I'm sure Thomas can help out."

Lucy just stares at him.

"Don't make a big deal out of it." He elbows her. "Just promise me that you'll go on this hike, get John out of your system, live a little, have fun, loosen up, and then come back. Skip, Tom, Squirt, and I will be waiting for you. Some donuts too."

Holy cow! Without saying it, Manny just said *it*. He's looking at Lucy like she's a big juicy bone.

Lucy faces forward and nudges her shoulder against his.

"And before you bring up that rescuing business again," Manny says, "I'm not rescuing you. I'm being here for you. That's what friends are for."

Yup, Manny. All for one and one for all.

63

SKIP

DON'T LOOK BACK

SPRING IS IN THE AIR. I can tell Lucy and I are going for a longer walk than usual because she brought her backpack with a water bottle pouch on the side. And it's full.

Yahoo! Getting ready for her hike totally agrees with me. I may not be going with her on the big trip, but I like how she's been including me in the preparation. We even stopped by Golden Years to pick up some shells and rocks from Enid to add to Lucy's backpack. Enid said, "Okay, now you're ready! Remember, when you throw these onto the trail at the end in Santiago de Compostela, shout, 'For June and Enid!' Don't forget to take pictures. Then eat one of those almond cakes for me that everyone talks about. Bring me back one if you can."

Lucy always finds us a new trail to train on. "Just like the trail will be new to me on the hike," she says.

So you know what this means; I have uncharted territory to mark.

But what I love most about our training is how light Lucy's steps are despite her giant backpack. It's been a month since she ran into Cecilia, then rescued me from the pound again. She always says, "We rescued each other." I like it when she reminds me that's how she sees things. Lucy never told me what happened with Cecilia after I ran away, and that's okay because more and more, I'm living in the bow-Now again.

That's why it's so ironic when a few minutes later, I smell him. I smell John.

I try to slow our pace and to smell which direction he might be coming from. I wonder how to let Lucy know. In the end, I think we all see each other at the same time, and we all freeze in our tracks. By "we" I mean me, Lucy, John, Cecilia, and Bunny. Bunny is ahead of John and Cecilia.

I don't move. I know how this alpha business works, so I wait for Bunny to come to me. *Bingo, got her.*

Lucy has been going to training with me, so I'm hoping she realizes she can't approach John. Not shouldn't, but can't. He has to come to her. But maybe humans are a bit different because while Cecilia calls for Bunny and tells John, "I'll give the two of you some privacy. See you later," John and Lucy meet halfway and stop two dog lengths apart.

Lucy keeps her chin up. She looks confident, and I have to say, she feels confident to me. I don't sense any tears coming on. Her energy is more like her energy in doga: present, calm, patient. I can't lie; my heart still got a little kick-start when I saw John. Part of me will always love him. I'm guessing it might be the same for Lucy.

But you should see how John's eyes light up. "Lucy," he says. And the way he says her name, it's like he's taken a breath for the first time in a long time or is about to drink a tall out-of-this-world glass of water.

"Hi, John."

Cecilia and Bunny should be gone by now. I don't even have time to look or care. I'm not taking my eyes off of my Lucy.

John says, "Skip, buddy. How about a hug?"

I look to Lucy, and she nods in approval.

John squats down and takes me in his arms. Yeah, I'm always going to love him.

"I miss you too," John says. He stands, sniffing. He wipes his eyes on his sleeve. "Damn," he says and then laughs. "I'm happy to see you both. Don't let the water-works confuse you."

Lucy smiles gently. I know she knows all about tears, but she knows more than tears now. "You look good."

"I feel," he hesitates, "good." He cocks his head and looks her up and down, ultimately resting his eyes on her face with such yearning I almost have to look away. "You look . . . different."

"I feel different."

He nods. "It suits you."

My Lucy doesn't break eye contact, but John looks away and then back. He clears his throat and swallows hard.

"That's quite a pack you're carrying," he says, but he's not really looking at her backpack. He's looking over every inch of her body again. And I ache for him. In that moment, I know he misses Lucy more than Lucy ever missed him.

Lucy doesn't move. She is playing this smart. She is letting him come to her without encouraging him.

He takes a step forward.

She doesn't budge.

He takes another step closer to her. Just three feet between them now.

"Australia?"

She shakes her head. "The Camino de Santiago. I'll start in the French Pyrenees and end in Spain. Skip is my training partner. I leave in October."

I'm not going to lie; John's face falls at first. Like he's lost something. Lucy. He brushes his hand through his hair. Half his mouth has a tilt; the other side is still turned down. I can tell he is sad, but he is trying to be happy for her.

"Wow," he says. He takes another step closer. Two feet left, just enough room for me. "Who are you going with?"

She is thoughtful but says, "I'm going alone. It's an organized group."

John looks over his shoulder, probably checking if Cecilia is gone. Another step. One step left between them. I'm being pushed out. He takes a deep breath of Lucy and closes his eyes. When he opens them, he's giving her the look. The you're-everything look. "I'm really happy for you." And then he pauses. "This is bittersweet, though."

He reaches out to adjust the strap on her shoulder.

Lucy doesn't react.

And just like that, after all these years, she has him. Lucy is alpha.

"So you're going alone. Have you been dating?"

"John."

"I know it's none of my business. After all I . . . I don't want to be the reason you're alone."

Lucy smiles, confidence oozing from her pores. "Being alone isn't the same as being lonely. Someone smart once told me he needed to be alone. I didn't want to make the same mistake and rush into a relationship."

"If *he* was truly smart, he'd have taken the time alone

before he met you, and he'd be with you today, maybe even planning a pilgrimage with you."

"Yes, but you're not."

"No, I'm not." He lifts one palm and cups her cheek. "I love you, you know."

"I know," she says.

"Be safe out there. Send me a postcard if you feel like it."

By now there isn't room for me between them. But it's clear there isn't room for John anymore either.

"Skip and I have to go. Take care of yourself." She turns to leave.

John is only half-joking when he points at me off-leash and calls after her, "Aren't you worried Skip will want to come home with me?"

Oh please, John. I love you and all, but Lucy and me? We be the bomb.

She answers without looking back. "He won't."

"What about you? What if you want to?" he calls after her.

"I won't," she says, laughter in her voice as she keeps walking.

I stop in front of John. Lucy isn't worried about me. She knows I'm all hers. John and I stare at each other, and he gets down on his knees and gives me the best rub and hug I've ever had from him.

"You take care of your lady, Skip. Trust me, she's a keeper." He wipes his wet face in my fur.

I know, I say by nudging his chin and licking away a few of his tears.

He pushes me. "Go before I turn into a puddle."

I lick him one last time and turn around and catch up to

Lucy. She's standing at the end of the block waiting for me, her back to us, with her thumbs hitched around her back-pack straps in front, shoulders rolled back with confidence. Her feet are planted and pointed straight ahead. And even though she has tears pouring down her face, she is smiling, and her chin is lifted. She won't be looking back. She set John free, and in so doing, she set herself free.

But I do look over my shoulder one last time. John hasn't moved and is watching us.

And then Lucy looks both ways and we cross the street, leaving John behind.

When we return to our apartment, Lucy sets down her back-pack, and we both slide onto the living room floor and catch our breath. I sprawl on the floor while she leans against the couch. We really hoofed the last mile, and San Francisco has some wicked hills. But we needed to walk off our confrontation with John. I imagine him still standing where we left him, staring after us like a lost puppy as we walked away.

I sit up to look back at Lucy to see how she is doing.

She scoots forward and faces me.

Sitting like this, I'm a little taller than her.

Her hair is damp around her face from our exertion. Her cheeks are flushed too. Just a few months ago, it was tears soaking her hair and grief reddening her face. Now look at her. She is so dog-damn beautiful.

She leans forward like she used to and says, "You're perfect for me."

And I want to say, "You're more perfect for me than ever."

"We're going to be just fine, you and me. We don't need John anymore. We have each other. Right?"

I bark. *You got that right, lady.*

"What do you say? Should we shake on it?"

And for the first time in my life, I make an exception. I put my paw in my Lucy's hand, and we seal the deal.

AUTHOR'S NOTE

No animals were harmed during the making of this novel. I did want to rescue at least a million dogs and cats, but due to frequent travel, I resisted the temptation.

Please forgive me for anthropomorphizing the canine species to write this book. In fact, dogs do not think or act like humans. Sadly, dogs also do not talk or narrate novels. I wish they could because the world would be a better place.

Woladors are part Timber Wolf and part Labrador and might be restricted or require a permit in some areas. Contact your State Department of Fish and Game, Restricted Species Permits Division for more information.

I know, I know. The dog on this book cover is not a Wolador. It is a Berger Blanc Suisse. When I first researched Woladors, the first image I found was a white dog that looked very much like this Berger Blanc Suisse. It was love at first sight for me. And I was unable to find a professional photograph of a Wolador for the cover.

This book is fiction, but Amanda Toler Woodward and Loki are real. With Dr. Woodward's permission, I included them in this book. I highly recommend you follow Dr. Woodward's newsletter at amandatolerwoodward.com.

Thomas is a fictional character on the autism spectrum. His capabilities do not represent all persons with autism.

*Love is Tox*ic is not a real book. I wish I could give appropriate credit for the information about how the five senses can influence your body chemistry during a breakup. I learned the information during an author's presentation at the RWA 2005 National Conference in Reno, Nevada. I have reached out to the RWA to learn more.

For my *Tiger Drive* fans, I hid an Easter egg of a character in this book. Did you find him or her? Email me: teri@tericase.com. For those of you who haven't read *Tiger Drive*, the first chapter is provided at the back of this book.

Thanks for being you.

ACKNOWLEDGMENTS

I've said it before, and I'll say it again: it takes a village to write and publish a book.

Thank you first and foremost to Ted Llana for everything. I heart your guts.

My dear friend, Elizabeth (aka, Vego), thank you for the years of endless discussions and epiphanies that ultimately shaped this story.

Without Ingrid Yocum Reisman's perspective and feedback, I wouldn't have dared to write a character with autism. You make me laugh through tears, Ingrid. Thank you.

Lisa Sinicki, thank you for inviting me to take the Story Genius workshop via Author Accelerator (and for being a beta reader).

On that note, thank you Lisa Cron and Jennie Nash for partnering up to offer the Story Genius workshop. Lisa, my paperback copy of *Story Genius* goes everywhere I go. And Lizette Clarke with Author Accelerator, thank you for your "genius" coaching and manuscript evaluation. I won't write a book without your help.

My drafts need beta readers and authors *extraordinaire*. Cathey Nickell and Lisa Manterfield you fit the bill.

Additional beta readers include the dynamic duo, Kate McKenzie and Buddy the Bull Dog, and authors Kim Hamilton, Kathryn Brown Ramsperger, Mary Incontro, Brian Joyner, Mary Jo Hazard, Peter Mires, and Lorie Schaefer. I'm grateful to my first ever beta book club, The DRBC, especially Christina H. Furasek, Dana Mauger, and of course, Larry and Thor.

Editor Paige Duke, your patience with my initial draft and your willingness to teach me and reread my changes differentiate you in your field. Follow-on editors Eddy Bank and Carrie Ann Lahain, I can sleep at night because of you.

A dog book needs dog people. Thank you, Donna Newman Wilczynski, Jessica Case, and Kristi Tristao Jensen for sharing, and letting me use, your dogs' peculiar habits.

Photographer Gretchen Lemay, everyone needs their headshots done by you.

DOGTV has years of scientific research behind its mission to entertain and comfort your dog when alone. You can learn more at DOGTV.com.

Special thanks to Dr. Amanda Toler Woodward and Loki (Chapter 38) for their dedication to the care and dignity of the elderly. Learn more about Dr. Woodward's work at amandatolerwoodward.com.

Thank you Rupert Davies-Cooke and the Original Writers Group, especially Nahid for her input on astrology and how it influences personalities. Special thanks to Publishing Pros, Creative Rock Stars, and IPTIA.

Guess who kicks ass? Kelsey Browning, Reva Benefiel, and the rest of the KicksAss Creations Inner Circle. Learn more at kicksasscreations.com. Matthew Wallace, you showed up each day for a year, and that made me want to show up too.

Thank you, Dan Blank. As I write this list, it doesn't escape me that I know at least 12 of these fantastic contributors because of you.

Dear Facebook friends, you chimed in whenever I asked for ideas or support. Where would I be without you?

Betty Crocker, thank you for creating the Cherry Chip Cake.

Greg Behrendt and Liz Tuccillo, thanks for writing *He's Just Not That Into You*. I also couldn't have lived without *It's Called A Breakup Because It's Broken* by Greg Behrendt and Amiira Ruotola-Behrendt.

Dear J.K. Rowling, I just . . . thank you for being you and for making life magical.

What good would a book be with the Backstreet Boys?

Finally, every book gets judged by a cover, and I'm grateful to have cover designer, Olya Vynnychenko on the team again. Original photo credits belong to:

Couple: Neustockimages, iStock #155072327
Berger Blanc Suisse: GlobalP, iStock #484845940
Tennis Ball: Bequest, Pixabay #1593518

Everyone, thanks for being you.

TIGER DRIVE
a novel

one family
too many secrets
four people who want to matter

TERI CASE

CHAPTER 1

HARRY

Hello, my name is Harry
—Sobriety meeting

Saturday morning, April 1, 1989

Harry opened his eyes and waited for his vision to clear. He was dressed and lying in bed—his bed. He recognized the quilt pattern on the damn twin mattress Janice had moved into their room six months before—and after seven kids and thirty years of marriage. The finality behind her action had made it one of the worst days of his life. They hadn't slept together since.

So he'd made it home, but how and when? He rolled onto his back and stared at the bedroom ceiling.

Another blackout.

What did he do last night? Or was it more than one night? He was no stranger to drinking binges and running blackouts that could last up to a week at a time. They had become part of his genetic makeup and bad habits over the past several years, increasing at a disastrous rate. He looked at his watch: April 1. So one night was lost forever, and he was waking up on April Fools' Day.

He was a fool.

What had he done between the blackout and bed? Part of him wanted to know, and part of him didn't. Nothing good ever came out of being so drunk he couldn't remember a damn thing.

His head pounded, and his ulcerated stomach gurgled with acid, rushing heat up his esophagus and burning his dry throat. His breath smelled and tasted of vomit and putrid mistakes. Waking up from a time warp was the worst feeling; he dreaded putting the pieces together because they were always wrapped in regret and guilt. Without fail, he'd always said or done something he shouldn't have. Something he could never take back.

Why did he keep doing this to himself? To his family?

The last thing he remembered was drinking beers at the Creek Bar.

Harry lifted his hand to his chest and then curled his fist over his heart. The skin over his knuckles stretched tight and began to burn.

What in the hell?

His knuckles were busted wide open, and dried blood caked his skin. A trail of bruises and scratches ran from his wrist to his elbow. His other arm didn't look any better.

He fought escalating panic. What happened last night? Who did he hurt? He eyed his hand. His best-case scenario would be that he had hit something, and his worst-case scenario would be that he'd hit someone. The scratches on his arms indicated the worst.

Janice was asleep in her bed, and her blankets pooled around her waist.

He eyed the plump skin of her upper arm. No obvious bruises. What a relief. Leaning across the two-foot chasm between their beds, he shook her shoulder.

"Janice. Janice," he said around small gasps of air. He cleared his throat and stroked her arm. "Janice."

"Leave me alone." She shrugged her shoulder away from him and buried the side of her face deeper into her pillow.

"Did I hurt you?"

"No, I was in bed when you came home and passed out." She tensed and started to turn to look at him. "Why?"

He nudged her shoulder to keep her in place. "Nothing to worry about, go back to sleep."

She tilted her head enough to squint at him. "Heard that before."

He couldn't bear to alarm her before he knew any details. Busted fists couldn't be good news, and it'd be best to let her remain oblivious, at least for now. He lay back on his bed. He looked again at his right hand and flexed his fingers, opening and closing them several times. Both hands were swollen and aching, but his dominant right hand was worse. Squeezing his eyes shut, he tried to remember. Waited. Nothing.

Think. Think. Think.

Okay. So he'd gone to the bar straight after work. He was stressed out, and he'd needed a drink because Janice would leave him for good if she found out about his gambling debt. And the damn debt had gone past due as of Friday morning. Anytime now, the asshole might call or show up on his and Janice's doorstep and claim the roof over their heads and take their cars. His stomach tightened as if he had just gone from cold to hot in that game his kids played. "Hotter," they'd say as he moved closer to what he needed to find.

Was that it? Was he getting hotter? Did his injuries have something to do with the pawnshop owner and lost titles?

He'd have to call Scotty at the Creek Bar to retrace his steps, and he prayed he hadn't brought more damage to his family than he already had. Had he gotten in a fight at the bar? No. He would've woken up in jail, or Janice would have heard about it. She was always there for the karaoke contest on Saturday nights. At one point, he'd thought he could scrape by and use her contest winnings to stay ahead of the loan, but she always told him she'd used the money to settle past due bills or buy groceries. He couldn't say, "Oh by the way, honey, I pawned our home and vehicles in a poker game." But one crisis at a time, he thought. First, what had he done?

Harry looked down at his T-shirt. It was splattered with reddish-brown stains. Blood—he hoped from his own damaged hands. His pants looked similar. He rolled over to the side of the bed. His top shirt was crumpled in a ball on the floor. He grabbed it, and an iron-like smell permeated his senses. Harry shook the shirt open. It was covered in dried blood—too much blood. He gagged and dropped it to the floor.

Invisible hands encircled Harry's neck. He struggled for oxygen. Spots blurred his vision. He sat up, putting his feet on the floor and dropped his head low between his knees.

Oh mother. What did he do last night?

As soon as his vision stopped spinning and he could breathe like a normal human being, Harry grabbed the bloody shirt and stumbled to the bathroom. He shoved the shirt in the small trash can, whipped off his T-shirt and pants, and added them to the garbage before tying the bag closed. He turned to the sink and scrubbed his face with soap and warm water. The yellow soap burned his wounds. He grabbed a towel from the floor and braced his hands on either side of the sink.

"What have you done?" he asked his reflection, a reflection he'd come to know as the self-sabotaging Jekyll to his broken-spirited Hyde. He reached for the glass of dentures on the counter. His upper teeth were soaking in the container. He ran his tongue around his toothless mouth. Where was his lower set of teeth? He shuffled toiletries around on the counter. They had to be there somewhere, but they weren't. He couldn't afford to lose those. Literally.

Damn it.

It wasn't funny how the sight of himself without his teeth could bring him to tears. He used to be a handsome man. A man going somewhere. A man people stared at for all the right reasons as he walked by.

Not anymore.

He turned his face from side to side. He just looked tired and old. Worn out. In trouble.

So he had hurt someone, lost his teeth, and gone to bed in bloody clothes. He glanced at the plastic boats and toy cars deserted in the drained tub. *Please—not his boys . . .*

Morning light from the windows guided his way as he raced in his boxers down the hall and through the living room to look for his four children who still lived at home. No one had fallen asleep on the couch. He made his way toward the two rooms at the far end of the main trailer. Nineteen-year-old Lisa was asleep in the first room, and he didn't see anything strange. He cut through the Jack and Jill bathroom to the second room.

His dog, Star, named after the white shape between her eyes, was lying on the bath mat and growled at him—nothing new about that. Star had been growling at him since they'd brought her home as a puppy. He'd grown up on a farm in Minnesota and had once been a natural with animals, but that was a long time and too many bad decisions ago. He ignored her and stepped into the adjoining bedroom. The bunk beds his nine- and ten-year-old boys treated like a fort were empty.

Oh God.

He pushed on and stepped over to the bedroom window. His station wagon was parked outside. So, yeah, he had either hurt someone, lost his teeth, and driven home; or driven home, lost his teeth, and hurt someone he loved. Where were Justin and Tommy?

His self-loathing grew with every step.

His college-bound daughter, Carrie, was asleep in her room. As usual, she had cotton stuffed in her ears to block any noise.

No sign of the boys. There was nowhere left to look.

Oh, shit. Harry spun on his heel and headed back to the Jack and Jill bathroom.

Star was a terrier mutt with a white belly and caramel-colored coat. She was fifteen pounds if she was lucky, but she stood to her full height and then bared her teeth like a mama bear.

If dogs could talk.

He forced her to the side. Her bark had always been bigger than her bite. With his heart doing a *thump-de-dump*, he opened the vinyl shower curtain.

Justin and Tommy were huddled sound asleep beneath a pile of ThunderCats blankets in the porcelain bathtub. Their heads were on opposite ends of the basin and lying at awkward angles. Their bare, twig-like legs stuck out from their cartoon-pic skivvies, and Justin's foot rested under Tommy's chin. Tommy hugged a yellow plastic Wiffle Ball bat to his side. A dying flashlight glowed under Justin's hand, creating a translucent pink glow between his pudgy fingers. The pajama shirt at Justin's wrist was smudged with blood.

If he had hurt them, he'd never forgive himself. Harry curled his lips and choked on a sob. "Boys? Boys. Wake up." He leaned over the tub and squeezed their shoulders.

His touch startled his children. Justin's eyes widened, and he shrank back. He hugged the flashlight to his chest, casting an eerie glance over his face.

"Get away!" Justin cried.

Tommy gripped the bat and struggled to his knees. Cocking his elbows, he lifted the bat just like Harry had taught him for Little League baseball.

Hell—they were scared of him.

Harry put up his hands and took a step back. "It's okay. I'm not going to hurt you. Justin, show me your wrist." He sat down on the toilet to be at their eye level. "Did I do that?"

Justin nodded and pulled back his sleeve.

"Oh no," Harry said.

Justin's small wrist and forearm had bruises matching the sizes of Harry's thumb and four fingers. "Does it hurt? Rotate your wrist for me."

Justin stuck out his lip. He wiggled his wrist and flinched. "You scared me."

It took Harry a few minutes to find his voice. Every time he tried to speak, an anguished keen threatened to escape, and he'd have to clear it like a bad cough. "I'm so sorry. What happened, Tom?"

Tommy's scrawny arms were shaking, but he tightened his hold on his bat. His lips quivered. "You said if we didn't get out of your way, you'd kill us. We ran, but Justin tripped. You grabbed his arm and swung him over there." He pointed across the room.

Harry leaned forward until he was kneeling next to the tub. "I'm so sorry. I didn't mean it." He tried to take the bat, but Tommy wouldn't let go.

"Okay, keep the bat until you feel safe. That's your right." He turned to Justin. "Did I do anything else?"

Justin nodded. "My shoulder hurts."

"Nobody hates me more than I do right now, son. It won't happen again. I swear on my life."

Star started to whine, and she put her front paws on the bathtub.

Harry smoothed the hair between her ears and looked at his sons. "See, I know how to be gentle and nice now. Star's forgiven me this time, and she doesn't even like me. Tom, I'm real proud of you for sticking up for your little brother. Now, how about we go to Winchell's and get some hot chocolate and donuts? Just us boys. Will that help?"

"With sprinkles?" Justin asked.

"Anything you want. Come on, let's get dressed."

The boys crawled out of the tub and shied away from Harry's helping hands.

As soon as Justin's bloodstained pajama top hit the floor, Harry wadded it up and shoved it under his arm.

Tommy asked, "What did you do that for?"

Harry couldn't look him in the eye. "I'm going to get him a new pair of PJs."

"But I like my Superman jammies," Justin said.

"I will get you new ones. Let's get your shoes on." Harry took Justin's foot and pushed the tennis shoe past his heel. He was tying Justin's shoe when Tommy spoke again.

"You had blood on you last night."

Harry cringed and focused on Justin's shoe. His poor sons deserved so much better. "That was wine, not blood. Maybe I should get a Superman shirt to replace mine."

Justin giggled. "You're too big for one."

Harry brushed the bangs off of Justin's forehead. *So forgiving.*

Crossing his arms and shaking his head, Tommy said, "It wasn't wine. I know what wine smells like."

"I know you do," *Jesus Christ, he was the worst dad ever*, "but let's not talk about it anymore. It's our secret, and we have some donuts to eat. I think I'll have sprinkles too."

Justin laughed again. "You're too old for sprinkles."

"No one is too old for sprinkles," Harry said. "Let's go."

Two hours later, Janice was waiting for him on the back porch when they returned with full stomachs and Kmart bags.

Harry could tell by her pursed lips she was annoyed. He slowed his pace. There'd been a time when she looked at him as her hero. He'd sunk so far. Man, if she only knew how much trouble he was in. He wished he could tell her about the title to their trailers, but he couldn't until he came up with a solution. And he still couldn't remember last night.

"What have you three been up to? What's in the bag?" she asked.

"The boys and I went out for breakfast, and I bought them a gift."

"Why didn't you take the girls too?" she asked.

Because he hadn't scared the crap out of the girls.

"Boys, go in the house," Harry said.

The bags bounced off their skinny legs as they ran up the steps.

"You, Lisa, and Carrie were sleeping like angels," he said.

Janice squinted and looked hard at him. He hated it when she did that; it felt like she could read his mind. And after thirty years, she was damn good at it too. Drinking made him too predictable.

"You asked me earlier if I was okay. Did you black out last night?" she asked.

He nodded.

Janice rolled her eyes and reached for his injured hands. "What happened?"

It was the first time she had touched him in weeks, and he hated himself for needing to break the contact and pull away before she touched the sores. "I don't remember, but don't worry. It wasn't you, or the kids. But I scared them last night. I just wanted to make it up to them."

"By buying them breakfast and a present? Jesus, Harry. You didn't hit them? Can you even remember? You better be honest with me. I'll ask them anyway. Unlike you, they don't like to lie."

Harry was ninety percent confident he'd bought the boys' secrecy, but they were kids after all. "They're okay," he said.

She stared at him for an eternity, then she looked away and crossed her arms over her chest. Her stance reminded him of Tommy's defiance a few hours before. "They looked happy."

And he thought he'd gotten away with one more bad day, but he hadn't. Janice moved on to another topic he wished he could avoid.

Extending her hand, palm up, she said, "Give me the rest of your money. Our lot rent is due this week. And we need groceries."

Harry hesitated. "Um, did you win anything at karaoke last night? Can you use the money for groceries?"

"Harry . . ."

He looked at his feet because they were the safest place to look.

"Damn it, Harry. You promised. I knew I shouldn't have trusted you with your paycheck yesterday, but I didn't have time to swing by the shop and pick it up. I was going to take it last night, but you left while I was singing. Please tell me you didn't blow it."

"Honey, I needed it for something else—"

"What for? Poker? Is that it? You never learn. What kind of a man are you? You want us to live on macaroni and government-issued cheese for the week? Don't you care if your kids have a roof over their heads? We need that money, Harry."

She was too close to the truth because, no, in the heat of the moment, he hadn't cared enough about a roof over their heads or food in their bellies. He'd been playing to win and to break even or at least catch up with the loan. He'd thought he'd win and nothing would be an issue. He clenched his jaw only to be reminded that he'd misplaced half his dentures. He hated how he looked without them. Nothing felt shittier than shame, and he felt what few hairs he had left on his balding head and the back of his neck rise like a damn dog who has been backed into a corner and is ready to fight his way out. His heart rate quickened, and sweat gathered on his forehead. "I can't handle this right now. Get out of my way!"

"Get out of *your* way?"

He didn't like the way she said "your"—like he'd been keeping her from something better than her life with him. Because he knew he had been, and that he'd done so for years. She'd always deserved better. The truth hurts that way. He couldn't handle any more truth right now.

"You've become a pathetic excuse of a man, do you know that? I wish I'd never met you!" Janice yelled.

And he definitely couldn't handle that.

Over the years, they'd argued more and more, and they often said stuff they didn't mean, but dammit, her eyes told him she meant it this time. She did think he was pathetic. He snapped. He grabbed her neck, slamming her against the side of the trailer, creating a rumble and vibration through the thin metal. It echoed, and shouts and running footsteps told him the children had heard. The folds of Janice's chin were like silk under his bruised and calloused hands, and he felt her throat spasm as she tried to swallow and suck in air all at once. As she struggled with him and his hands tightened, images of another person flashed through Harry's mind. A different struggle. He shook his head to try to clear his thoughts. *What was happening to him?*

Janice clasped his hands and raked her nails across his injured knuckles.

Harry swore, released her throat, and slapped her. The

force of his beefy palm threw her off balance, and she landed on the porch with a scream and a thud. Harry jumped back. Appalled by his own actions, he cried, "Janice. No, Janice." He took three steps back and looked from his hands to his wife.

He'd never forget Janice's expression, his betrayal radiating from her blue eyes. The set of her lips and jaw spoke of a finality that far surpassed any divide between a set of twin beds. He'd never laid his hands on Janice's neck before. She'd made him promise not to touch her neck years ago because it made her feel vulnerable. He'd never known her reason, but her fear had been reason enough for him. And now, he'd broken his promise to her.

A fragmented memory of his two hands choking some man flashed again. Was it from last night? Had he strangled someone? Shit. What had he done? Was he both a murderer and an abusive husband now? His forehead was dripping sweat now. Janice and his home swam before his eyes. His anxiety almost overwhelmed him.

"Janice, I need your help—"

"Leave. God help me, but I never want to set eyes on you again." Janice curled her lip in a sneer and climbed to her feet. She rubbed her hand over her neck and then her cheek. "You promised never to touch me like that." Her voice reverberated between clenched teeth. "Never. Come. Back." She walked away from him, and without sparing him so much as another glance, she went into the trailer and slammed the door behind her.

Harry heard the distinct click of the lock, and Janice's voice carried through the cracked window as she called the police. Numb inside, he turned and stumbled to his car. He drove around town for a few hours in a daze and then began to retrace his steps from the night before. With each step, he knew he had lost his family forever. He registered for a kitchenette on Green Street, his usual location of exile and the one place that would let him pay in arrears.

A day later, there was a restraining order in place to stay away from his family, and Harry had figured out he'd beaten a man into a coma.

Available now in hardcover, paperback, and ebook

www.tericase.com

ABOUT THE AUTHOR

Teri Case is the award-winning author of *Tiger Drive*. A native Nevadan, she lives in Washington, D.C., during the summer and in Clearwater, Florida, for the winter. She often travels—watching, learning, and writing about people who want to matter. *In the Doghouse* is her second novel.

Teri runs the Tiger Drive Scholarship for students who want to reach, learn, and grow beyond their familiar environment by attending college.

www.tericase.com

photo by Gretchen Lemay Photography

facebook.com/tericaseauthor

twitter.com/tericase_author

instagram.com/terilcase

Made in the USA
Middletown, DE
10 June 2019